Fighting for Peace

SOCIAL MOVEMENTS, PROTEST, AND CONTENTION

Series Editor: Bert Klandermans, Free University, Amsterdam

Associate Editors: Ron R. Aminzade, University of Minnesota
David S. Meyer, University of California, Irvine
Verta A. Taylor, University of California, Santa Barbara

(continued on page 308)

Fighting for Peace

Veterans and Military Families in the Anti–Iraq War Movement

LISA LEITZ

Social Movements, Protest, and Contention, Volume 40

University of Minnesota
Minneapolis | London

Published with assistance from the Margaret S. Harding Memorial Endowment, honoring the first director of the University of Minnesota Press.

Published by the University of Minnesota Press
111 Third Avenue South, Suite 290
Minneapolis, MN 55401-2520
http://www.upress.umn.edu

Library of Congress Cataloging-in-Publication Data
Leitz, Lisa.
    Fighting for peace : veterans and military families in the anti–Iraq War movement / Lisa Leitz.
    (Social movements, protest, and contention ; volume 40)
    Includes bibliographical references and index.
    ISBN 978-0-8166-8045-0 (hc : alk. paper)
    ISBN 978-0-8166-8046-7 (pb : alk. paper)
1. Iraq War, 2003–2011—Moral and ethical aspects. 2. Veterans—Political activity—United States. 3. Peace movements—United States. I. Title.
    DS79.767.M67L45   2014
    956.7044'31—dc23

                                             2013028410

Printed in the United States of America on acid-free paper

The University of Minnesota is an equal-opportunity educator and employer.

20 19 18 17 16 15 14   10 9 8 7 6 5 4 3 2 1

To all the veterans and military families seeking peace

This does not mean that you are warmongers. On the contrary, the soldier above all other people prays for peace, for he must suffer and bear the deepest wounds and scars of war. But always in our ears ring the ominous words of Plato, that wisest of all philosophers, "Only the dead have seen the end of war."

—General Douglas MacArthur
in his speech at West Point
on May 12, 1962

Contents

Contradictions

Peace/War and Observer/Participant

The U.S. military is largely hostile to protest and protestors. Like militaries in many other countries, it has been called on to control, dispel, and end protest both in the United States and abroad. People who participate in the military are less likely than civilians to take part in protest.[1] Therefore, an examination of military community members who take on identities as protestors, especially peace protestors, is a study in contradictions. Thousands of U.S. military servicemembers, veterans, and their families protested the Iraq War; they not only managed this identity incongruity but also used this perceived inconsistency to their advantage.[2] Like them, I also lived and utilized this contradiction.

When I met my husband, he was a bookstore clerk using the GI Bill from his service in the U.S. Army Reserve to pay for college, and I was a graduate student examining and taking part in peace protest. Before we met, David had committed himself to over a decade of more military service by applying to transition from his nearly complete Army Reserve service to becoming an active duty naval aviator. As he became an officer I helped organize protests in Santa Barbara, California, against the impending and, then, the existing Iraq War. During our early years the contradictions of our chosen paths as a war protestor and an elite military asset seemed insurmountable and even caused a brief breakup. We grew intellectually and personally from our supposed contradictions, however, developing nuanced ideas about war, peace, and service.

Moving from California, where I was surrounded by overwhelmingly left-leaning and antiwar friends and colleagues, to a military base near Pensacola, Florida, provided further lessons in understanding

FIGURE 1. Tim Kahlor speaks in Santa Barbara, California, on December 10, 2006, at the Honor the Warrior, End the War rally. Author (*second adult from right*) stands with other members of Military Families Speak Out. Photograph courtesy of the author.

supposed contradictions. My perspective on American foreign policy alienated me from many of the formal and informal family support groups, so that summer of 2004, I scoured the Web looking for others in the military community who were outspoken in their opposition to the Iraq War. I found and joined Military Families Speak Out (MFSO). At first, I had no interaction with them, as there was little infrastructure to the organization and no active members in my area. In search of local allies, I volunteered with Panhandle for Kerry, where I worked alongside Vietnam War veterans and a Coast Guard spouse to elect Senator John Kerry as president of the United States. When Elizabeth Edwards, wife of Democratic vice-presidential candidate John Edwards and the daughter of a naval aviator, came to Pensacola, I was asked to introduce her and to sit on a panel with her because of my military-spouse status. She appointed me to a whirlwind speaking tour of the country as a national spokesperson for the Kerry/Edwards 2004 campaign. During what was referred to as the "Moms on a Mission" tour, I participated with mothers and wives of American servicemembers in town hall meetings, political rallies, and media events aimed at questioning President George W. Bush's policies in the Iraq War and for the military. In October the tour brought me into contact with the first MFSO activists I met, Stacey Bannerman, the wife of a National Guard soldier who was at that time in Iraq, and Lietta Ruger, the mother-in-law of an Iraq War veteran with numerous other family connections to the military.

During the campaign I was fascinated with the deference both conservatives and liberals gave to military veterans and families and thus decided to focus my research on members of the military community who questioned the Iraq War. Studying the military peace movement afforded me a way to stay sane while facing the enormous pressures of military deployments, the book process, and the job market. While my close friends never saw me as holding onto contradictions as a peace activist and a military spouse, strangers and acquaintances sometimes questioned my loyalty to one group or the other, suggesting I had to choose between my love for and support of military members and my antiwar sentiments. It is this seeming contradiction of identity and its role in social movements that this book explores.

EXAMINING A COMPLEX SUBJECT

The seemingly conflicted existence of this movement and the constantly shifting realities of social movements lend themselves to ethnographic methods. In this book I draw on intensive participant observation from 2006 to 2008, followed by continued attendance at major movement events and observation from a distance via online technologies through 2012.[3] My data include ethnographic fieldnotes from a variety of protest events and organizational meetings in every region of the United States, in-depth interviews with participants and leaders in the movement, a qualitative follow-up survey with participants in 2011, and thousands of organizational and media materials on the movement. The fluidity offered by participant observation, in-depth interviewing, and qualitative content analysis is well suited to the study of deviant cases that are absent from mainstream discussions of the military and past research on this subject. In-depth analysis of those who differ from expectations of much of society and who embody both sides of a dichotomy, such as peace/war or male/ female, pushes us to grapple with the complexity of the lived experience whereby the two sides of a dichotomy come to be understood as ideal types that are never as separate as we imagine.

Ethnography allowed me to enter this research without presupposing who the players in the military peace movement were. I immersed myself in peace movement protest and materials on this movement to discover what military identity–based organizations and individuals were involved in peace activism. From the sheer numbers of people in these organizations, the presence of these organizations on speakers' lists and at other events, and the repeated references to them in the media, I determined that MFSO, Veterans for Peace (VFP), Iraq Veterans Against the War (IVAW), and Gold Star Families for Peace (GSFP)/Gold Star Families Speak Out (GSFSO) operated as the primary homes for the military community within the peace movement. Vietnam Veterans Against the War (VVAW) was also a visible player (though not as visible or integrated with the others as VFP), but since most of the members of that organization I observed were also involved with VFP, I limited my interviews with veterans from past wars to VFP. As I describe in chapter 1, while other military peace movement organizations and some prominent members of the military community critiqued the war, most existed outside the broader peace movement entirely, and many did not directly oppose the war. Many others operated only in a locality, and a few organizations were only one or two individuals who operated a website. In addition to providing space for me to locate the major forces in the movement, the flexibility built into ethnography also allowed me to shift focus as one organization, GFSP, largely died and another, GSFSO, arose.

My use of an ethnographic extended case method analysis pushed me to pay close attention to the context in which actors moved, and for understanding the military peace movement, context is key.[4] Not only was the movement surrounded by a country deeply divided over a war, but these people navigated their way through two very different landscapes in the peace movement and the military. These subjects were pushed and pulled by their competing loyalties and the intensive demands of war deployments and postwar reintegration. I captured personal narratives describing the navigation of competing identities by recording speeches at movement events and through informal questioning of activists in the course of observation and thirty semistructured interviews with movement activists.[5] I also used a primarily qualitative online survey with fifty-six respondents to follow up with activists to examine the ongoing effects of the wars in 2011 and the changes in antiwar activism of these military veterans and families.[6] Since military peace movement activities often operated simultaneously in numerous locations and since I was unable to be at every event or interview all activists, I used thousands of pages of media and movement materials to provide a more complete picture of the movement, including transcriptions of speeches, blog posts, videos of events, poems, books by movement activists, emails from movement leaders, organizational newsletters, website materials, and press releases.[7] Although imperfect in other ways, these documents allowed me to overcome some of the limitations inherent in the subjective nature of qualitative research.

I do not use pseudonyms in this book. When I name activists, it is largely because they gave me permission to identify them. Most activists prefer that the world know who they are and what they stand for. Other names that I use are from public actions that one can easily find information about in the media or on the Web; these activists gave their information to journalists and crowds freely, so I use their names. Each person who agreed to a formal interview gave permission for the use of his or her name and likeness. What might get lost, though, are the several hundred unnamed activists whose individual statements or actions are described in this book. These people are referred to in ways that do not reveal their identity, often by their military branch and their rank or affiliation (e.g., Air Force mom or Marine sergeant). When I have other nonunique details, I use phrases such as "a young Army wife" or "a National Guard soldier from Michigan." Recounting the experiences of these unnamed actors provides a lay perspective that may be different from those of the leadership or of full-time activists, whose names appear in print. I believe it is important to include those activists I encountered only once in my eight years of ethnographic research, and including details from events and meetings I attended, as well as materials given to me by organizations or available on the Web, provides a richer picture of this movement. It was impossible, however, to obtain informed consent from many of these people, and I do not use names or identifying information unless an action was public or I have permission.[8]

THE MOVEMENT AND I

As a participant-researcher I was given nearly complete access to movement materials and events. My personal experiences straddling the two worlds of the military and peace activism informed my questions about and investigation into these organizations. While this research was certainly not "autoethnography," my identity as a military spouse granted me knowledge of the military and its culture, and this allowed me easy access to and increased rapport with movement subjects.[9] Emotional movement activities were personally draining, however, and often made it difficult to summon the additional energy for writing fieldnotes and/or conducting interviews. I avoided leadership positions in the movement until I was done with most of the data collection, but I spoke occasionally to the press or addressed crowds. Although I tried to limit my impact on the movement, my actions did influence the direction and outcomes of movement strategies and tactics. I attempt to offer an objective analysis of the military peace movement, but like the other members of this movement, I believed my activism was necessary because the lives and souls of my loved ones were at stake.

Like most members of the movement, the other people in these organizations became a part of my wider family. I took late-night calls from stressed-out parents and spouses, and I sat through the night with veterans traumatized by the war and with their families who worried about them. Since the movement concerns were also personal concerns, I was rarely able to escape the war and its consequences. I shared activists' fear, guilt, anger, pride, and joy. Some days, I could not stop crying while I wrote this book, and I had a very hard time coming out of the field. It was painful to stop engaging with the peace movement at the level I had from 2003 to 2008 because the wars continued taking the lives and health of friends and family.

Similar to the subjects of this book, I wrestled with the public perception of the seeming contradiction in being both an antiwar protestor and connected to the military, so on Veteran's Day November 17, 2006, at a candlelight vigil in Santa Barbara, I gave a speech describing how I combined my activism and my military family identity. The crowd of fewer than two hundred gathered around the memorial discussed in chapter 5. I am asked regularly how someone could be both an antiwar protestor and connected to the military, and some readers, as well, may have a hard time understanding how the two could go together. As I described that night:

I often feel that I am straddling two worlds. When I am with my colleagues or with members of the general peace movement, lots of people want to know how I, someone who is seen as an advocate for peace, can be married to someone in the military. . . . While the Army Reserves helped David pay for college life, when he became an officer it was because he has always wanted to fly, which is an expensive dream. David believes in the ability of the U.S. military to do good in the world, and like me he hopes it could be used to end human rights abuses not perpetrate them. . . . It is important that we distinguish those in the military from those that have made the horrific decisions to use indiscriminate weapons against civilians and to invade and occupy countries.

When I am with other military spouses or others my husband serves with, people wonder how I can protest this war. . . . I ask you how, given the stakes with my beautiful husband and friends on the line, I could not protest this war? . . . Our military has done all that was asked of it, but the plans of this war were shot from the beginning. . . . If he doesn't make it home, I will be stuck correcting people who tell me he died a hero. I will have to say, "No, he died for lies and greed." If he makes it home, he will forever have to live with the knowledge that he killed people—again, for lies and greed.

I am proud to be both a peace activist and a military spouse. I am working to make the U.S. a country that treats its military better and that involves being a more peaceful country ourselves. Support for the troops is not a yellow magnet on a car and ignorance about this war. No, real support for the troops involves making sure that we only send troops when it is truly necessary, not when it is politically or economically expedient.

The Military Peace Movement

I n response to a 2011 survey, veterans and military families who considered themselves antiwar activists bemoaned the United States' continuing wars in Iraq and Afghanistan. They pointed to a divide between the military community and the civilian populace as a reason for the wars' continuation. Larry Syverson, whose three sons served six deployments to Iraq and Afghanistan, explained the wars' impact on his family:

> Because of the stress generated by deployment, my wife had a difficult time working while our sons were deployed. As a result, before our youngest son's second deployment to Iraq, she took early retirement. It is the only way she has been able to deal with multiple deployments. Our youngest son was recently divorced. It was a result of his recurring PTSD [posttraumatic stress disorder]. His wife would not accept the mental problems he was having. Twice he has been admitted to a psychiatric ward. It was after the second admission that they were divorced.

As Syverson explained, both military servicemembers and their families were emotionally and psychologically devastated by the wars. Like Syverson, many in the military blamed the wars for marital, employment, and other social consequences. What separated Syverson from many in the military was, however, that he had long engaged in protest of the American-led Iraq War that began in 2003 and, later, of the U.S.-led war in Afghanistan.

Syverson was quoted in dozens of media outlets, spoke at rallies, and marched in many of the major East Coast protests, but the action that gave him the most pride was his vigil in front of the Richmond, Virginia, federal courthouse, where he held signs that displayed pictures of his sons and messages such as "Iraqi Oil Isn't Worth My Sons'

FIGURE 2. Members of the military peace movement pose for a picture after five hundred of them marched from their national convention near the convention center to the Gateway Arch in St. Louis, Missouri, on August 19, 2007. Photograph by the author.

Blood." He explained, "I protested over two hundred times. For many, including the newspaper, I was the face of the antiwar movement in Richmond. I felt—I hope—I influenced other Richmond residents' views of the wars." Syverson believed that people paid attention to his view of the wars in Iraq and Afghanistan because he was a military parent. Like Syverson, most veterans and military families in the anti–Iraq War movement intended to bring the war home to Americans, who were largely unaffected by these wars because the country had an all-volunteer force (AVF) that comprised less than one-half percent of the overall population. Activists believed this personalization helped turn the tide of public opinion in the United States against the Iraq War.

Many activists point to the summer 2005 media storm that was generated when many veterans and military families held a vigil outside President George W. Bush's ranch in Crawford, Texas. For one month that summer, while the president vacationed, White House media correspondents were restless, and this protest, led by the mother of a nineteen-year-old soldier who died in Iraq, offered a counterpoint to coverage of the president's policies.[1] Newspapers across the United States and around the globe described the protest, even on their front pages, and the twenty-four-hour news networks made it a part of their daily news loops. The mother, Cindy Sheehan, demanded a meeting with President Bush so that she could ask him for "what noble cause" her son, Casey, died.[2] She set up camp in a roadside ditch and, later, on donated rural property, where she and other activists waited for that meeting. The vigil supporting this request brought over ten thousand people throughout the month to the small rural town of Crawford. Most who came supported Sheehan and stayed multiple days, living in primitive camping conditions on the side of the road leading to the ranch.[3] These people, many of whom were veterans and military families, developed a sophisticated system for not only feeding and sheltering each other but also working with the media and getting messages out to supporters across the country. Bumper stickers and T-shirts supporting the vigil cropped up in peace movement communities across the country, with sayings such as "What Noble Cause?" or "Texas Is Bush Cindy Country," and the protest became known as Camp Casey in honor of Sheehan's son. Although the media attention focused on one woman, Sheehan—using the trope of the grieving mother—the vigil was the product of hundreds of veterans and military family members who interacted with each other within the peace movement.[4] Like the leading figures of all movements, Sheehan was linked into and supported by thousands of individuals, many with their own stories of grievances and activism.

This 2005 protest in Crawford and the resulting media coverage was a watershed moment for this movement. While Sheehan did not achieve her immediate goal, a face-to-face meeting with President Bush, this vigil succeeded in electrifying the peace movement and obtaining media coverage for antiwar sentiments, which had been lacking since the start of the war. In addition, the vigil brought together veterans of the current wars, veterans of past wars, families of dead military servicemembers, and families of current servicemembers who were all critical of the Iraq War. Before the media coverage of the Sheehan vigil, many of these people were unaware of other military-connected individuals who were willing to protest the Iraq War. Most activists involved in this protest described the Crawford protests as an important time for building a sense of community within this section of the peace movement and strengthening ties between the military antiwar organizations. Although I do not have the data to determine whether the sagging polls on the war that followed the vigil were directly attributed to this event and/or the involvement of veterans and military families in the antiwar movement more broadly, the timing allows for such conjecture.[5]

Thousands of military-affiliated people critiqued the war through activities such as media interviews, public presentations, marches, encampments, memorial displays, and street theater. The involvement of veterans and military families in the anti–Iraq War movement in part grew out of established veterans' peace organizations, but Iraq War veterans and their families also created new organizations. The veterans and military families who worked with each other inside the broader peace movement from 2002 to 2013 comprised what I call the Iraq War military peace movement. This subsection of the wider peace/antiwar movement distinguished itself from the broader movement by focusing on activists' identities that connected them to the military. While the Iraq War generated numerous critics, few spoke with the authority or garnered the media attention of American veterans and military family members. These activists' visibility challenged the widespread assumption that military veterans and families unquestioningly supported the Iraq War, and media outlets covered these activists disproportionately to their numbers. In fact, such deference was given to the military community that in a column for the *New York Times* Maureen Dowd described them as having "moral authority" when speaking about the Iraq War.[6] The involvement of veterans and military families in antiwar protest was both novel and significant for the peace/antiwar movement. Activists attempted to reframe popular debates around patriotism and troop support and to mobilize bystanders by calling attention to their military identities. As such, activists used their identities strategically to challenge hegemonic ideas about the war.

By 2010, however, much of this movement was frustrated that the attention generated by the Crawford protests and subsequent tactical repertoires had dissipated. Activists in the military peace movement were facing issues related not only to reintegration into civilian life, war wounds, and war deaths but also to new and continuing deployments. According to Department of Defense (DoD) figures, as of March 2011 over 110,000 troops remained in and around Afghanistan; over 90,000 were in and around Iraq; and over 100,000 additional personnel were stationed aboard various ships, many in supporting roles for these wars.[7] While the deployments continued, the recession that began in December 2007 reduced personal, foundational, and other resources from which activists could draw. Although polls from 2010 to 2012 showed that few Americans were concerned by the wars in Iraq or Afghanistan, these wars continued to dictate military families' lives.[8] While troops officially withdrew from Iraq at the end of 2011, U.S. involvement and anticipation of conflicts related to the global war on terror kept up the quick deployment pace and the strain on military families. Without support from foundations or the public, one of the military peace movement organizations closed its main operations in 2013, but during that summer the United States had over ten thousand military contractors still in Iraq, over one hundred thousand contractors in Afghanistan, and over sixty thousand uniformed servicemembers in Afghanistan.[9]

In various polls, military veterans and families were asked whether most American civilians understood the sacrifices made by military servicemembers and their families, and nearly all believed they did not. My 2011 survey of military peace movement activists mirrored that answer. Most said something similar to Debbie Caruth, the mother of an Army soldier who served four tours in Iraq: "No! No one understands." Like the wife of Larry Syverson, Caruth suffered serious psychological consequences from the stress of these multiple deployments, and so did her son. Syverson, who in 2011 was the chairman of the board of directors of the antiwar organization Military Families Speak Out (MFSO), expounded on the isolation that many military families felt:

> Because such a small number of troops are being subjected to multiple deployments, the effects of the war directly impact an extremely small group of Americans. I don't think the other 99 percent have any idea

what the 1 percent of us that deal with these multiple deployments are going through over and over and over. My three sons have had six deployments: five Iraq and one Afghanistan. . . . We need to continue to link the wars with the economy. The public doesn't care about our loved ones being deployed. But they do care about their pocketbooks and government programs. I hate having to do it, but it appears that is the only way to get many people's attention.

Although their personal stories initially attracted media attention to the problems of the Iraq War, 2011 had little to no media coverage of either that war or the Afghanistan War.[10]

The military peace movement was tired and struggling with the long-term consequences of the wars, but the issues that had brought them together in 2003 had only gotten worse as servicemembers came home to face a backlogged and ineffective Department of Veterans Affairs. For example, Joan Najbar, a mother of an Iraq War soldier, said:

Reintegration after extended warfare is complete hell for soldiers and families. For National Guard soldiers and their families, you are without support services. As a result, deployment and reintegration are very isolating experiences. Most community members are disconnected and ignorant about the realities of war. As a result, "unknowingly" many community members say hurtful things without any understanding of modern warfare and deployment. As a result, soldiers and family members feel even more isolated, because the American public lacks real compassion. The following is a list of comments said to myself and other moms of deployed soldiers: "I know just how you feel [having a loved one deployed] because my son is away at college." "You need to get over it." "So do you talk to your sons every day when he's deployed?" "Is it true that the guys on the front lines in the war have low IQs?" This was actually said to me by a mental health coworker: "I bet they all have personality disorders." . . . This makes even the process of reconnecting in your community even harder because Americans totally don't have even the most basic understanding of the human impact of war. . . . Most citizens, politicians, and the press regard war as some kind of Disneyland experience. This disconnect makes feelings of pain and isolation even worse. It's as if we exist in some parallel universe and we are the people that carried the burden of these wars while Americans watched reality TV. So I find the lack of connection, the detachment, to be a bizarre commentary on our culture: our culture which has been comfortable with 1 percent of our nation carrying the burden of war for ten years. It's very cruel.

Najbar expressed the heartache of many in the military peace movement. While most Americans believed the Iraq War and the Afghanistan War were drawing to a close, for veterans and military families the wars and their long-term consequences remained a grueling part of everyday life. The military peace movement hoped to showcase the consequences veterans and military families faced in order to personalize the wars and encourage opposition to them.

The military peace movement played an important role in shaping public opinion to oppose and question policies in Iraq and Afghanistan. This book focuses on the development, maintenance, tactics, and strategies of this movement. I describe how identity and emotion are factors both in the internal workings of social movements and for movements' external actions and consequences. My focus on identity not only highlights micromobilization and solidarity processes but also illuminates how movements frame their arguments and interact with bystanders. By exploring this intriguing movement, I demonstrate the critical importance of identity and emotion for all major aspects of social movements. Examination of this particular movement also provides insight into the divide between the military and civilians in the United States, as well as the relationship between warfare and peace activism.

THE MILITARY AND PEACE MOVEMENT CONTEXT

Americans often award veterans and their families an elevated social position, which has been particularly true during the wars in Iraq and Afghanistan.[11] In its development during the Iraq War, the modern military peace movement combined cultural and structural elements of both the military community and the American peace movement. As such, it is important to understand the historical and the cultural contexts of that war and of the U.S. military and the U.S. peace movement.

The Wars in Iraq and Afghanistan

Although the military peace movement developed largely in response to the 2003–11 Iraq War, the Afghanistan War played an increasingly important role in the movement, and by 2009 all organizations in the movement had developed positions against it. Though these two wars are conceptually and tactically distinct, their timelines overlap (as seen in the appendix), and many people in the military served in both wars. Despite lengthy American military involvement in these countries, both Iraq and Afghanistan are considered failed states and have high levels of economic instability, infrastructure failures, out-migration, corruption, and violence, and in both countries governmental leaders are regularly accused of using the military and police to intimidate or eliminate political rivals. Whereas the U.S.-led war in Afghanistan had widespread international and domestic support for its mission of countering terrorism and retaliating against the terrorist attacks of September 11, 2001 (9/11), the Iraq War had less support for its rationale and was more contentious at home and abroad.

The al-Qaeda suicide attacks on the Pentagon and the World Trade Center and the downed flight in Pennsylvania killed nearly three thousand people, heightened patriotic fervor in the United States, and brought increased international denouncement of the Islamic terrorist organization al-Qaeda, which was believed to be responsible for those attacks and others against Americans. President Bush demanded that Afghanistan's governmental leadership, the Taliban, hand over the al-Qaeda leaders, who were staging attacks from rural areas of Afghanistan. When the Taliban refused, America began airstrikes on October 7, 2001, starting a war that was aided primarily by forces from the United Kingdom and the Afghan Northern Alliance fighters. Although the majority of cities were captured by these forces and a new government was put into place by summer 2002, the NATO-led International Security Assistance Force, with the United States continuing to provide most troops and services, battled against Taliban and other fighters for over a decade. Although Afghanistan began holding presidential and parliamentary elections in 2004 and 2005, respectively, the elected government continued to battle Taliban forces for control of the country, particularly in rural areas. Troop levels and U.S. casualty numbers were limited in Afghanistan until President Obama dramatically increased troop levels in 2010, hoping to stabilize the country. By the fall of 2013, American troops remained in Afghanistan, battling largely guerrilla-style attacks from various groups.

In his January 29, 2002, State of the Union address, President Bush declared Iraq part of an "axis of evil" that aided terrorists and sought "weapons of mass destruction" (WMDs) to use against the United States.[12] For a little more than a year, his administration built a case against Iraqi president Saddam Hussein, and the U.S. Congress authorized a war in Iraq that began on March 20, 2003. The lack of an attack by Hussein's government on the United States before the war led many to label this war a preemptive attack, and the legality of this war has since been challenged in the United States and abroad. As in Afghanistan, American and coalition forces were able to obtain a quick victory over the military, but they were unable to fully secure peace in Iraq as sectarian and insurgent violence continued for the duration of the war. Although Saddam Hussein's Ba'athist regime fell in April 2003, U.S. forces did not catch him until that December, and in 2005 Iraqi courts convicted and hung him for crimes against humanity, particularly for the mass murder of Iraqi citizens. The 2005 Iraqi elections were followed by an increase in insurgent violence, so President Bush ordered a surge of additional troops into the country. In 2007, changes in military tactics and the addition of troops led to the deadliest year for American servicemembers, but sectarian violence was significantly reduced in the following years.

By 2007, President Bush and numerous cabinet, intelligence, and Pentagon sources had confirmed that Iraq had no WMDs or ties to al-Qaeda. Although those initial reasons for the war were unsubstantiated, many, including President Bush, defended the war because it removed a dictator from power and brought democracy, however limited and fragile, to Iraq. During his election campaign, President Obama promised to end the Iraq War, which he did, but on a timeline that had been agreed to under President Bush within the Status of Forces Agreement with Iraq. President Obama's administration and Iraqi officials worked to create a new agreement that would have left American troops in Iraq as trainers for the Iraqi military for several more years. After that fell through over Iraq's unwillingness to grant U.S. servicemembers and contractors immunity, American forces left Iraq on December 15, 2011.

Although other militaries, especially the British Armed Forces, supplied troops to Iraq and Afghanistan, U.S. servicemembers made up the bulk of the forces in those wars. Many more nations sent forces to serve with the United States in Afghanistan than in Iraq. From 2001 to 2012, over two million American servicemembers served in the wars in Iraq and Afghanistan. Although the war in Iraq likely distracted political, aid, and military attention from Afghanistan, it did not reduce troop levels.[13] In fact, during the course of the Iraq War, troop levels in Afghanistan went up from an average of just over five thousand in 2002 to almost one hundred thousand in 2010. The United States put significantly more "boots on the ground" (servicemembers who served in country) in Iraq, however, for most of the time it fought these simultaneous wars. Beginning in 2009 under President Obama, troop levels in Iraq wound down while troop levels in Afghanistan went up. By the summer of 2010, more U.S. troops were in Afghanistan than in Iraq. At its conclusion the Iraq War had claimed the lives of 4,474 American servicemembers, and as of September 13, 2013, 2,194 American servicemembers had died in Afghanistan's Operation Enduring Freedom.

The wars in Iraq and Afghanistan stretched American military and financial capacities. Senior government officials such as Defense Secretary Robert Gates and Admiral Michael Mullen, chairman of the Joint Chiefs of Staff, raised concerns about the operational tempo (OPTEMPO) of, or the pace of deployments to, Iraq and Afghanistan, as well as the length of deployments, which reached nearly two years at their lengthiest. These officials were concerned about these factors' effects on the fighting capacities of the military, military retention, the psychological health of servicemembers, and military families. During the wars in Iraq and Afghanistan, dwell time, or the time between deployments, was regularly less than twelve months, the military's own suggested minimum. The cost of these wars to the United States through 2012 is estimated at $1.4 trillion if one examines only direct outlays,[14] but analysis puts the full costs of the wars, including veterans' care, interest on loans used to pay for the war, and some war-related aid, between $4 and $6 trillion.[15]

The Iraq War: Repeating History?

Numerous people, including President George W. Bush and former secretary of state Henry Kissinger, have compared the Iraq War to the Vietnam War.[16,17] Both wars involved unconventional (guerrilla or insurgent) warfare used against U.S. forces that produced an uncertain battleground for military personnel and thwarted traditional tactics. Both conflicts had broad support at the beginning that dropped significantly over the course of the wars.[18] Vietnam was touted as a war to halt the spread of communism, while Iraq was described as an important battlefield in the fight against radical Islamic terrorism. More important for understanding the military peace movement are the Vietnam veterans who became instrumental in antiwar protests of that time and the involvement of the military community after 2001. Despite the similarities, Iraq was not Vietnam, and the military of the 2000s was very different from the one the United States fielded in Vietnam. These differences led to dissimilarities between these two eras' military mobilization against the war.

The Iraq War and the Vietnam War began with 59 to 75 percent of Americans approving of them, and these numbers held during the first few months of intense combat for both wars.[19] In the later years of both wars, however, when asked whether they had been a mistake, over half of Americans believed they had been. By August 1968, over half of Americans believed the Vietnam War was a mistake. Beginning in the summer of 2004, a few polls were finding that half of Americans believed the Iraq War was a mistake, and by August 2005, a majority of Americans were consistently holding this opinion. Three years into the large-scale ground wars of each conflict when Americans were asked if they approved of the presidents' handling of the wars, significantly more disapproved of President Bush's handling of Iraq than disapproved of Johnson's handling of Vietnam.[20] Although both wars became unpopular with the majority of Americans, the Iraq War was disapproved of more quickly than was Vietnam.

The Vietnam War represented a departure from past conflicts because the military community was a visible part of the antiwar movement. Veterans of wars before Vietnam, primarily World War II veterans, actively protested the Vietnam War through an organization called Veterans for Peace, or Veterans for Peace in Viet-Nam (which has no affiliation with the organization I focus on in this book). In 1967 six Vietnam veterans organized Vietnam Veterans Against the War (VVAW), the first and most visible organization of military members protesting the war in which they had fought.[21] Beyond VVAW, soldiers organized protests in Vietnam beginning in 1968 and created a variety of other formal and informal organizations.[22] Although military life traditionally cut off soldiers from forces critical of war, in the late 1960s antiwar activists brought antiwar literature, the counterculture, and radical politics to soldiers through coffeehouses they opened near military bases.[23] Military personnel demonstrated opposition to the Vietnam War also through desertion, intentional sabotage of equipment or paperwork, the use of symbols such as the peace sign, and underground newspapers.[24] By 1971 troop morale in Vietnam was very low, and instances of drug abuse, the murders of officers, or "fragging," and combat refusals or mutinies were on the rise.[25] Estimates of Vietnam-era servicemembers who participated in antiwar activities range from 20 to 37 percent.[26,27] While soldiers were important participants in the anti–Vietnam War movement, scholars began only recently to examine the actions of the military community to end the war.[28] Therefore, mythology that suggests Vietnam-era peace protestors and veterans were at odds has persisted.[29]

Although veteran–activists have been prominently featured in discussions of antiwar movements, little has been written about military families who protest wars. In his extensive illustration of the Vietnam-era military community's protests, Gerald Nicosia uses only one page to describe the involvement of Gold Star Mothers (mothers whose children were killed in war) and the girlfriends of soldiers and veterans in antiwar protests.[30] From Vietnam to the Gulf War, the military actively enforced a media silence on spouses of servicemembers and prisoners of war.[31] The earliest evidence of an antiwar military family organization that I found was for one that developed in the lead-up to the 1991 Gulf War.[32] Military families opposed to that war formed the Military Family Support Network, and when the war ended after less than two months of American combat operations, the organization regrouped as a service organization focused on Gulf War syndrome. It lasted, however, for only a short time after the war. The prominence of military families' antiwar organizations during the 2003 Iraq War and the longevity of MFSO certainly represented a departure from the past.

There were dramatic differences between the U.S forces fighting the Vietnam War and those that fought the Iraq War, and these differences led to striking dissimilarities in the military opposition to those wars. First, the Iraq War occurred while the United States was already engaged in ground combat and nation-building operations in Afghanistan; the military was also engaged in operations in Libya and other places through its broader global war on terror. Second, significant aspects of the anti–Vietnam War protests within the military could be attributed to racial unrest in the United States, whereas the Iraq War's military leadership was more racially diverse and movements for racial equality were less prominent and perhaps less relevant to American soldiers.[33] Third and, I believe, most important, the Iraq War's military included only those servicemembers who chose to enlist. While the voluntary nature of the U.S. AVF military can be debated since it draws few members from the middle and upper classes, no one was drafted into the Iraq War. Only Americans already associated with the military faced immediate war consequences. Without a draft, or a fear of a draft, there was no draft-opposition movement working in concert with the broader antiwar movement, as there was during the Vietnam War. Whereas the military would draw in a broad range of people during a draft, including many with left-leaning politics, those who served during the Iraq War and their families had more-positive attitudes toward the use of force in American foreign relations than did other civilians in the United States.[34]

Without a draft many in the military served multiple tours in war zones, often beyond the parameters of their initial contracts. In fact, by 2011 it was not unusual for military families to describe a servicemember going on a fifth or sixth deployment. In contrast, Vietnam draftees and enlistees served only one tour unless they reenlisted. Without the draft, the U.S. military, particularly the Army, faced shortfalls in enlistment numbers as the wars dragged on, and from 2006 to 2012, standards were lowered to allow for the enlistment of older individuals and people who had been convicted of various crimes. Reenlistment rates remained at historically high rates, however, during the wars in Iraq and Afghanistan, even though the more months a person was deployed, the less likely they were to believe they wanted to reenlist.[35]

Despite these constraints, Iraq veterans organized resistance faster than did veterans during the Vietnam era. Military resistance to the Iraq War developed quickly, in part, due to previous military-community activism, which peaked during the Vietnam War. Although a couple of the leaders of VVAW tried to learn from the older veterans involved in antiwar protest, most Vietnam veterans felt alienated from World War II veterans, who largely did not have misgivings about the causes of their war.[36] Iraq veterans, however, benefited from protest during the Vietnam era because VVAW and related groups created a cultural climate in which veterans could critique a war, and they offered tangible resources to the younger generation. In fact, leading Vietnam veterans in the antiwar movement of the 1970s, such as Bobby Muller and Ron Kovic, were influential in part because they personally mentored their younger counterparts in Iraq Veterans Against the War (IVAW).[37,38] The relationship between today's veterans and past veterans was evident in organizational structures and emotional bonds.

Although the changing demographics of the military created barriers to mobilization for the modern veterans' movement, demographic shifts positively influenced the creation of military-family organizations. Military members during the Iraq War were significantly more likely to be married or have dependents than those at any other point in U.S. history.[39] During previous wars, when anyone could have been drafted and wider swaths of the population served, virtually every family was or could be a military family.[40] During the Iraq War, however, the burdens of military family life rested on fewer than 2 percent of American families. These changes likely influenced the proliferation of military-family organizations, including antiwar organizations.

In his extensive work studying the Vietnam veterans' movement both before and after that war ended, Nicosia describes veterans' feelings of alienation from civilians who did not understand their military experiences and its lingering trauma.[41] Similarly, I found that the civilian/military divide continued to influence the formation of the Iraq War military peace movement, and the relatively small number of military veterans from 2001 to 2011 intensified this divide.

The Military and Civilians

The section of the peace movement illustrated in this book drew its distinctiveness from its relationship to the military. Since a military's primary function is to enact war, widespread opposition to war from inside this community is unusual. In his book describing Vietnam-era military activism, David Cortwright points out that "political activism is difficult under the best of circumstances, but within the Draconian legal structure of the military it can be suicidal."[42] Americans, however, have often objected to conscription, and conscientious objection, which, historically, was religiously based, has existed since the Revolutionary War.[43] Both in past wars and during the Iraq War, the military overtly discouraged antiwar sentiments through regulations and covertly created acceptance of war by demanding conformity and obedience to those who directed American foreign policy. Military culture separates military members and their families from civilians, and the military community regularly opposes antiwar protest. The military not only shapes people's experiences so that they are supportive of wars but also attracts individuals with a greater propensity to support them.

Regulations stemming from the U.S. Constitution's establishment of civilian control over military policy intentionally limit military members' free speech, particularly during wartime. Six primary military regulations limit servicemembers' participation in antiwar activities. First, Department of Defense Directive (DoDD) 1325.6 establishes servicemembers' right to expression but limits this right to speech that is compatible with the effectiveness of their military unit. Second, DoDD 1344.1 forbids military members from wearing their uniforms to political events or engaging in any other behavior that indicates military endorsement of political activities. Third, DoDD 1344.10 prohibits military personnel from speaking at political events in favor of political candidates or issues, such as war. Fourth, Article

88 of the Uniform Code of Military Justice (UCMJ) bans military officers from using "contemptuous" language in reference to the U.S. president or "other military officials." Fifth, UCMJ Article 133 further limits military officers' actions through the vague prohibition against "conduct unbecoming an officer." Finally, military members, particularly enlisted servicemembers not bound by the previous two regulations, can be charged under a catch-all provision in UCMJ Article 134 that forbids any action or speech that the military deems contrary to "good order and discipline."[44] These formal regulations establish fairly severe punishments for military members who participate in antiwar protest, as I describe in chapter 1.

The differences between military and civilian culture are so great that the For Dummies series of guidebooks published *A Family's Guide to the Military for Dummies*.[45] Military life requires an extensive commitment not only from its workers but also from their families, which further separates this community from civilians, resulting in conformity and loyalty to the military's missions. The military community has their own slang, and military parlance involves numerous acronyms. Military rituals involve secretive events, including violent hazing, and formal public traditions, such as parade marches or military funerals. The military regulates its members' and their families' bodies through numerous strict rules about clothing, hairstyles, physical fitness, and even makeup. Military members are frequently unable to communicate with their families or friends outside their military group for weeks or months at a time. The military also requires its members and their families to move frequently, on average every two to three years, regularly affecting family members' occupations, earnings, and networks. Military community members daily face the likelihood of death, injury, or psychological damage. Military bases operate like miniature cities, with their own stores, restaurants, recreational facilities, and even car washes. Additionally, most military members and their families are required to and are rewarded for obtaining services such as health care, insurance, and banking on base and within the military system. The unique culture and constraints of military life lead its members to believe they are different from and, in some cases, better than most civilians.[46]

At times, journalists and some members of the military have been alarmed by the increasing gap between the U.S. military and U.S. civilian society.[47] Reasons for alarm over this gap include fear that civilians might become so uninvolved with the military that they stopped funding and supporting it or that military personnel might become so disillusioned with their fellow Americans that their loyalty to civilian leadership diminished or disappeared, which at its worst would lead to a military coup. Military personnel are more likely than civilians and civilian leadership to be conservative, vote Republican, and hold nationalistic or hawkish prowar attitudes.[48] Although some data found that this gap was narrowing before the Iraq War, it also found significant political-affiliation differences.[49] Additionally, veterans and military families have had significantly more-positive evaluations of the wars in Iraq and Afghanistan than have civilians.[50] These voting and attitudinal trends suggest that the military community would be less ripe for antiwar protest than would be civilians.

In fact, many military members widely disparage or, at least, mistrust protest activism and protestors. Some soldiers and their families have negative feelings about peace protests because they believe such protest is aimed at them.[51] This likely stems from a revisionist interpretation of history that, in part, blames war protestors for the U.S. failure in Vietnam. Vitriolic treatment of peace protestors spills over into at least one of the songs, or cadences, military members sing while marching; the cadence titled "Jesse James" describes the desire to kill a "long-haired hippie." In military communities during the Iraq War, Jane Fonda was still referred to as "Hanoi Jane," and her high-profile status as a Vietnam War protestor made her an example of the misguided, enemy-loving peace protester.[52] Individuals who participate in military service are significantly less likely to participate in social-movement activism or other untraditional political actions.[53]

Despite the constraints of military culture, between ten and fifteen thousand members of the American military community joined anti–Iraq War protests. This portion of the military community was small considering nearly twenty-four million veterans were in the United States in 2010 and over two million people served in Iraq and Afghanistan. This book does not attempt, however, to describe the entire military community's opinions about the Iraq War. It instead focuses on those individuals who from a veteran's, a soldier's, or a military family member's perspective stepped beyond norms and publicly spoke their opposition to these wars. Given military culture and the consequences for activism, it was surprising that opposition to policies the military was charged with enacting came from inside the military community. Military family members and veterans had to negotiate competing identities in order to criticize American military policy while also participating in or supporting loved ones in the military. Military peace organizations provided spaces where people could reconstruct their understanding of themselves and even the social understandings of peace and the military. Furthermore, these organizations provided collective identity and kinship for many people in the military community, some of whom were explicitly ostracized by other military organizations because of their political beliefs. All of this made the people in the movement exceptional, and research on them offers insight into a state-focused movement where occupational and other forms of identity clearly mattered.

The Anti–Iraq War Movement

During the Iraq War the antiwar movement comprised numerous individuals and organizations that often worked together, though, as in most large movements, they frequently disagreed over tactics and strategies.[54] In addition, the movement was divided by cognitive differences in their constructions of the scope, causes, and cures for the war. For instance, the movement included pacifists and hawks, people who linked peace to larger social-justice issues and those more narrowly focused on international conflicts, and people focused on world peace and those focused exclusively on the Middle East, as well as those interested only in ending the Iraq War.

Following the Vietnam War, the peace movement focused on issues of nuclear disarmament and, briefly, the Gulf War, but neither of those issues attracted the large-scale demonstrations or the broad base of participants of the Vietnam War's peace movement.[55] Although the war in Afghanistan reenergized peace movement organizations, they struggled to mobilize large numbers of participants until President Bush focused military attention on Iraq.[56]

On October 2, 2002, one of the first demonstrations against the Iraq

War occurred when several thousand people rallied in Federal Plaza in Chicago to hear speakers, including the then senator Barack Obama, denounce the war.[57] Three days later, several hundred protesters marched down the shopping and tourist main street of Santa Barbara, California, led by veterans of World War II, the Korean War, the Vietnam War, and the Gulf War. By the end of the month, a rally in Washington, D.C., attracted over one hundred thousand protestors. Localized protest continued until transnational organizing sparked protests in over sixty countries on February 15, 2003.[58] These actions were inspired by fears of war created when Colin Powell described the supposed stockpile of WMDs in Iraq at a meeting of the United Nations (UN) on February 3, 2003. After the war began, most national antiwar protest marches happened in Washington, D.C., with many coinciding with anniversaries of the first day of the invasion.[59] Large protests in 2004 and 2008 also coincided with the Republican and Democratic national conventions.[60] In April 2009 activists sought to connect the war to the economy with a large march aimed at Wall Street in New York.

In the initial protests against the Iraq War, peace movement leaders responded strategically to the intensified patriotic pride and nationalism among Americans in the wake of 9/11.[61] They made claims to American identity and American values such as democracy and civil liberties.[62] They also redefined patriotism through commonly used phrases such as "peace is patriotic."[63] Since politicians and others encouraging U.S. involvement in Iraq linked patriotism and troop support to backing the Iraq War, veterans and military families were often pushed to the front of peace movement activism.[64] As I describe in chapter 4, military peace movement activists used their military credentials to lay claims to troop support and patriotism for the peace movement.

From 2007 to the end of the Iraq War in December 2011, peace protests were significantly smaller and less regular than they had been at the height of the anti–Iraq War movement (2003–6), when national marches attracted hundreds of thousands. Until 2008, however, organizations continued to build up their infrastructures and regularly engaged in lobbying and advertising. After January 2007 national protests were no larger than tens of thousands, and by 2009 most protests were in the hundreds.[65] Much of this can be attributed to a changing political landscape in which Democrats made significant gains in the

2006 and the 2008 elections. Activists affiliated with the Democratic Party left antiwar activism, and the remaining movement became radicalized.[66] Numerous activists within the peace movement celebrated the election of President Barack Obama, and many expressed sentiments similar to those of an Army mother from my research: "We need to give Obama a chance to bring the troops home. I think we should wait to protest." As activists and organizations waited to see what the new president would do about the wars in Afghanistan and Iraq, the movement demobilized. They did so while large troop deployments were still being made, some larger than those made during President George W. Bush's administration. Simultaneously, the global recession of 2007 took its toll, reducing foundational and other organizational funding sources and individual activists' financial availability.

IDENTITY AND EMOTION IN A UNIQUE CULTURE OF ACTION

Within the broader peace movement, people with connections to the military created a unique subsection that was cognitively, emotionally, and physically different from other segments of the movement. Maren Klawiter offers the term *culture of action* to describe how movement segments differ not just by ideology but also by norms, symbols, and language.[67] Whereas other works on cultures of action focus on movement segments' different choices of tactics and frames, in this book I describe the way cultures of action are separated by mobilization, maintenance, and influence. I examine the role of identity and emotion in the internal processes of cultures of action (those between participants), as well as in their external processes (those aimed at a wide audience). By examining how identities and emotions are intimately tied to a host of movement processes, I demonstrate how a culture of action has consequences for the activists within it and the movement's broader goals.

Identity

The current resurgence of activity by the military community has opened numerous avenues for sociological research on identity processes in social movements. Most research on identity in social movements focuses on identity-based movements that center on the recognition of or equality for people with particular gender, racial/ethnic, religious, sexual, or other identities. This book demonstrates how identity affected a wide range of movement processes within a state-focused movement.[68] The military peace movement developed a shared identity and used their identities to challenge cultural understandings about wars, militarism, and peace protestors. Examining identity at the culture-of-action level allows scholars to understand the importance of divisions and connections between organizations in movements. Activists within a movement interact with members of various organizations, and they frequently develop strong bonds with people beyond their own organizations, but not with all members of a wider movement. An exploration of collective identity at the culture-of-action level can better explain the totality of relationships that facilitates mobilization, sustains participation, and transforms activists' lives.

Identity within the Movement

In order to get sustained involvement from their members, social movement organizations must do more than convince people of their side of an issue or that there is a possibility of winning. They must also develop a sense of belonging, community, or we-ness among participants, or what social movement scholars call *collective identity*.[69] In their review of social movement literature, Francesca Polletta and James Jasper provide the following definition of collective identity: "an individual's cognitive, moral and emotional connection with a broader community, category, practice, or institution."[70] Participants construct collective identity through interactions with other activists and with the opposition.[71] Social movements are often spaces where people reconstruct their identities and the meanings of fundamental identity categories.[72] David Snow and Doug McAdam suggest that several processes are involved in how people align themselves with a collective identity, and this book offers an in-depth examination of the identity-consolidation process whereby activists create a single identity that blends two identities that were previously thought to be incompatible.[73]

Collective-identity construction happens at a variety of levels, and as described by William Gamson, collective identity has three "embedded layers: organizational, movement, and solidary."[74] A person's identification with one of these layers need not mean that one identifies with the others. For example, a person may identify with an organization but not the broader movement within which that organization is embedded. A person may also develop identification with a broad status group (e.g., race, gender, sexual orientation, work group, and social or labor class) but not a collective identity in a movement or organization that seeks to better that group's position. An array of data on the social psychology of movements demonstrates that before people will cooperatively work to change their disadvantaged situations, they must develop a collective identity that links them to a cause.[75] Much of this data suggests that collective-identity formation at the level of the disadvantaged solidary group is not as effective at leading to activism as identification at the organizational or movement level, because movements provide a context that politicizes disadvantage.[76] As one aligns his or her identity with a movement or an organization, that person internalizes the group's norms and consciousness (e.g., goals and understanding of the situation), thus further compelling them to actively participate in protest.[77] By focusing my analysis on collective-identity formation at the submovement or culture-of-action level, I illustrate an important additional layer of this embedded collective identity. In the military peace movement, the culture-of-action level of identity was often as and, in some cases, more important than organizational or movement levels of identity. The culture-of-action level of identity is important for examining how multiple intersecting identities affect the choices activists make, their experience in a movement, and the effects of activism over the life course.

The military peace movement activists I studied built their collective identity by recognizing and appreciating their unique insider–outsider status. They were insiders on war, patriotism, and the troops, and yet their antiwar beliefs and activist tendencies located them outside the mainstream military community. At the same time, they operated inside the peace movement, but their military connections and history made them outsiders to a space in which many distrusted the military and sought to end the need for and use of it. In the military peace movement, veterans came to grips with their participation in the military and their understanding of peace, while military family members felt both love for people wearing military uniforms and disgust at what the military was doing. This research contributes to sociological understandings of how identity develops through social interactions rather than as a part of an innate self, and I demonstrate how social movements influence the construction of identities based on apparently conflicting loyalties. Rather than focusing on how their outsider status separated them from the mainstream military community and the wider peace movement, activists built a positive identity that combined these two distinct aspects of themselves through collective action. Their collective identity was built on a shared definition of the Iraq War as a problem for the military, and they demonstrated how military experiences required antiwar activism.

Identity for an Audience

Social movement participants make calculated choices about how to present themselves through appearance and actions, thus strategically deploying their identities.[78] When movement actors deploy identity, they strategically highlight particular aspects of their history, bodies, and life in order to influence external audiences. Using research on gay and lesbian activists, as well as examples from other movements, Mary Bernstein theorizes that activists deploy identities either for education by highlighting their similarities to the majority or for critique by stressing their differences from the majority.[79] I add to these categories of identity deployment by laying out two other ways that movements strategically display their identities. First, activists deploy oppositional identities that attract attention and counter claims by their critics.[80] When activists use this strategy, they highlight aspects of themselves that might lead people to think they are on the other side of an issue. The military peace movement activists garnered attention for the peace movement and helped to counter the prowar arguments that the peace movement was unpatriotic and that troop support required believing in the Iraq War's mission. Second, activists deploy identities for authority whereby participants present themselves or some of their members as experts in an effort to mold public opinion. Movement participants use this strategy because presenting these identities accords them greater legitimacy in the discourses surrounding a topic.[81] Military peace movement activists garnered authority when protesting the Iraq War because their military association conferred standing on this issue.

The strategies of oppositional and authoritative identities are rooted in the very bodies and core identities of movement activists. Thus, I expand the notion of personalized political strategies in order to reveal the importance of the everyday deployment of identity through clothing, symbols, affiliation, rhetoric, and bodily movement.[82] Activists use these things to emphasize their identities not only at protest events but also in their everyday activities. By embodying identities that contradict mainstream ideas or suggest authority in a cultural or political contest, these personalized political strategies can become more palatable to segments of the population who dislike traditional protest. Embodied protest demonstrates how strategically important it is for movements to link the personal and the political. State and other institutional policies often seem disconnected from everyday lives, but these identity strategies use personalization to connect bystanders to the issues in both cognitive and emotional ways. Thus, military peace movement activists built a collective identity around their connection to the military and their unique position from which to criticize the war, and their strategies and rhetoric drew on a variety of identity claims to assert legitimacy.

Emotion

Over the past two decades, social movement scholars have paid increasing attention to the critical roles of emotion in social movements.[83] This work contrasts with collective-behavior theories that link emotions to irrationality and adds complexity to insights from dominant social-movement models of resource mobilization and political process that focus on structural resources or political opportunities, narrowly defined, as determinants of protest.[84] I demonstrate that emotion can be utilized to affect both movement participants and audiences.

Emotions within the Movement

Activists are often mobilized because of the strong emotional draw of a cause. Social psychologists find that emotions, particularly anger,

motivate people to identify with a movement.[85] Solidarity and collective identities must be built on affective ties; they do not merely
arise.[86] Feelings of injustice often mobilize participants, and the construction of a movement collective identity channels anger and con-
verts shame to pride.[87]

Emotions are a part of collective-identity construction.[88] Strong
emotional attachments foster solidarity and mobilize actors to join
together for a cause.[89] Participants often feel reciprocal emotions or
positive affective bonds such as love, respect, and trust for one another.[90] These reciprocal emotions maintain movement ties and assist
in the development of collective identities.[91] Activists frequently draw
pleasure from their participation, which helps maintain their activism during trying times.[92] The emotional bonds and friendships of a
movement can even cut across other potentially divisive identity categories such as race and gender.[93]

Activism involves emotion work, which entails managing, direct-
ing, transforming, and legitimating participants' emotions in ways
that facilitate movement goals.[94] Activists must manage negative
emotions such as shame, fear, and guilt in order to overcome despair
and act to change their situation.[95] Developing a consciousness that
challenges mainstream interpretations of a situation such as a war can
take vast amounts of emotional energy, and even more is required to
participate in tactics aimed at changing society.[96] The tight-knit multi-
organizational structure found in the military peace movement grew
from the anger and negative emotions of war, and this culture of action facilitated reciprocal emotions that made activism possible.

Participation in activism can also transform the emotions experienced by activists.[97] In the course of working with others and locating
the source of their troubles outside themselves, activists move from
feeling shame, fear, and guilt about their situation to anger at the other
people or the structures that caused their pain.[98] Veterans and military families who opposed the Iraq War often experience guilt and
internalized anger over their participation in war or their inability to
stop the participation of others; loneliness as military and peace movement outsiders; and fear over the war's consequences for friends and
family. The family-like structure of the military peace movement and
its resulting emotional attachment helps activists face and channel

negative emotions brought on by the Iraq War. The construction of a movement family identity alters activists' emotions so that they express group pride, love for and protectiveness of fellow activists, and anger directed at structures and authorities. Activism can transform *emotions of powerlessness* into *emotions of resistance*.[99]

Emotions for an Audience

Emotions play a role in movements' ability to make change, and tactics and strategies often derive power from their ability to elicit desired emotions. Activists hope not only to make arguments that people accept but also to provoke emotional responses that lead people to take action for the cause or further bind them to the movement. Nancy Whittier's research on the movement against child sexual abuse and Deborah Gould's on AIDS activism demonstrate the strategic use of emotion to aid social-movement framing and outcomes.[100] Activists intentionally evoke feelings of grief and anger through tactics that use narrative, theater, and other art forms, such as the antirape Take Back the Night marches and rallies, the anti–domestic violence Clothesline Project, and the AIDS Memorial Quilt project.[101] These tactics elicit strong emotions, educate the public, and affect institutional policies. The emotional element is not accidental. In fact, activists strategize about which emotions to stimulate in others in particular contexts.[102] While movements attempt to elicit many different emotions, grief— particularly, maternal grief—has been a critical tool in organizing against militarized violence because it resonates with the public.[103,104]

Military peace movement activists publicly demonstrated the emotions brought on by war in order to motivate the wider American public, who was largely unaffected by war. Participants regularly attempted to stimulate grief, which would bind people to the movement and its cause, particularly through politicized memorials. They moved their audience also to act on their anger toward policy makers who continued the wars. This book describes the role identity plays in emotion strategies by examining how activists deployed a military identity in ways that heightened bystanders' emotional response to their tactics. By exploring more fully how movements strategically elicit emotions, I push social movement scholars to grapple directly with the emotional meanings of tactics and strategies in order to explore their effects on movement contests and outcomes.

FOLLOWING THE MILITARY PEACE MOVEMENT

As I describe in the preface, the following chapters are based on extensive ethnographic data I collected between 2005 and 2012. Chapter 1 lays out the history and context of the military peace movement. I explain how veterans and military families carved out a unique culture of action within the wider peace movement and how activists within this culture faced greater risks for peace movement participation than did their civilian counterparts. These risks not only made this movement significantly more novel than other segments of the peace movement but also drove members of the military community together to form this culture of action.

Chapter 2 shows how military-affiliated individuals who faced the risks described in chapter 1 and the military's antiprotest culture moved from being soldiers and their supporters to becoming peace activists. These activists adopted a collective identity based on a shared sense of being both insiders and outsiders. I describe what set these activists apart from others in the military and the peace movement and how their unique identities placed them in an important position.

Chapter 3 moves from identity to emotion and examines how the military peace movement identity helped to transform activists' emotional states. The family structure of the military peace movement allowed activists to move beyond the negative emotions of powerlessness—the fear, guilt, shame, and unfocused anger brought on by war—and develop emotions of resistance—those of righteous anger, love, and group pride. As such, the construction of a military peace-movement identity had important consequences for sustaining and enabling movement participation.

Chapters 4 and 5 turn from identity and emotion in the internal workings of the movement to a discussion of their use in the military peace movement's attempts to change American perceptions of the Iraq War. Chapter 4 illustrates how the movement made use of their unique identities both as people connected to the military and as antiwar activists.[105] Activists within this movement recognized and exploited their combined military and peace-activist identities in order to attract attention from the media, the American public, and government officials; demonstrate legitimacy in the debate over war; undermine prowar rhetoric; and reach those unconvinced by traditional peace-movement claims. Though these identity strategies were often effective, they were controversial within this culture of action and for its relationship to the broader peace movement. Chapter 5 examines the intentional use of emotion by the movement, focusing on the movement's use of antiwar war memorials to elicit grief and sadness. Activists used these emotions to draw people who supported the war into the tactic and to encourage greater participation in antiwar activities. They also deployed their military peace movement identities in order to assert authority about the Iraq War and enhance emotional responses to the tactic.

The conclusion provides a picture of the continuing activism in this movement after the Iraq War ended in 2011, as well as a summary of what we can learn from the movement. This research on the military peace movement provides rich data about the ways that the dichotomy between peace and war affected peace-movement participation and attempts at change. Examining the microprocesses in the military peace movement contributes to social movement theory on how collective identities develop, are sustained, and influence other movement outcomes. I build upon and add to social movement theory's understanding of the interconnectedness of identity, culture, emotions, and political opportunities. My research on the overlapping and interconnected organizations of military community members demonstrates the importance of social movement research that recognizes a meso-level between a movement and its organizations, or the culture-of-action level.

1

Joining the Military Peace Movement

Risky Business

Sweating profusely in the Texas summer heat of 2006, about thirty members of IVAW, GSFP, MFSO, and VFP, buoyed by smaller numbers of other peace organizations such as CodePink, worked frantically to create a space to stage events on a vacant lot that Cindy Sheehan purchased in Crawford approximately seven miles from President Bush's ranch. Activists readied the rural space by building roads, clearing brush, planting gardens, setting up memorials, constructing a stage, installing generators and bathrooms, and rigging a sound system and lights. The work became especially hectic as September 1 approached because the activists had called for a press conference that they hoped would attract attention to the peace movement in a way that Sheehan's own original protest had in 2005. Twenty-two-year-old Army Specialist Mark Wilkerson was to announce his surrender to military authorities at the Army's Fort Hood base in Killeen, Texas. Wilkerson went AWOL (absent without leave) when he was supposed to redeploy to Iraq, and he had hid from military authorities for eighteen months.

In the days leading up to this press conference, military peace movement activists taking part in these Camp Casey III protests spoke excitedly about finally drawing attention to the uniquely difficult decisions that military members had to make about the wars. The activists were in agreement that if a war was illegal and immoral, then soldiers had the right to resist deployment to that war. Although MFSO had not officially backed this position at that point (it would in just a matter of months), many members of MFSO were heavily involved in planning the press conference and supporting war resisters such as Wilkerson. In calling attention to his story, activists hoped

FIGURE 3. Mark Wilkerson (*center, holding microphone*) announces his surrender to military authorities at a press conference at Camp Casey near Crawford, Texas, on August 31, 2006. He had been AWOL for one and a half years. In the front row with him are the other speakers including (*left to right*) Geoff Millard, Charlie Anderson, Cindy Sheehan, Ann Wright, and Chaz Davis. In the background are many other members of MFSO, GSFP, and VFP. Photograph by the author.

that the spotlight would smooth his transition into military custody and Americans would learn more about the risks that military members faced in trying to oppose the war.

Before Wilkerson spoke at the press conference, other members of the movement called attention to the difficulties of being both connected to the military and opposed to the Iraq War. Colonel (Mary) Ann Wright (Retired) explained that federal employees and other civilians faced limited consequences for protesting the Iraq War, whereas on that day at least twelve soldiers were facing courts-martial for doing so and that, depending on the numbers used, between 8,000 and 40,000 other servicemembers had gone AWOL. Those actions demonstrated the inherent riskiness of protest for military individuals. Wright said:

In no way should anyone dispraise what he has done in going AWOL or turning himself in to military authority. He wants to get on with his life. He wants to be able to speak about the reasons that he went AWOL in the first place. And the way to do that is to subject himself back to military authority, take what happens, and then come out of whatever happens as a whole person, as a person of conscience. . . . So I, as a senior military officer, am extraordinarily proud of Mark for standing up for [his] conscience to say, "I know the difference between right and wrong, and it is my duty as a military personnel to obey that. I do not have to obey illegal orders. I do not have to go to an illegal war. I will take the consequences." So if we are people of courage, if we are people of conviction, we must stand by these men and women that are doing exactly that.

In her speech Wright sought to use her status as a retired high-ranking military officer to quiet the fears of soldiers who felt it was disloyal to disobey orders and to encourage others to resist following "illegal orders." She fully acknowledged, however, the unique risks that military members faced as a result of such actions of conscience, since military members could not choose which wars to fight. As Wright spoke she illuminated how members of the peace movement needed to come together to support what she and the movement called "war resisters."

All of the speakers called for civilian peace protesters to find ways to support those soldiers whose consciences led them to cut ties with or run from the military. In doing so, they brought attention to one of the greatest differences between the military peace movement and the civilian peace movement: military members faced much higher risks for their opposition to the war. TruthOut contributor and Iraq War veteran Geoff Millard prepared a series of exclusive interviews with Wilkerson, with which he hoped to call attention to the resistance inside the military to the war. He spoke about this resistance during the press conference and announced that he would no longer follow his obligations as a member of the Army Reserve, to which he owed several more months of duty. Millard also described organizing the IVAW chapter in Toronto, which was primarily populated by military members who had gone AWOL and fled to Canada. Millard suggested that the wider peace movement needed to do more to support military members whose conscience would not allow them to serve in these illegal and immoral wars. He spoke of the legal and material needs that this war resistance created.

Protesting the Iraq War meant something very different to Wilkerson, Millard, and the thousands of soldiers who Wright referenced than what it did to most Americans. Military individuals faced three main controls on their activism: military regulations of free speech, prowar rhetoric that suggested the military was unified in its support of the current war, and the U.S. military community's generally negative perception of protestors. In spite of these constraints, thousands of veterans, soldiers, and military family members took part in national and local protests for peace.

Although these constraints set the military apart during any conflict, the lack of a draft and the intense pace of combat deployments, as described in the introduction, meant only a small subsection of Americans were directly affected by the wars. This created a sense of isolation, which I further elaborate in chapter 2, and led to a unique culture of action within the peace movement comprising people whose daily lives were at some point regulated by the U.S. military. This subsection, the military peace movement, was primarily composed of four interconnected organizations within the broader peace movement. This subculture within the peace movement developed out of shared identities, experiences, and risks.

This chapter begins with a description of the increased military involvement in political action since 2001 and then focuses on the military peace movement. I detail the origins and demographic makeup of four military peace movement organizations that differed from similar organizations that did not overtly critique the war. I also describe how the military identities of activists increased the risk of their peace movement participation and how these risks separated the military peace movement from the wider peace movement. In general, peace activism is a low-risk activity, but the military connections of these activists made much of their activism high risk, involving actions that were likely to cost them physically, legally, financially, and/or socially.[1] Although these consequences varied depending on a person's relationship to the military—for example, the veterans of past wars faced far fewer consequences than did the veterans of current wars

and their families—activists faced three broad categories of consequences in this culture of action: (1) official risks, (2) estrangement
risks, and (3) psychological risks.

MILITARY ACTIVISM AND THE IRAQ WAR

During the wars in Iraq and Afghanistan, groups that focused on
issues facing the military flourished. The military community's activism drew on established veterans' peace organizations, as well as
nearly a dozen new organizations created by post-9/11 veterans and
their families. The military community actively sought to alter U.S.
foreign policy through groups that campaigned for John Kerry and
Barack Obama during the 2004 and the 2008 presidential campaigns
and through these groups' successors, which included political action
committees (PACs) of various types. The explosion of new antiwar
organizations and renewed mobilization against military intervention
in the Middle East from within the military community made up the
military peace movement. This movement developed out of a larger
political field of critical military politics during the Iraq War. These
critical voices from inside the military provided a context of discon-
tent with the status quo, which allowed the military peace movement
to emerge and be heard.

During the Iraq War a unique phenomenon occurred: numerous
people with long military careers spoke against U.S. policy there.
Many of the senior officers who made their opposition to the war
public, including General Anthony Zinni, Lieutenant General Greg
Newbold, Major General John Riggs, Major General Paul D. Eaton,
and Major General Charles Swannack Jr., did not join forces with antiwar organizations. A few prominent veterans—namely, General
Wesley Clark and Major General John Batiste (the latter an Iraq War
veteran)—worked with the PACs but not in protest organizations per
se. Their highly publicized critiques of the Iraq War demonstrated,
however, that cracks existed in the U.S. military's "green wall" of support for global military interventions. Additionally, critique coming
from men of their stature—as senior military officials who gave their
whole careers in support of their country—likely encouraged other
military members to critically consider the current political landscape.

In the first decade of the 2000s, there were three broad types of critical military-affiliated political organizations: service organizations, PACs, and antiwar organizations. Military community members engaged in critical politics within these types, and they arranged themselves according to their relationship to the military (Figure 4). This section offers a general overview of this protest field.

Political Action Committees

The military community engaged in critical politics that critiqued some of the policies in Iraq and Afghanistan through standard lobbying and candidate support by PACs. While these organizations often criticized the war, most were not completely opposed to it or its continuation. Some of these groups worked for specific candidates. Presidential candidates John Kerry and Barack Obama harnessed groups of veterans and military families who opposed the war's handling by crafting speaking tours of and events for veterans and military families. These were aimed at reducing the perception that the Democratic Party was soft on issues of war or disdainful of the military while allowing these candidates to oppose current war policies.

Many of the veterans and military families involved in the 2004 political races on behalf of the Democrats formed the nonpartisan progressive lobbying organization Veterans and Military Families for Progress (VMFP) in February 2005. VMFP focuses on both foreign-policy issues and domestic policy concerning the military and veterans and, unlike many of the peace movement organizations, is recognized by the VA.

Since 2004, many veterans critical of aspects of post-9/11 war policies have created technically nonpartisan PACs, such as Vote-Vets, which targeted primarily Republican lawmakers for their votes against funding body armor and improved veterans' benefits. In the 2012 election, VetPAC: Veteran's Alliance for Security and Democracy actively took on an anti–President Obama PAC created by a retired Navy SEAL. Additional veteran-affiliated PACs, such as Operation Free, worked on issues such as renewable energy, which they linked to their veteran status by pointing out the role of oil in recent American wars

	Veterans of All Wars	Vietnam Veterans	Iraq Veterans	Military Families	Gold Star Families
Service organizations	Veterans for Common Sense; Veterans United for Truth	Vietnam Veterans of America	Iraq and Afghanistan Veterans of America; Operation Truth	Military Spouses for Change	
Political action committees	VoteVets; Vets for Kerry; Vets for Obama; Veterans and Military Families for Progress			Moms on a Mission; Blue Star Families for Obama; Blue Star Families of America; Veterans and Military Families for Progress	
Antiwar organizations	Veterans for Peace; Veterans Against the Iraq War; West Point Graduates Against the War; Service Academy Graduates Against the War	Vietnam Veterans Against War	Iraq Veterans Against the War	Military Families Speak Out	Gold Star Families for Peace; Gold Star Families Speak Out

FIGURE 4. Critical Military Organizations from 2003 to 2009.

Critical Veterans' Nonprofit Organizations

Military veterans were involved in protesting the Iraq War starting in 2002, when President Bush threatened to intensify U.S. activity against the Iraqi government. Members of Veterans for Peace (VFP), an organization of veterans of all conflicts and peacetime soldiers, founded in 1985, and Vietnam Veterans Against War (VVAW), an organization of veterans from only the Vietnam conflict, founded in 1967, marched and took part in educational efforts against the war.[2] A number of smaller veterans' organizations that operated primarily online and organized around particular veteran identities were founded in response to the Iraq War. Most of these organizations focused on the Iraq War in particular, as opposed to peace and militarism more broadly.

Other veterans' organizations developed to focus on veterans' care and demanded a more responsible use of military force. These organizations are better understood as critical military service organizations than as antiwar organizations. For example, Veterans for Common Sense (VCS), founded in September 2002 by Gulf War veterans, argued that the Iraq War was unnecessary, but the organization focused on veterans' care issues rather than protest of the Iraq War itself. Others, like Veterans United for Truth (VUFT), called for war to be used as a last resort and had a vague position on Iraq but spent their efforts on helping veterans secure benefits.

As veterans returned home in the years after the invasion of Iraq, they formed new social movement organizations and joined with older veterans, particularly Vietnam-era veterans. VFP helped returning vets from Iraq and from Afghanistan form IVAW. Other veterans' organizations criticized the Iraq War but were not specifically or primarily focused on ending it. For example, Operation Truth, which in 2005 became Iraq and Afghanistan Veterans of America (IAVA), concentrated on exploring the daily problems facing the troops and expressed limited criticism of the wars. IAVA was more focused on the wars' handling and veterans' reintegration issues rather than on the Iraq War's legality or morality.

Critical Military Families' Nonprofit Organizations

During the lead-up to the Iraq War and as the war continued, military family members formed new social movement organizations in an attempt to stop the war and to have their perspectives on war heard. Military families can join veterans' organizations only as associate or guest members, despite their connection to the war. In November 2002 military parents began Military Families Speak Out (MFSO) to oppose the impending Iraq War. A handful of families of slain servicemembers found each other through connections made by MFSO leaders in January 2005 and formed their own organization, Gold Star

Families for Peace (GSFP), using the military distinction Gold Star, which is given to families whose loved ones have died in war. A number of Gold Star parents later left GSFP and formed the MFSO chapter Gold Star Families Speak Out (GSFSO) in late 2005 and early 2006.

In 2007 a small group of military spouses in Texas formed Military Spouses for Change. While this organization was critical of the Iraq War, it is difficult to label it an antiwar organization, as the group's public information was vague about their position on the war and they chose instead to monitor politicians' stances on a variety of issues related to military families, including the war. Its strongest language about the Iraq War suggested that the United States was "hemorrhaging funds on the war." The organization remained small and focused its energy on helping spouses cope with deployments, employment challenges, military stressors, and the transition back to civilian life.

In December 2008, Blue Star Families for Obama reorganized, dropped the "for Obama" from their name, and became more of a critical military service organization. According to their website, they sought to raise "awareness of the challenges of military family life with . . . civilian communities and leaders" because military families made up "only one percent of the country's total population," so most Americans did not have "firsthand knowledge of the military experience." This organization continues to work closely with Michelle Obama and Jill Biden in Joining Forces, an effort to cross the civilian–military divide.

The increase in the public engagement of the military community in critical politics demonstrated the increasing political diversity of this community and the rising criticism of the military status quo. Within this context a number of organizations and online communities made up of veterans and military families spoke out against the war in Iraq. While some service organizations and a number of individuals also engaged in outspoken criticism of the war, military people who actively *protested* war after 9/11 faced the greatest risks for their political engagement.

THE MILITARY PEACE MOVEMENT ORGANIZATIONS

Although a number of antiwar organizations contributed to the military peace movement's culture of action, the most visible in the media and at protest events were VFP, MFSO, IVAW, and GSFP/GSFSO. These organizations frequently worked together on various strategies and tactics, but each had its specific identity-based constituency and political positions. Although veterans and military families shared an intimate connection to war, the difference between being in a war or having one's family members in war and in *which* war led to a need for separate organizations that distinctly spoke to each group's concerns. For instance, MFSO provided a space for military families to discuss the difficulties of caring for and reconnecting with loved ones injured in war while not fearing that those loved ones would take offense. Similarly, although IVAW members shared military training and in many cases combat experiences with VFP members, the unique circumstances of the current wars and the age differences between most Iraq War and Afghanistan War veterans and Korean War and Vietnam War veterans created distinct differences between these organizations. Although these four organizations formed coalitions, they differed politically on peace issues. For instance, whereas IVAW and MFSO focused almost exclusively on the Iraq War and, by 2009, the Afghanistan War, VFP and GSFP advocated for a broader focus on world peace.

Veterans for Peace

American foreign policy in Central America during the twentieth century led Jerry Genesio to seek out other veterans who were angry with American foreign policy and who could speak from experience about the horrors of war. Genesio was a Marine veteran whose brother died in Vietnam, a war he believed in at the time. His son and one stepson were also in the military. In the winter of 1984–85, Genesio and his wife, Judy, presented slideshows on their peace trip to Nicaragua to churches and other organizations. As they traveled they met other veterans interested in a veterans' peace group. This led to the first VFP meeting on April 6, 1985. This meeting brought together veterans of World War II, the Korean War, and the Vietnam War.

That first meeting resembled today's VFP membership in that it was open to all U.S. veterans and active duty servicemembers no matter where they served, whether in conflict or in peacetime. Civilians, typically military family members, were allowed to join as associate members with nonvoting status. By the Iraq War, VFP was a UN-recognized nongovernmental organization. It moved its national office from Washington, D.C., to Saint Louis, Missouri, in 2001, and had over 144 chapters nationwide. The wars in Iraq and Afghanistan contributed to membership growth in VFP. According to reports of VFP executive directors, in 2001 the organization had approximately seven hundred members, and by the fall of 2007, the paid membership was over seven thousand. During observation I found that the ranks of today's VFP included a number of people who considered themselves members but who failed to pay their yearly dues. Hundreds of new members joined each year, but as members admitted to me, they often forgot to pay their current dues.

Although not a pacifist organization, in its twenty-three-year history VFP has protested nearly all U.S. military actions during, including the first Gulf War and the 1990s' conflicts in eastern Europe. VFP's mission statement clarifies that the organization is an "educational and humanitarian organization dedicated to the abolishment of war." While the organizational mission defines itself as a peace rather than an antiwar organization, VFP leaves open the option of supporting a war, particularly defensive actions taken by the United States or other countries. In November 2002, VFP released a statement critiquing what they saw as President George W. Bush's "relentless drive for war with Iraq." The organization had earlier that year called for an end to the war on terror, believing that war encouraged rather than reined in terrorism. Activists in VFP were heavily engaged in prewar protest action, and they founded a number of weekly events across the United States, such as vigils and marches. The organization has a long tradition of public works projects in countries with which the United States has previously warred and has worked to hinder U.S. military recruitment through their truth-in-recruiting campaigns. It continued its opposition throughout the course of the Iraq War, and in August 2008 VFP's members voted to also oppose the U.S. occupation of Afghanistan.

Military Families Speak Out

In August 2002 a young man told his father, Charlie Richardson, and his stepmother, Nancy Lessin, that his Marine unit was headed to

Iraq. He had confirmed his parents' fears that the United States was preparing to invade Iraq. His parents realized that they needed to personalize the war in the fall of 2002 when Richardson overheard two men arguing over whether the United States should invade Iraq. He felt that he should have "put a picture of my son right on the counter" and said, "If you're going to have this discussion about what should happen with Iraq, why don't you do it looking into the eyes of someone whose life may be at risk because of this war? Why don't you think about that instead of some abstract notion of an invasion?" That incident left Richardson and his wife with a desire to force people to face the sacrifices of military families. They sent an email with a picture of their son to everyone they knew and asked people to help prevent the war. Since their email traveled the Internet and was posted in various locations, they received dozens of replies from people in the United States and on other continents. Some they did not even know. This led Lessin to the sense that their "voice as a military family with someone close at risk had a power to it." As a labor organizer, Lessin understood the power of personalizing stories in order to maximize tactics' impacts. In the following months, Lessin and her whole family decided to put the message of their letter on signs at antiwar rallies. The signs read, "Our son is a Marine. Don't send him to war for oil." They received thanks and praise from members of the peace movement and attention from local media.

One family does not constitute an organization, however. Lessin and Richardson researched the history of the short-lived Military Family Support Network, an organization of military families that opposed the Gulf War and was active from late 1990 until 1992. Lessin and Richardson looked for other families with whom to form a new antiwar organization. In late October 2002, they met Jeffrey McKenzie of New York at a Washington, D.C., protest of the Iraq War. McKenzie's son was an Army helicopter pilot who had orders to deploy in January 2003 to Kuwait. The two families worked by phone and email to put together a press conference to announce the organization's founding in Washington, D.C., on January 15, 2003. According to Lessin, over two hundred people from military families joined the organization within twenty-four to forty-eight hours after the press conference. Although Lessin was concerned that the organization might fall apart after the war began, as the Gulf War military families organization had, she said that membership doubled within a week of the start of the invasion.

MFSO grew from two families, a home-phone line, and a rudimentary website in January 2003 to over four thousand families, an office with three full-time staff, and a much more sophisticated Web presence by March 2008. Although McKenzie continued to be part of MFSO, like many in the organization, his activism decreased sharply after the return of his loved one from the war.[3] Lessin and Richardson took on the bulk of MFSO's initial work, and they continued to be active as the recognized founders of the organization. In 2006, MFSO elected a board of directors to lead the organization. MFSO membership was open to "relatives or loved ones who are currently in the military or who have served in the military since the buildup to the Iraq war in the fall of 2002." This definition of a military family is much broader than the definitions found in most research on military families. Scholarship and the military's own research tend to address only those who are current military dependents and who are the spouses and children of servicemembers serving at the time of data collection. MFSO's expanded definition included parents, siblings, gay and lesbian partners, girlfriends and boyfriends, grandparents, aunts, uncles, and families of veterans (not just servicemembers).

Though the organization mainly comprised outspoken parents, spouses made up a significant percentage of the group's membership, as well, and the organization was open to gay or lesbian partners of military members, who were not recognized by any other military service organization at the time. While MFSO counted all four thousand families who voluntarily joined the organization as members, only a few hundred could be considered active at any time, and some who were counted in the membership may have no longer considered themselves members.

MFSO focused on the Iraq War, and its primary mission was expressed in their tag line "Support the Troops, Bring them Home NOW!" In order to maintain a broad coalition of members, Lessin and Richardson initially kept the focus on the single issue of the Iraq War, and the organization did not take a stand on more controversial issues such as war resisters, which included individuals who went AWOL or who refused to deploy for political reasons. In the fall of 2007, how-ever, MFSO polled its members, who overwhelmingly voiced support for war resisters, and it joined with other organizations in the military peace movement on this issue. Like VFP, MFSO moved to include opposition to Afghanistan in the organization's goals following a vote among its membership in April 2009. In August 2013, however, MFSO announced that due to its dwindling human and financial resources, it would "dissolve as a legal entity" at the end of the year.

Iraq Veterans Against the War

Former Air Force technician Tim Goodrich met Marine Lance Corpo-ral Mike Hoffman at a protest against the Iraq War at Dover Air Force Base during the first anniversary of the war in March 2004. According to my interview with Goodrich, the two began to "talk about the idea of an organization [for Iraq War veterans] and went through various iterations of name and mission statement." These conversations contin-ued as the two met additional Iraq War–era veterans at antiwar events across the United States. In July 2004, six Iraq War veterans took the stage at the VFP annual convention at the historic Faneuil Hall in Bos-ton to announce the official formation of IVAW. The founders of this new organization included four Marines (Mike Hoffman, Alex Ryabov, Jimmy Massey, and Isaiah Pallos), two Army soldiers (Kelly Dough-erty and Diana Morrison), and one member of the Air Force (Tim Goodrich).[4] Each of them served in the Middle East in some capacity supporting the war on terror, and while many of them initially sup-ported the war, by 2004 these individuals believed the war was wrong.

In the months preceding the 2004 VFP convention, these activists found each other through VFP and MFSO, as well as other peace or-ganizations and events. Several of them, such as Hoffman, whose Ma-rine artillery unit entered Iraq with the initial invasion, had already spoken at numerous antiwar events. According to Goodrich, IVAW founders were political novices: "[IVAW] was an extremely loose or-ganization, and to tell you the truth, we didn't know what the hell we were doing. None of us. I mean, we were all fresh out of the military, and we were all still in shock from our experience. We were trying to figure out what to do. Organizing was this new thing for us. It was just completely on-the-job training." The first IVAW members had recently left a rigid institution that disparaged protest and were reeling from the consequences of war. The mentorship by and connections to VFP, MFSO, and VVAW members were important for these individuals and this organization's development (see chapter 3).

The organization grew from eight members in July 2004 to over one hundred in November. IVAW expanded steadily to eight hundred members in March 2008, when it experienced a growth spurt following the organization's March 13–16, 2008, Winter Soldier: Iraq and Afghanistan events.[5] Following these events, as IVAW executive director Kelly Dougherty described in a newsletter, the organization processed a deluge of applications. In the fall of 2008, IVAW claimed over 1,300 members in forty-nine states. IVAW membership was open to anyone who had served in the U.S. Armed Forces, including the National Guard and the Reserve forces, since 9/11.

At the end of 2008, IVAW had fifty-six chapters, including one in Canada and one in Germany. The first IVAW international chapter was established in 2006 when IVAW members recognized and helped organize servicemembers who resisted war deployments by fleeing to Canada. At or near Army bases, IVAW founded five chapters primarily comprising active duty personnel. IVAW members were stationed at U.S. military bases in Iraq, Afghanistan, and many other countries. Chris Capps founded the first chapter outside North America. Capps went AWOL while stationed in Germany when he was ordered to Afghanistan not even a year after returning from a ten-month tour in Iraq with the Army's 440th Signal Battalion. Capps turned himself in at Fort Sill, Oklahoma, and he was fortunate to be quickly discharged from the military without having to serve time in a military prison. Upon release from the military, Capps joined his wife in Germany, where he established an IVAW chapter near the U.S. military installations in Frankfurt, and in 2009 he was working to help U.S. soldiers stationed there find IVAW and to help end the German government's attempts to send Iraqi refugees back to Iraq.

IVAW began with the following three points of unity: (1) the United States and its allies should immediately withdraw from Iraq; (2) American governmental and corporate control of Iraq's resources should end, and America should provide reparations for the human and other damages caused by the war; and (3) returning American servicemembers should receive full benefits, including both mental and physical health care. Although IVAW activists initially debated whether to support war resisters, they made this support an important component of the organization's antiwar strategy. In early 2009, IVAW members voted to add a resolution opposing the war in Afghanistan. The organization also added a resolution against the military's Don't Ask, Don't Tell policy, which restricted gays and lesbians from serving openly. IVAW had difficulties with radicalization and what a few members called an attempted "take over by the International Socialist Organization" from 2008 to 2009, but by 2010 the most-radical members had left to form March Forward! a veterans' organization affiliated with Act Now to Stop War and End Racism (ANSWER), which was begun by the Workers World Party, a U.S. communist organization.

Gold Star Families for Peace and Gold Star Families Speak Out

In January 2005, Cindy Sheehan and nine other family members of slain servicemembers found each other through MFSO and online searches. Cindy Sheehan's son, Army Specialist Casey Sheehan, was killed in the Sadr City suburb of Baghdad on April 4, 2004, and she was joined by her then husband, Patrick Sheehan, and her sister, Dede Miller, in founding Gold Star Families for Peace (GSFP). Sheehan was joined by Lila Lipscomb and Sue Niederer, two women whose criticism of the Iraq War had also made the news. Michael Moore's film *Fahrenheit 9/11* featured Lipscomb because her support for the war eroded when her son, Army Sergeant Michael Pederson, died in Iraq. Niederer gained national notoriety when she was arrested for interrupting a campaign speech by Laura Bush in September 2004 and asking why her son, Army Second Lieutenant Seth Dvorin, "had to die" in Iraq. Other founding members included Bill Mitchell (whose son, Army Sergeant Michael Mitchell, died in the attack that killed Casey Sheehan), Jane and Jim Bright (whose son, Army Sergeant Evan Ashcroft, died in Iraq in 2003), and Celeste Zappala (whose son, Sergeant Sherwood Baker, was the first Pennsylvania Army National Guard soldier to die in war since 1945). They formed GSFP to be both a political organization and a support group for families who had paid the ultimate price for the war. They used the military distinction Gold Star, which is designated for families whose loved ones have died in war. At the organization's peak, it claimed a membership of one hundred Gold Star family members.

In the summer of 2005, the organization received tremendous media coverage, and Cindy Sheehan's name became synonymous with antiwar protests. At the VFP convention in Dallas, Sheehan was a featured speaker. She called for people to join her in protesting outside President Bush's ranch in Crawford about two hours away. On August 6, 2004, a caravan of twenty vehicles, which included VFP's white-and-blue Impeachment Tour bus, carrying Sheehan and a number of Iraq and Vietnam veterans arrived in Crawford. Sheehan, the veterans, Gold Star and military families, and other activists stayed in what they refer to as "the ditch" for a protest that lasted twenty-six days and brought tens of thousands of people to this rural section of Texas. Sheehan's status as a mother who had lost her son in the war was an important element for both the media coverage and reenergizing the peace movement, which had lost steam after failing to stop the war and after President Bush's 2004 reelection.[6] The image of a grieving mother was a powerful symbol in war protests worldwide and could be seen in Madres de Plaza de Mayo in Argentina and in various Women in Black protests from Israel to the Balkans.[7]

By the fall of 2005, personality differences, disputes about Sheehan's statements on a wide variety of conflicts, and the media's exclusive focus on Sheehan led a number of Gold Star parents to leave GSFP and form a chapter of MFSO exclusively for those whose family members died as a result of their military service. Whereas GSFP had initially focused on ending the Iraq War, Sheehan developed a wider focus on conflicts around the world, including Venezuela and Israel. These statements were heavily criticized by right-wing members of the media and Internet bloggers, as well as by some of the Gold Star families. Although Gold Star families were active in the anti–Iraq War movement before Sheehan, the media attention on her and her ability to travel full time as a peace activist meant that her every action or speech was seen as a statement by GSFP. Furthermore, whereas the other organizations in this movement became professionalized, with boards, staffs, votes, and other forms of communication, Sheehan maintained almost total control of GSFP. Many Gold Star families' feelings toward Sheehan remained raw throughout my research.

By 2008, GSFP existed largely in name only (even the website disappeared for a few years), and most organizing of families whose loved ones had died as a result of war was coordinated by Gold Star Families Speak Out (GSFSO). Two stated goals of GSFSO separated it from GSFP. First, the organization was committed to all of its members' stories being told, which stemmed from frustration with the media's focus on Sheehan. Second, the organization paid more attention to providing support than did GSFP. Its website read:

> The first place we seek peace is in our own hearts, recognizing our own and our nation's need to grieve. All of us in this group have suffered a tremendous loss and as long as we stick together, we can and will make a difference.

This statement outlines how GSFSO sought to overcome the elements of GSFP and Sheehan that frustrated members. During my fieldwork a number of Gold Star mothers expressed their concern that in the rush of events and speaking out involved in the Crawford protests and their aftermath in 2005, people were not able to properly grieve and did not receive the necessary emotional support. GSFSO was open to people whose loved ones had served in the military since September 2001 and who were killed or had died, including from suicide. In the fall of 2008, GSFSO had 125 members and was represented on the MFSO board by Karen Meredith, whose only child, First Lieutenant Kenneth Ballard, died in Najaf, Iraq, from small-arms fire on May 30, 2004. In 2011 communications, however, GSFSO activists expressed a need for more attention from the larger peace movement, writing that families whose loved ones had died were "often utilized for protest participation but then forgotten when it [came] time for their needs."

Working Together: Bring Them Home Now Bus Tour, September 2005

These military peace movement organizations frequently acted as a coalition, and the members developed strong bonds that crossed organizational affiliation (see chapter 4). They shared many focuses and addressed many issues simultaneously, and their members often shared physical spaces as well as similar concerns. The historical overview in this chapter separates these organizations, but by examining one of their early tactics, traveling speaking tours of military peace movement activists, one can see how they functioned collectively as a culture of action.

When President Bush finished his vacation and left Crawford at the end of August 2005, the month-long protest associated with Sheehan outside his ranch did not simply end. Rather, members of IVAW, VFP, MFSO, and GSFP organized three bus tours that traveled the United States before converging in Washington, D.C., for a massive protest with the broader peace movement. This series of events was called the Bring Them Home Now Tour and comprised over fifty-eight speaking events in twenty-eight states.[8] Each bus was staffed with organizers who helped coordinate media and arrange speaking events, as well as with members from each of the organizations. Local members of these organizations and other peace movement activists in each different locale helped organize events that included memorials (see chapter 5), media interviews and appearances, town hall–style speaking engagements, prayer vigils, visits to politician's offices, marches, and other activities.

The tour coincided with the immediate aftermath of Hurricane Katrina, which had devastated New Orleans and Mississippi and Alabama's Gulf Coast. Members of the tour frequently linked the use of the National Guard and Reserves in Iraq and the financial costs of that war to the inadequate government response to the hurricane. That was not, however, the primary message of the tour. It was designed to build on the media attention afforded to the Crawford protests and mobilize people to join peace movement activities in order to put pressure on the national government to quickly end the war in Iraq. The events in Crawford had gained national media attention on nearly every day of the protests, prior to which the U.S. peace movement had been out of the national spotlight since the early days of the war. Members of the military peace movement saw the bus tour as a way to bring their personal stories of the war to people who could not get to remote Crawford.

Tour members believed that when people heard these personal stories of the horrors of war, they would be motivated to spend more time in peace movement activism. This message was clear in the Evanston, Illinois, rally held by the northern bus tour. Members of local peace organizations constructed a cross display to symbolize the deaths of American soldiers in Iraq. Gold Star mother Karen Meredith spoke first and was followed by Al Zappala. Zappala described how his son was killed in Iraq and told the crowd that the bus tour was not intended for preaching to the choir. He said, "Now it's time for the choir to start preaching to America. Talk to your neighbor; talk to your congressman. Try to get into the media as much as you can, but talk." Zappala related his visit with Meredith to the office of Walter Jones, a conservative North Carolina Republican who had famously led the effort to redesignate the U.S. Capitol cafeteria's french fries as "freedom fries" in protest of France's decision to oppose the U.S. invasion of Iraq. Zappala said that these Gold Star parents had moved Jones to tears and that Jones had changed his mind about the war and now opposed it. He said, "If he can change, anybody can change. That's what I am asking you to do: change those people." At the time of the tour, American public opinion continued to favor the war, but the tide was turning. Tour members believed that if they could change public perception of the war, they could end it.

At that stop in Evanston, two military wives, an MFSO member with multiple ties to the military, a male Iraq War veteran, and two other Gold Star parents also offered emotional testimonies about how the war had affected them. After giving a speech about the war tearing her marriage apart and about her fears that the war would change her husband physically, emotionally, and mentally, MFSO member Tammara Rosenleaf explained the importance of the military peace movement, saying, "People listen to us because we have skin in the game." Rosenleaf meant that military families literally had their loved ones on the line in the war, unlike most Americans. She continued by telling the audience that the seventy-six crosses honoring the lives of Illinois servicemembers who had died in Iraq represented their communities' skin in the game—that the good those people could have brought to their communities was lost. She said, "The lives they could have touched will forever remain untouched." The local organizer said that the speakers were "inspirational" and that people now had "more reasons to end the war."

The Bring Them Home Now Tour concluded when these organizations joined the rest of the United for Peace and Justice Coalition in a march on Washington, D.C. They arranged for Camp Casey DC to be set up on the National Mall, a space that included not only tents used in Crawford, as well as signs and pictures from there, but also a display of boots that represented American lives lost in the war. Inside the main tent were tables for each of the organizations. When I arrived at the tent, a gray-haired woman asked if I was a military family member, and when I replied affirmatively, I was given my first MFSO T-shirt. I was told that there were safe spaces for military veterans and families away from other peace activists, and another military spouse pointed me toward where to gather. As she did so, she pointed out the other organizations in the Bring Them Home Now Coalition and explained that we, as military families, needed to march together with the veterans, though with IVAW "going first, of course." I watched as members of these four organizations interacted with a lot of hugging and bantering. People ran back and forth between the four organizations' gathering spots to pass on information about where to meet up after the march for meetings as well as social events. Members of each organization decided to march with their friends in other organizations from this culture of action. I watched, however, as some members shielded each other from activists thought to be from nonmilitary groups. In fact, before I put the T-shirt on, every time I tried to talk to a veteran or a military family member, I was asked to explain who I was.

That September 26, 2005, march drew between 100,000 and 300,000 people. By my count, over two hundred military families marched with MFSO, nearly one hundred Gold Star families (several dozen from one southern family of an African American killed in Iraq), a few dozen veterans from IVAW, and several hundred VFP members. Certainly, the military peace movement's activities in Crawford and the bus tour had had an effect—this antiwar protest was the largest since the invasion of Iraq. The obvious links between the military peace movement organizations at this event demonstrated that the organizations operated as a unique culture of action within the broader peace movement. Activists distinguished themselves as separate in part because they recognized that they shared unique costs and risks in this war and for their activism.

MILITARY-STYLE HIGH-RISK ACTIVISM

The majority of Americans faced few consequences for engaging in peace activism during the Iraq War.[9] Most peace activists faced, if anything, short-term arrest and minimal criminal punishment for civil-disobedience activism. Some peace activists had their privacy invaded when they were monitored by U.S. intelligence services throughout the war.[10] For many members of the military peace movement, however, particularly veterans of recent wars and their families, the consequences of their activism separated them from the rest of the U.S. peace movement. Military connections turned what would otherwise be low-risk activism into high-risk activism.

Many veterans of the post-9/11 wars faced intense consequences if they engaged in activism, including military imprisonment, life on the run (sometimes with spouses and children), and giving up military careers. The majority of MFSO and IVAW activists to whom I spoke expressed fears about their activism, including harming their own or their loved ones' careers, receiving negative repercussions from the military such as loss of pay or being deployed, and being ostracized from their family or the military community, upon whom they were very reliant due to the isolated and demanding nature of the military. Some of these activists lost jobs, homes, and relationships because of their commitment or overcommitment to activism. A number of activists, both veterans and families, described how peace activism reopened psychological war wounds. These fears, emotions, and realities fell into three broad categories of risk: official, estrangement, and psychological.

Although these categories of risk applied to members of all four organizations, the risk that each activist took varied. IVAW members faced the most serious consequences for anti–Iraq War activism—particularly, those who decided to protest while still on active duty military status. Some VFP members had confronted similar consequences during Vietnam or other war periods, but during the Iraq War most members faced less official risk for protest. For MFSO members, the official risks they faced were often secondhand, such as the loss of a job or a promotion for their military family member; these losses had real consequences, though, such as strains on budgets and depression. For GSFP and GSFSO members, much of the official or estrangement risk was gone because their loved ones had already died. Protest did mean, however, that the psychological wounds caused by these deaths were continually reopened. Thus in the discussion of two types of risk, official and estrangement, I focus on IVAW and MFSO members. I then demonstrate how peace activism had psychological risks for all members of the military peace movement.

Official Risks

I categorize the possibility of institutional sanctions for activity in this movement, mainly from the military, as official risks. Military regulations required most Iraq and Afghanistan veterans to leave the military in order to protest the war. As explained in the introduction, military members during the Iraq War were more likely to have families, or what the military called "dependents," than were military members during previous long-term conflicts. Due to the frequent moves, geographic isolation, and other requirements of military life, many military members' families depended on military income for their financial well-being.[11] Additionally, military training was not always applicable to the civilian workforce, so when protest meant a lost job, the risk was serious for the whole family.

Vietnam veteran and Army Special Forces Master Sergeant Stan Goff (Retired) described this risk in VFP's fall 2003 newsletter:

> Soldiers in uniform do not have the First Amendment freedom to criticize their superior officers about war-related matters, and that goes right up to the Commander-in-Chief. The families, of course, have their First Amendment freedom, but the reality is that the officer and enlisted personnel management systems control a soldier's career, and they can be extremely subjective. One bad line in your file can ruin your career.

As Goff made clear, the military monitored not only the public but also some private speech of its members. Speech or actions that were openly critical of military and political leadership could subject servicemembers to a variety of punishments, including courts-martial. Although military family members' speech and actions were theoretically not subject to this monitoring and these consequences, numerous servicemembers faced consequences for their family members' public antiwar declarations. Military members and their families thus confronted serious official risks for antiwar protest.

Conscientious and Selective Objectors

A number of military peace movement participants were conscientious objectors (COs) or selective objectors who risked their careers and their freedom by going public with their antiwar views while in the service. During the Iraq War, military regulations determined that COs were individuals whose moral, religious, or ethical belief systems caused them to refuse to participate in any and all wars. The U.S. military offered an honorable or a general discharge to members of the military who proved through an application process that they were COs and that they shifted to those beliefs after they joined the military. Because the U.S. military was an AVF, an individual who was believed to have developed CO beliefs before entering the military was seen as having joined the military under false pretenses to gain various benefits and was subject to a variety of punishments, including military imprisonment.[12] Selective objectors were those who refused participation in a particular war or wars because the individual's religious, moral, or ethical beliefs found fault with that particular war, in this case the Iraq War and/or the Afghanistan War. The military did not recognize selective objection as a valid reason for obtaining a discharge. In fact, the military often rejected CO applications that included political or policy critique of a particular war, even when coupled with a significant moral objection to all wars. Servicemembers accused by the military of using the CO application to obtain a discharge for other reasons, including selective objection, were subject to imprisonment, fines, courts-martial, and other punishments.

Some IVAW members, such as Michael Blake, Stephen Potts, and Joshua Casteel, applied for CO status and had their applications approved after a lengthy and varyingly burdensome process. The military often waited until after a deployment to announce approval of a CO application, as they did for Peter Brown, a 2004 West Point graduate who sued the Army in federal court in 2007 with the help of the ACLU after his initial CO application was denied. Although some members of IVAW were able to achieve CO status, this process often alienated these individuals from their friends and coworkers and caused the individuals to lose their military benefits and careers.

For others who believed that they were COs, including Augustin Aguayo, Camillo Mejía, and Mark Wilkerson, this discharge never came. The military denied these men's applications. Some of these men were provided bogus information about how to apply for CO status from senior officials and harassed during the process of their application. Wilkerson's superior told him he had only two weeks from the time he began talking to other members of his unit about his belief that war was wrong to submit his application packet, which meant he turned in a rushed application without any guidance from organizations and individuals who specialized in this process.

In addition, many CO applicants reported being harassed by the people required to interview CO applicants and to assess them. According to Wilkerson, during his interviews with the military psychologist, this medical professional called him a coward and explained that as a Vietnam veteran, the psychologist did not believe in conscientious objection. Although Wilkerson's CO application claimed moral opposition to war not based in any particular faith denomination, he was also interviewed by a military chaplain. The chaplain asked him how he could know that war was wrong without "consulting the Bible" and explained that what the United States was doing in Iraq was "justified by God." Not surprising, these men's evaluations were not favorable toward Wilkerson's application.

Mark Wilkerson, like many others, believed the denial of his CO application meant that he had no other choice but to serve in Iraq for a second tour, which directly conflicted with his conscience. Wilkerson described the result of the application's denial as follows:

> I found out at the end of November that it was denied and that they would expect me to return to Iraq. Keep in mind that this entire time I'd been going under the assumption I would be getting out. So I didn't

do weapons training. I didn't prepare myself financially, emotionally for this impending return to Iraq. It hit me like a ton of bricks, and I didn't really know what to do at that point. I thought maybe I could do a rebuttal and find a way to stay behind. Those oral appeals did not work. So I was left with the decision to go unprepared emotionally, physically, mentally, every, every way possible unprepared, or do I go AWOL and stick with these, these new beliefs that I had found, I had discovered, and keep them intact by choosing not to go? So after some very, very careful deliberations, as good as I could give it, we [Wilkerson and his wife] made the decision that it was best that I left.

Wilkerson was shocked and upset when his application was denied. He felt that he was left with few options. During this time Wilkerson also faced harassment for his CO application, and some of the harassment felt like threats against his life. He recounted, "A staff sergeant told me he was passing on a message to me from high above. If I embarrassed the unit or made them look foolish, I might not find myself returning from Iraq a second time." Since Wilkerson felt trapped and endangered, he went on the run.

Wilkerson evaded the military for a year and a half. He had only a few weeks to plan his departure. He made it look like he was preparing to move his wife home during his deployment, so he and members of his unit packed their belongings into a moving truck.[13] Daily, he withdrew cash from an ATM, and initially, Wilkerson and his wife tried to stay off the military's radar. They lived in a hotel booked in a friend's name, and he did not tell his parents where he and his wife were staying. Going on the run meant giving up his paycheck and not being able to get a new job or rent an apartment for fear of background checks. This was stressful, and Wilkerson described how simple things became complicated: "I was driving, knowing that I could be pulled over for speeding and be arrested at any minute. I had to be extra careful. I couldn't just kind of zone out like so many people do when they drive." As time went on, Wilkerson became braver as his wife and then he got a job. The situation strained his marriage, however, and he eventually moved into his parents' house without her.

In the end, Wilkerson saw that his life was deteriorating because he was AWOL, and he decided to turn himself in. He said: "I didn't like the situation I was in. I was already kind of separating and drifting apart from my wife. And I wanted to go to school and make something of myself. I wanted to have a better job that required a background check. So I decided that was the right time for me to go back [to the military], so I did." Being AWOL meant that Wilkerson had to put his personal, financial, and educational goals on hold. While AWOL, Wilkerson befriended members of IVAW and other military peace movement organizations, and they helped him arrange the press conference described at the start of this chapter. As he prepared to surrender at Fort Hood in Killeen, Texas, he was gaunt and appeared frightened. Life on the run had not been easy, and he knew the military was likely to imprison him for desertion at a time of war. The August 31, 2006, press conference attracted significant attention to the issue of AWOL soldiers who, like a growing number of Americans, had become disillusioned with the mission in Iraq.

Wilkerson waited six months, mostly in the brig at Fort Hood, before his court-martial. Wilkerson's civilian lawyer, who specialized in these cases and had been contacted through the military peace movement, got him a sentence that was shorter than those of most other soldiers who had gone AWOL. He was sentenced to seven months in the military prison at Fort Sill, Oklahoma, and was given one month off for his work in the prison and for prior good behavior. Wilkerson said, "So my original release date was sometime in September, and I was released on July 13—*greatest day of my life*." After Wilkerson left military prison in 2007, he became an active IVAW member and spoke about his moral opposition to the Iraq War and his experiences in Iraq. Few modern-day U.S. activists, particularly in the peace movement, faced consequences like Wilkerson's and those of others in the military. At the time of his interview, nearly one year after he left prison, the Army had not officially discharged Wilkerson, and the strain of this process had left him separated from his wife.

Family members of AWOL soldiers explained the stress of the process from their perspective, as well. One parent described having her son, an Army corporal, on the run as "agonizing and paranoia inducing." Several discussed the financial and personal burdens that the AWOL process, the trial, and prison induced.

Conscientious objection has been an acceptable reason for potential soldiers to avoid war throughout American history and the histories of many other countries.[14] Objection to specific wars, as opposed to war in general, has typically resulted, however, in jail time.[15] Selective objection disrupts the chain of command in a military and challenges the foundations of a war, as well as civilian authority over militaries.

Military Punishment

Some members of IVAW and most of the loved ones of MFSO members stayed in the military and faced other consequences. The most common fear these members of the military peace movement expressed about their activism was that they or their loved ones could lose their military careers. Many others were afraid they or their servicemembers would be passed up for promotion or be arbitrarily sent to a more dangerous or difficult situation.

In 2008, MFSO began an initiative to encourage spouses to publicly critique the wars their wives or husbands were being asked to fight. The planning committee discussed this fear as the number-one reason most military spouses who opposed the war did not speak publicly or join MFSO. In a speech in 2006, Tammara Rosenleaf described how her husband was harassed in Iraq by his superiors for her activism. He was threatened with extended time in the war zone, and various measures were taken to hinder his communication with Tammara or to otherwise make his life more miserable. Parents also reported that their servicemembers were told they would face punishment for their parents' antiwar activism. MFSO founder Nancy Lessin said, however, that one man's superior was supposed to order him to get his "wife under control." Instead, the superior asked him to pass on the message, "You go girl!" Some MFSO members did, though, cut back their activism after their loved one was threatened or missed a promotion.

The military cut ties with some IVAW members who decided to protest. As discussed in the introduction, military members faced various consequences, including imprisonment and discharge, for speech based on vague and broadly interpreted rules in the UCMJ. IVAW member Thomas J. Buonomo, a former Army intelligence officer, was involuntarily discharged from the Army because he expressed his belief that Vice President Dick Cheney should be impeached for "deliberately deceiving members of Congress regarding prewar intelligence on Iraq." Buonomo was charged with numerous violations of the UCMJ resulting from conversations he had with fellow officers and open letters he sent to Congress about the Iraq War. He was convicted of violating UCMJ Article 88, which prohibits making contemptuous statements against the vice president, and was discharged from the Army.

In addition to losing their careers, activists were threatened with downgraded discharges, and sometimes the threat was carried out. Military discharges affect a veteran's access to benefits, and dishonorable discharges can carry the stigma of a felony conviction. The Marine Corps made these threats against members of IVAW on Individual Ready Reserve (IRR) status who wore their uniforms to a March 2007 protest. Servicemembers on IRR status are already discharged from active duty, not on the military payroll, and generally not considered military personnel. Technically, though, they can be called back to active duty should the military need them. IVAW member Adam Kokesh, who had been honorably discharged the previous year after serving in Iraq, was contacted by the Marines about his activism. Kokesh wrote a strongly worded response to the Marine investigator, admonishing the major for wasting the military's time and money during war and telling him, "Please, kindly, go fuck yourself." Shortly thereafter, Kokesh was informed that the Marines were holding a hearing to downgrade his discharge status to Other Than Honorable. That change would have stripped Kokesh's access to veterans' health care services, and he would have been required to pay the military in excess of $10,000 for veterans' educational benefits he received. The hearing resulted in a downgraded discharge status, but not to the level suggested, allowing Kokseh to retain most of his benefits.

Military threats of discharge changes or forced return to Iraq were sometimes successful in limiting or ending military peace movement members' protests. At least one member of IVAW who was threatened with changes to his discharge status agreed to not wear his uniform in future protests in order to keep his veterans' benefits, which included health care and payments for being physically and psychologically

disabled during the Iraq War. Later, this activist decided to quit protesting because he feared being sent back to Iraq, since the military
had restored him to active duty from the IRR.

Risk of Estrangement

Activists had to step beyond their communities' and, often, their own
prejudices in order to join the peace movement. Military-affiliated individuals understood that military culture stereotyped peace activists
and that their decision to join peace activism meant leaving behind
many connections to the military world. Because they engaged in antiwar activism, many military peace movement activists were accused
of not being "real veterans" or part of "actual military families" by
conservative commentators, in public comments in the media, and by
right-wing blogs. Rather than recount this negative treatment of veterans and military family members, this section focuses on activists'
own descriptions of this estrangement from the military community.

Lost Community

Concerns about leaving their brothers and sisters in arms behind or
hung out to dry were common among military peace activists. Many
activists understood that by joining in peace activism, they would
be estranged from the family-like atmosphere of the military. Liam
Madden, a Marine who left active duty twenty-two days before our
interview, described military assumptions about protestors. He said,
"There is a whole culture of [protest] being taboo or being disloyal, a
hippie or whatever they want to label you, and its partly based on fear,
not based on what is actually permissible." Although veterans and
active duty members were allowed to join peace organizations, Madden said that doing so was outside the norm because of a pervasive
feeling that protest demonstrated unfaithfulness to military brothers and sisters. These veterans and military families recognized how
difficult military life was and expressed concerns that activism could
cause stress in addition to that already brought on by the war. Some
feared that as one Afghanistan veteran described it, activism might
"put troops in a bad place," causing low morale or other conditions

that could lead to deaths or injuries on the battlefield. These apprehensions revealed their fears that antiwar participation could harm their connections to the military community.

A number of military peace movement members held stereotypes of peace protestors prior to their activism. Before his activism, Cloy Richards thought peace activists were "a bunch of long-haired hippy freaks" that "just hate the man . . . hate the government." The military commonly stereotyped peace activists as hippies, possibly because of stories of military members being spat on by protestors during the Vietnam War.[16] These stereotypes made it difficult for military-affiliated individuals to develop solidarity with the peace movement.

Although they agreed with their organizations, many members of the movement were afraid of the consequences of their activism. A senior officer's wife joined MFSO but asked that all her information remain anonymous. She feared that her activism would not only hurt her husband's career but also ostracize her from the only community she had known for the past twenty-plus years. Activists were concerned with the way they would be perceived by the military community if their activism was made public. This may explain why military peace movement organizations had significantly more enrolled members than they had people involved in public forms of protest.

For people in the military peace movement, it was often painful to have their loyalty to the military called into question. Richards recalled an incident in which people questioned his combined Marine peace activist identity:

But sometimes it does get hard. I was out protesting in my dress blues one time, and I was on a street corner. I was standing next to my mom, and she was just holding a sign saying "bring them home now," and I was standing next to her and a guy who was in the Marine Corps for twenty-some years. He was a colonel or something, and he pulls over and comes up to me and says, "Marine, what are you doing? You're a disgrace to your uniform." And I was just like, I stood there, and he said, "You come over here right now." And I said, "You can't order me what to do. You're retired, and I'm already out." He's like, "You need to take that off right now! You're disgracing your country and your Corps." And I said, "Why? By standing next to my mom in my uniform?" I was like, "I'm a Marine. I'll always be a Marine, and just because I don't have the same viewpoint as you doesn't mean, do you think that every Marine should agree with every Marine? What do you think that everyone who serves in the military agrees with everybody else and their ideologies and everything? No!"

When Richards described this confrontation, he wore a pained expression on his face. Being a Marine was a key element of his identity. To have this questioned by a stranger was hurtful. As he and other veteran activists explained during interviews, speeches, and other activist moments, they were frustrated by people's expectations that military members "toe the line" on the war and remain silent about their misgivings and their negative experiences. These frustrations led to feelings of estrangement from a community that was an important part of their identity.

Lost Resources and Services

Many MFSO and GSFP members were ostracized by military family organizations on which they depended for information about their loved ones' deployments and for support during difficult times. A few spouses and mothers who spoke openly about their antiwar beliefs were asked to leave military-initiated and civilian-initiated support organizations. Several mothers of military members told me they were asked to leave websites and Internet chat rooms that provided support, information, and other resources to them and their servicemember. Tina Richards, who had joined MarineMom.com, spoke at length about how important this group was for her when her son first enlisted in the Marines. She engaged in actions that encouraged the children of others on the site, and she and her son benefited from the group's care packages and other support. When she questioned President Bush's axis of evil speech and, later, the grounds for the Iraq War, however, she said they decided that she could either shut up or get out, and she lost those resources and that support network. When military family members criticized the Iraq War within spousal or family support groups affiliated with military units, they were often asked to keep their opinions to themselves, while others in the groups were allowed to support the policies of the war.

Many activists in the movement could not stay silent and were thus estranged from the resources of the military community. Stacy Hafley, whose husband was in the active duty Army, described her estrangement during his deployment to Iraq as follows:

> I pretty much got ousted from [the Family Readiness Group] and was told not to attend any more. . . . I don't make any qualms of just telling people flat out [that I am against the war], and I figured I was just going to let it out beginning with the deployment so all these wives would understand that I don't want this rah, rah, rah, hoo-ahh, you know, uber-patriotic crap around me, 'cause it makes me sick. So . . . I wasn't going to lie to these people and be someone I wasn't and be the good little Army wife, which I never was, so . . . they pretty much asked me not to come anymore.

As Hafley described, military communities were typically intolerant of pubic criticism of the war. When MFSO activists were cut off from these groups, they missed critical support and information that helped sustain families while their loved ones were at war. These organizations provided a sense of community in a military life that was filled with frequent moves and long-distance relationships. The group from which Hafley was estranged organized a variety of morale- and community-boosting events for the families of those deployed, including video calls to deployed servicemembers and holiday parties for their children. These organizations offered information on how to navigate military bureaucracy and about the deployments themselves, including return dates. While a number of military spouses felt "OK with being kicked out" of these groups, they gave up a sense of community with military members in order to be activists.

Although Hafley and many other MFSO activists believed they did not miss interacting with these people who unquestioningly supported the war, this estrangement had critical consequences. Without these groups, MFSO spouses were left unaided while they lived without their servicemembers on or near bases, which were usually far from family and other friends. This made them vulnerable when unforeseen circumstances, such as their own illness or a child's injury, arose. During her husband's deployment, Hafley's family lost their house and everything in it due to a severe black mold infestation. While other military families could have reached out to military support groups for help finding a place to stay or preparing meals, Hafley's ostracism placed her out of that network, leaving her family briefly homeless. A few months later, while her husband was still deployed, Hafley became very ill. When she asked the military for help, they threatened to have her children taken away by the state unless she found someone else to care for them. Hafley turned to a variety of military-focused charities and NGOs but received virtually no help. In the meantime, the money she was spending on babysitters forced her family to seek charity for food. Had Hafley forwent activism and maintained a bond with a military family support group, the group would have likely stepped in to help, as they often did when other members fell ill or when someone had a new baby.

Even more extraordinary, her activist beliefs kept her husband's military command from sending him home to help. Hafley said that her inability to be a stereotypical military wife made her unafraid to seek help from her U.S. congressman. He began two investigations that recommended her husband be reassigned to an Army Reserve command near his family in order to help care for the children. His commanding officer, however, ignored these recommendations and, at least five times, denied his requests for emergency leave. Hafley said of the officer:

> He just thought I was faking it. Because he knew I was against the war. Because I made no bones about telling people in the unit, you know, that I'm against the war. So basically, he thought that I was doing this; this was my ploy to get my husband out of Iraq because we're both against the war. And unfortunately, I wish it was, 'cause it would have been crafty, but unfortunately, this is really what happened.

Hafley's antiwar activism almost led to the military intentionally letting her family fall apart. The commanding officer ignored recommendations by politicians and a variety of school and medical officials because he was unsympathetic to individuals who opposed the war. Fortunately, Hafley once again ignored the military chain of command and, this time, called the Pentagon, where she was transferred to the Army Inspector General. By this time, Hafley was incredibly angry with the entire situation, and she did not expect to do much more than "rant and cuss" into a recording. The inspector general admonished her, "Wives don't usually call the Pentagon." However, he personally saw to her husband's return from Iraq. Five days after the call, her husband telephoned from Kuwait to tell her he was on his way home. While Hafley was able to overcome the worst of what her activism cost her, veterans and military family activists were regularly denied services and connections that were vital to those facing deployments and war.

Disconnect from Families

In addition to being estranged from the military, some activists were alienated from their families because of their antiwar beliefs and activism. One MFSO mother told a crowd at a peace march in the Northeast that her son had not spoken to her in over a year because of her activism. She explained, "I had to do what was right, though, because I am still his mother, and I need to protect him." Some activist wives told me that their activism strained their relationships with deployed husbands, and a few activists divorced nonactivist spouses.

Some veterans who decided to protest also experienced strained relationships with their families. Stephen Potts's family reacted negatively to his decision to become a CO during the lead-up to the Iraq War. He described his mother's reaction to his decision as follows:

> My mother was angry and disappointed and all sorts of things. She still feels like the Iraq War and any sort of war that we would ever enter into is necessarily good. She believes in America. She believes in Bush. She believes in war. . . . She actually told me I was lying about [my pacifist beliefs]. She did not believe my sincerity in it, which was even more damning than disagreeing with me. She thought somehow that I was delusional. It was a bizarre reaction. And in fact, it was interesting comparing the reaction of my commander, who had known me for five years and told me, "You know, Stephen, I disagree with

you, but this seems like you, and I support you, and I believe you're sincere." And my own mother did not believe that I was sincere. And that hurt, that my own mother would be so caught up in her own beliefs that she couldn't or wouldn't see how I felt about it, you know, whereas a commander, who should have been so much more upset, was so much more loving to me. That was exceptionally hard.

Potts's decision to leave the military destroyed his relationship with his parents. It also strained his other family relationships. His grandmother sent him "a fairly nasty letter" criticizing his decision, and his CO application hurt his relationship with his brother, who otherwise agreed with him about the war and the military.

Antiwar activism caused military peace movement members to be estranged from some parts of the military community and from their families. This estrangement had a number of consequences. It challenged people's sense of identity. It separated them from friends and colleagues who were affiliated with the military. Additionally, activists were often ostracized from the community support systems that the military had put in place to help veterans and military families cope with deployments and war injuries.

Psychological Risks

Beyond the official risks and the risks of estrangement, activism opened military peace movement participants to the risk of deepening the psychological wounds of war. Antiwar activism required many military peace movement members to relive horrible events in the hope of challenging Americans' positive opinions of the Iraq War. Young veterans recounted stories of their own guilt and pain. Gold Star family members repeatedly talked about their dead loved ones and the sadness brought on by those losses. MFSO members narrated painful stories of children, spouses, and parents forever and negatively changed by war. Veterans of past wars were reminded of their own war experiences, and their own posttraumatic stress often worsened in connection with their activism. Some members of these organizations expressed concerns that their emotional struggles were being used by the antiwar movement, but even these people believed that the military peace movement had to continue "sharing [their] pain" in order to end the wars.

Painful Memories

Activism caused some participants, particularly IVAW members, significant emotional and psychological distress. An IVAW member who was an Iraq War veteran described in his writings how difficult it was for him to be a part of the Operation First Casualty protests. Operation First Casualty involved the enactment of scenes from the war in Iraq as a form of street theater in major U.S. cities.[17] IVAW members wore their uniforms and carried themselves as if on patrols through Iraqi streets, and members of other peace groups, often MFSO, GSFO, GSFP, and VFP, acted as Iraqi civilians or passed out flyers about the protest tactic. An Army Reservist wrote about his difficulty with this tactic in New York City:

> Upon performing the action and seeing the faces of confused bystanders, apparently shocked by the way in which the action went down, I began to wonder if anyone understood what sacrifice it took to do what we were doing. Personally, as soon as we began patrolling the streets, I caught myself slowly shifting into the role I had once performed on the streets of Iraq. Perhaps people saw us and thought us to be acting, but I can only say of myself, after a short period I found myself honestly checking windows of tall buildings looking for snipers. My arms had become rigid, as if they were made to hold a rifle. No longer was an alley just that; they all became danger areas I needed to use increased vigilance while crossing. In short, within just a short while I was reliving a nightmare. It was frightening to realize how easily I could reassume that role I had once performed in Iraq, and quite frankly, it bothered me slightly that some people assumed us to be actors, because I can assure those people we were not acting.

His activism brought him back to his time in the war zone, exacerbating his lingering emotional and psychological trauma. It made him hypervigilant and caused him to feel "dehumanized" and "degraded." This tactic was a particularly moving experience for many activists. A

FIGURE 5. IVAW members perform the guerrilla street theater Operation First Casualty in Washington, D.C., in March 2007 in order to demonstrate to U.S. citizens what war entails. Photograph by Lovella Calica.

number of the activists involved, especially IVAW members, described how enacting war "hit close to home," in the words of a Vietnam veteran. At the end of the tactic, many activists were moved to tears.

Many military peace movement activists were asked to tell their stories at events, which involved explaining their connection to the military and the Iraq War and telling intensely painful stories. On the Iraq War's fourth anniversary, Anne Roesler told a crowd in California about the war's effect on her son:

I walked into his apartment in the middle of the day. All of the blinds were shut against the daylight, and the air conditioning was set to meat locker–like temperatures. I had to put sweat clothes on for warmth, and I had to wake him from a sound sleep. I learned that this was how he spent his days. He had a memorial built to a close friend who had died during the second deployment, and later he showed me memorabilia from another close friend who'd died. He carries the memorabilia in his wallet. When I gently asked him about it, he began screaming that I wouldn't understand. He's right. Although I've seen photos and videotapes and heard some of the stories, I can't even begin to imagine what he's been through. At times, he exhibits a vulnerability that breaks my heart, telling me that he doesn't know who he is anymore and crying in my arms. At other times, I've seen a dark side that keeps me awake at night—a side that is so filled with rage and hate that all he can talk about is killing people. I barely dare to breathe when I talk with him for fear of unleashing this dark side, but it doesn't matter. It comes forth with a fury that is indescribable and without any provocation at all.

Family members like Roesler told deeply personal stories of the war's devastating effects on their family members' states of mind. As they did so, these activists expressed their own pain, as well.

Activists and their audiences often cried during these stories, and several described being "physically and emotionally drained" afterward. Some IVAW and VFP activists told me that when they first started speaking about their experiences, they had increased nightmares and other PTSD reactions. The emotional toll of activism was also visible on activists' bodies. After speeches in Crawford and in Washington, D.C., I watched as members of IVAW went still and became unresponsive. Other activists had to take a break and step away from the movement in order to "recover," in the words of one military spouse. She said, "I can't keep focusing on war and the trauma it caused or I'm never going to heal, and I'll certainly never be able to help my husband [an Iraq War veteran whose PTSD left him with severe anger issues]."

Betrayal's Sting and Costs

For many activists, recognizing that the war was wrong and becoming a protestor were made painful because of their military connections. One Army wife wrote an open letter to MFSO in which she described her frustration that people assumed her personal connection made it easier for her to become a protestor. She wrote the letter to demonstrate "how much harder it [was] to oppose the war and policies that started it when personally involved." She wished she could take pride in her patriotism and be reassured that her family's sacrifice during her husband's deployment would produce a better world and a safer country. Instead, the fruitlessness of the war made her pain more intense. She expressed how difficult activism was for military families:

> Of course, military families rarely oppose wars: we have the most to lose. It is too painful to add the knowledge that we are suffering pointlessly to our loneliness and worry. It is so much easier to believe the rhetoric, to sing the songs and wave the flags. But to do so is to deny reality; to obey our leaders unquestioningly is to betray the spirit of democracy and freedom. Neither I nor America can afford to pay that price.

Although her activism and her belief that the Iraq War was wrong caused her emotional distress, she continued to protest the war because she believed that, unlike the war, the risks involved were worth it.

Activists felt betrayed by "the American people, the military, and our political leaders," as one Southern California Army veteran in VFP said. A desire to oppose the war overtook other aspects of their lives and led some to develop a deep commitment to, or what he called a "need" for, activism. Gold Star family members Carlos and Mélida Arredondo lost jobs and came close to losing cars and their home because of their intense schedule of activism. The Arredondos believed that these consequences were acceptable given the intense pain brought on by the loss of their son and stepson, Lance Corporal Alexander S. Arredondo. That pain was most evident when during a family celebration of Carlos's forty-fifth birthday, Marines notified Carlos of Alex's death in Najaf, Iraq. Carlos was so despondent that he ran to the Marines' van, doused it and himself with gasoline, and nearly committed suicide.[18] Carlos suffered severe second-degree burns and had to be wheeled into the church on a hospital bed for his son's funeral. After he physically healed ten months later, Carlos, often with Mélida, traveled the country full time in order to, in his words, "talk about Alex so other parents won't have to go through this." Looking at the pictures of his son, the coffin, the flags, and the other funeral and military memorabilia that were a part of the memorial display that accompanied Carlos on his antiwar travels, he continued, "This is my burden."

FIGURE 6. Two versions of
GSFSO member Carlos
Arredondo's traveling
memorial to his son, Lance
Corporal Alex Arredondo,
who was killed in Iraq.
In the top photograph,
he speaks to C-Span in
Santa Barbara, and in the
left-hand photograph,
he pulls a coffin and
carries a picture of his
son in Washington, D.C.
Photographs by the author.

On December 19, 2011, Alex's brother, Brian Arredondo, committed suicide. According to statements by the family, he had battled depression stemming from his brother's death. Brian had been a regular at East Coast antiwar events. Statements by Cindy Sheehan and others called Brian "another innocent victim" of the Iraq "war of choice for profit." Emotional reactions to military casualties are common in military families, including those not designated by the military as dependents.[19]

Families whose servicemembers returned from war also experienced intense psychological trauma that caused them to seek out activism in spite of its physical and financial costs. In a blog entry on the MFSO website describing a vigil outside Congress from June 22 to August 4, 2006, one mother of an Iraq veteran explained that she was facing being fired for her participation in that vigil:

> When I returned home from my trip to Washington, DC where I met with various Senators, Representatives, and the Speaker of the House as part of MFSO's Operation House Call, I received a notice of pending termination of my employment on Aug. 31st. It seems I have been distracted. My priorities in life have changed since the war began. It has become my passion, my mission to be part of the frontline of peace. How can I not be? On a personal level my son is still suffering from his participation in this war. He has killed men, women and children.

This mother's personal connection to the war kept her from focusing on her job, and her activism got in the way of a normal life. As the mother of a veteran who experienced "flashbacks" and struggled with his role in the war, however, she saw no possibility other than being preoccupied with the war. In fact, she went on to describe how her activism made it difficult for her to obtain the basics of life, such as shelter and food. Although she faced these consequences her identity as a mother kept her focused on her antiwar activism.

Military peace movement activists often rationalized their desire for protest as a religious calling. Their connection to the war meant, however, that they faced tremendous psychological costs for heeding this call. Military peace movement activism often involved repeatedly reliving painful moments in front of audiences and the media, and I suspect that the psychological costs were similar to those faced by those who describe their own rape or abuse.[20] These psychological risks discouraged some from participating in activism and encouraged the exit of others.

CONCLUSION

The Iraq War caused the proliferation of organizations populated by veterans and military families, and a handful of these organizations assertively protested the war. MFSO, IVAW, VFP, GSFP, and GSFSO formed a unique culture of action within the larger U.S. antiwar movement. This culture of action was unique in both its protests and its organizations' connections to each other. Although this movement comprised four separate groups, each with its own connection to the military, these organizations often operated together. Maren Klawiter describes cultures of action as local phenomena, but this concept can also illuminate national subsections of movements.[21] In the case of the military peace movement, the geographic separation of activists led to an important national culture of action within the broader peace movement. This geographic isolation of activists at times facilitated cross-organization interaction. When only a handful of individuals in a town were in one organization, they tended to interact frequently with active chapters of other organizations in the military peace movement. MFSO had, for example, a strong chapter in Orange County that frequently incorporated IVAW and VFP members into their activities. More often, though, MFSO or IVAW members worked with VFP, which had a much larger membership.

Military connections increased the level of risk involved in peace movement activism, so that many military peace movement participants were involved in high-risk activism involving considerable physical, legal, financial, and social costs. Military personnel on active duty faced substantial physical risks, since activism could result in a superior's decision to send them to a war zone or place them in a dangerous position in that war zone. Additionally, the military was by its nature a violent institution, and the unpopularity of antiwar activism among the military could lead to physical fights or attacks. Military personnel had to be cautious of their speech and actions regarding the war, as some types of activities allowed to civilians could result in courts-martial, imprisonment, and other legal actions. Military veterans and families faced the social consequences of estrangement, job loss, and financial costs. Activists in the military peace movement expressed fears of these risks, and they were likely significant barriers to activism, as other risks can be for those in different movements.[22] These risks were an important aspect of the novelty of and the solidarity within this culture of action.

While imprisonment and the loss of work are among the risks identified in the literature on high-risk activism, such activism can also lead to estrangement and psychological harm. Although the psychological risks of activism are rarely described as such, social movement scholars should be attentive to the ways in which these risks affect mobilization, endurance, and other movement qualities. Military peace movement activism carried tremendous emotional burdens that activists had to overcome in order to stay active. By recognizing the isolating and emotional risks of activism, I broaden and suggest new categories within the concept of high-risk activism. When activists tell raw, personal stories, they are reliving painful events, which takes a significant toll that is every bit as damaging as the physical, legal, financial, and social costs already accepted as parts of high-risk activism. When people challenge the fundamental beliefs of their communities, they risk losing necessary connections to others, resulting in losses of information, access and support. These risks account for limited mobilization within and departures from a movement. All of these risks are community specific and differ by culture of action. Chapter 2 describes how the family community created by the military peace movement's culture of action helped activists handle these costs.

2

Insider–Outsiders

From Warriors to War Protestors

ormer Army Specialist Mike Blake served in Iraq during the initial invasion and then filed for and obtained an honorable discharge as a CO in February 2005. Blake learned things from his military service that brought him to the conclusion that he was more patriotic when he protested than when he was in the Army. Through Blake's story we see that idealism often ran head on into the realities of war, causing activists to experience disillusionment with the Iraq War.

Blake's reasons for joining were not unlike those of many enlisted personnel and officers in the military. He was "eighteen and thick-headed" when he joined the military. He enlisted because he liked the idea of "serving [his] country, and traveling to new places, and all these great things." He believed that "the Army was a really great idea" for his future. Blake described growing up in the "hunky-dory days of Bill Clinton," which was a time of limited large-scale military usage and few military personnel being killed. Of his thoughts on the military at the time, Blake said, "The military was mostly used for peace keeping—you know, Bosnia or Kosovo. . . . I just thought I would be doing something positive." His perspective changed with the wars in Afghanistan and Iraq. Blake said, "We weren't creating peace or being peaceful, and it was not what I wanted to be a part of." This realization was painful for him because he believed he had placed his loyalty with the wrong people and that he and "his brothers," other military personnel, were being betrayed. Blake's ideas of what America and its military should be were challenged by the Iraq War, and he sought out activism as a way to better demonstrate his patriotism.

A post of his on IVAW's website showed how Blake's transition and education about the war had created personal grievances. He wrote

FIGURE 7. Mike Blake (*third from right*) helps IVAW lead the March 14–19, 2006, Walkin' to New Orleans march along the U.S. Gulf of Mexico. Photograph by the author.

about meeting a prowar, nonveteran civilian at an event who asked him, "If you didn't want to go to war, why did you sign up in the first place, huh?" That question triggered a number of thoughts for Blake:

> Like many of my brothers and sisters in IVAW I signed up before Iraq, before Afghanistan, and before September 11th. There was no way we could have known that the government was going to launch us into an illegal and immoral war with no clear objectives and no end in sight. There's no way we could have known that they would poison us with experimental vaccines, larium, depleted uranium, and lies. There's no way we could have known that we would be used and abused on the battlefield, wounded, traumatized, and then dumped back into society without any counseling or reintegration training. How could we have known that we would have to fend for ourselves in the job market, without health care, with PTSD, with substance abuse, and with trying to reclaim a semblance of the life we had before all this mess started?[1] There is no way anyone can know what war is like until

you have been there, until you have smelled the stench and seen the bodies; until you feel death following you wherever you go. . . . I had seen shit that [the civilian] could never comprehend; and I had done shit that he would never, in a million years, have the courage to do. A part of me died in Iraq, it will forever be buried with the men we lost and the people we killed.

Blake outlined a process of becoming a military peace activist that involved various steps of education in the war. Blake described becoming disillusioned with the war because of politicians' or the military's "lies" and the harsh realities of the battlefield. In antiwar speeches and writings, military peace movement activists like Blake frequently addressed the issue of volunteering for service in Iraq. They separated the Iraq War from the type of military service in which they had intended to engage by calling the Iraq War illegal and immoral. This distinction allowed for an integration of their military and antiwar-activist identities. By blaming the government for problems such as PTSD, Blake broadened his personal grievances to a social problem.

In many ways, Blake was fortunate that his parents raised him in a progressive and liberal household. He portrayed his father as a hippie and his mother as a feminist. Although as a child Blake played war and was fascinated with war in school, he understood that "joining the military was a strange step." Blake's decision to enter the Army was not well accepted by his family, as he recalled in his interview:

My dad took it especially hard. I mean, he was a hippie; he lived the hippie lifestyle. . . . It was hard for him because when I was a child he told me that he didn't want his son going off and dying in an oil war. Yeah, I remember that. My mom, she took it hard as well, but she understood what I needed to do at the time.

Unlike those of many of his IVAW compatriots, Blake's parents had not raised him to seek out military service; instead, they had actively discouraged him from this path. Because of his parents' left-leaning political beliefs, he openly told them of his doubts about the Iraq War and wars in general, and they were sympathetic with his shift from combat soldier to activist. Each IVAW activist had his or her own journey to peace activism, but those with liberal parents had a greater exposure and access to critiques of the Iraq War. They also had critical support through a difficult identity process that could cause cognitive dissonance.

Although Blake was exposed to left-wing political ideals, received a firsthand education in war, developed grievances with the military, and redefined patriotism to include activism, his identity reorientation was not easy, and he even contemplated suicide:

> There was really a breaking moment when I went on midtour leave. I was in Iraq for a year, and eight months in, I got to go home on leave.[2] I came home, and I was all of a sudden surrounded by people who loved and cared about me rather than being around cold, callous people in a terrible place. It was such a shock to have all that around me again. See, my body was in the states, but my mind was still back there. I couldn't get out of that mentality, and I gradually started to realize how terrible it was what we were doing there and how sick that I had to be a part of it, that I had to go back to it. And when I got back to Iraq, the first night I called home and was just crying on the phone for like twenty minutes. And I went back to my tent, and just for a moment, I thought about chambering a round and putting a bullet in my skull. And that scared the shit out of me. It really did. And so I knew once I got back to the states, I knew that I could not be a part of it anymore, and that's when I filed for my CO discharge that I eventually got out on.

Many war veterans struggled to make sense of their experiences, and during the Iraq and Afghanistan wars, military suicide rates increased dramatically.[3] Blake, however, had family members with whom he could talk about his changing beliefs in war. He also received help filing his CO paperwork, and the military accepted his CO application, which was rare. Blake talked openly about living with the emotional pain and PTSD caused by his time in Iraq and chose to share his story through his participation in the peace movement. This sharing was important because it helped him make sense of his complicated identity as both a military-connected individual and a peace activist. In part, Blake felt compelled to publically protest because he felt loyalty to his "brothers and sisters in IVAW," as he wrote in a Web post. Blake's close connection to this group, which connected both his military and antiwar activist identities, made him feel supported and allowed him to commit to activism, which he might not have done on his own.

Blake's narrative illuminated the complicated and seemingly contradictory collective identity of the military peace movement, which combined both a military connection and an opposition to the Iraq War, as well as other conflicts. In addition to the shared risks of activism described in chapter 1, many military peace movement activists shared a consciousness, or a world view, and identity that separated them from both people in the military and the wider peace movement. Although the military peace movement pulled together activists from a variety of backgrounds, all activists shared some kind of intimate connection to the military. Some spent a few years in the military as a young man or woman. For others the military was a career they had held for over twenty years, a career that had controlled virtually every aspect of their lives. Some in family organizations experienced the military as their spouses' all-encompassing job that often dictated their own work opportunities and their social lives. While some parents in the family organizations were occasionally veterans themselves, others' only connection to the military came as their son or daughter decided to join. Suddenly, these parents found themselves frequenting websites such as MothersofMilitary.org and sending packages to boost their child's morale. Whatever way they came to it, for these activists their military connection was central to their subsequent peace activism.

Military peace movement activists bonded over their shared identities as both individuals connected to the military and advocates against war. While movement activists were able to reconcile these aspects of their identity, this unique combination situated them both inside and outside military and activist communities. Activists' intimate connection to the military made them insiders on aspects of the war, but as activists they remained outside the mainstream military community, which valued following orders and distrusted protestors. This chapter outlines the following four social-psychological motivations, as found in Blake's story, that led activists to become outsiders within the larger military community: (1) information literacy about the Iraq War, (2) a redefinition of patriotism, (3) personal grievances with the military care system, and (4) connections to left-wing politics. Similarly, while military peace movement members participated as insiders within the wider peace movement, they were often viewed as outsiders and critiqued by activists within that movement because of their military affiliation. Because members of the military peace movement did not sit comfortably in either community, these individuals worked to build a collective identity as insider–outsiders. The outcome was a military peace movement identity that activists believed was uniquely situated to reach both the military community and a mainstream audience.

Military peace movement activists shared a world view that embraced both the military, or at least military individuals, and activism in the peace movement. Rather than focus on how their outsider status separated them from the mainstream military community and the wider peace movement, activists built a positive identity that set them apart as more enlightened than others in the military and more effective than many in the peace movement. As such, the military peace movement's collective identity not only interwove their military and antiwar identities but privileged such an identity over other peace movement identities.

THE MILITARY PEACE MOVEMENT:
A CONTRADICTION IN TERMS

People outside this movement often assumed that it was a contradiction to say there was a *military* peace movement. Many asked, How did these people go from being connected to and supporting the military to protesting military actions? Conservatives often wondered whether these activists were malcontents and assumed the activists were inadequate soldiers. Liberals pondered how these military members "wised up" and assumed that individuals underwent a dramatic moral transformation. Neither of these extremes encapsulates all of the stories that I heard in my interviews and at activist events. Although the modern military community favored military intervention and was broadly more conservative than the general public in the United States, diverse opinions and life experiences led people to join the military.[4] Those servicemembers and their families who joined or led the military peace movement were neither all malcontents nor all newly enlightened individuals. Their stories wove together personal moral beliefs and grievances in ways not uncommon to people who have joined hundreds of other movements.[5] The military peace movement identity exemplifies the process of identity consolidation, whereby two seemingly incongruent identities are brought together in a movement collective identity.[6]

Veterans and military families did not see a contradiction in claiming both a military identity and a peace activist identity. Most interviewees believed, however, that other people, including the general public and the broader military community, viewed their dual identification as contradictory if not hypocritical. None of the thirty veterans or military family members I interviewed thought it was a contradiction to be both a veteran or a military family member and an antiwar activist. I suspect that most of the military peace movement activists felt this way or they would not have participated in the movement. Those who thought it was a contradiction would have avoided associating with the movement until they no longer felt that way. Like others who hold two seemingly contradictory sides of themselves together, such as queer Christians, military peace activists saw both sides of this identity as an intrinsic part of themselves rather than as opposing elements.[7] Although it might have been difficult for members of the military who were not activists or the general public to understand how people made sense of being both military affiliated and a peace activist, most activists felt it was not a contradiction at all. Activists made a decision to be vocal about their antiwar political leanings and thus were unlikely to see this as a contradiction within their senses of self. Additionally, as I discuss in later chapters, linking military affiliation and antiwar sentiments was central to strategies and tactics of the movement. While all of the activists I interviewed agreed that these two identities were not contradictory, most thought it was difficult to assume both identities. They understood how some could see it as a contradiction, and as discussed in chapter 1, some were directly confronted by members of the military community who firmly believed you could not be a good veteran or supportive military family member and, at the same time, be an antiwar activist.

Experience Necessitates Action

In spite of a cultural perception of contradiction, veterans and military families described their activism in the military peace movement as normal and complementary to their connection to the military. When I asked Rowland "Lane" Anderson, who served in the Navy during Vietnam, if he found it difficult to be both a veteran and a peace protestor, he answered, "No, I'm comfortable with it." While it may not surprise people that Vietnam-era veterans, most of whom were drafted into the military, saw no problem with being both military affiliated and peace activists, Iraq and Afghanistan veterans had similar feelings. All of the IVAW members did not see a contradiction between being a veteran and being an antiwar activist. Former Air Force Captain Stephen Potts explained, "I think they fit together more than most people would expect." Potts recognized that most people found it striking that veterans were antiwar activists, but he believed these things worked together rather than contradicted.

Some of the activists thought it was possible to balance being both a veteran or a military family member and an activist because they considered the world to be complicated, and they were happy with their intricate politics as long as they had others around who understood it. Many MFSO and Gold Star members portrayed their activism as a natural outgrowth of their familial duties. In interviews, letters, and speeches, activists described their protest participation as their duty as parents or spouses. When I asked Rich Moniak, whose son served two tours in Iraq and another tour in Afghanistan, whether he thought it was contradictory to be both a military family member and an antiwar activist, he said, "Not at all. I look at them [activism and being a military parent] together. I was a parent first. . . . I've never separated them." Moniak, a shy and soft-spoken Alaskan, explained that although speaking as an activist wasn't his "nature," because he was the parent of a soldier he felt he had to overcome that. When military families gave speeches, they often referred to their children, parents, spouses, or siblings who were military servicemembers as the reason they held their antiwar beliefs. One mother of a National Guard soldier wrote an open letter to MFSO members entitled "A Parent's Concerns," and in this letter she concluded, "For our children's sake, let's act." This mother, like many of the MFSO parents, sought to encourage antiwar activism among military parents by drawing on parental obligations to protect their children. Familial duties caused MFSO members to see military affiliation as necessitating antiwar activism during the Iraq War. In speeches, letters, and protest signs, MFSO members described their love for their military member in the same paragraphs or the same breath as their antiwar positions.

Compared with the VFP veterans I interviewed, who served mostly in Vietnam, veterans and family members of servicemembers who had fought since 2001 were significantly more likely to point out that others would likely see military affiliation and peace activism as contradictory. I suspect that veterans of past wars had more time to reconcile their military past and their activism. Also, those who were new to political activism, as more MFSO and IVAW members were, did not have the previous social movement experiences that might have led them to be less invested in how those on the opposite side of the issue perceived them. Since I knew that many VFP members were antiwar activists before Iraq, I probed further in interviews to understand their original decisions to combine being a veteran and an antiwar activist. I knew that Anderson had been an activist during the Vietnam War, so I asked a follow-up question about whether it was difficult for him during that war. He replied, "No. Especially once I found the Vietnam Vets Against the War. I always had some veterans around me." Anderson's answer demonstrated not only how activists saw their military identities as congruent with their peace activism but also the importance for these individuals to speak as members of a larger group of military-affiliated activists. Similarly, a number of Iraq veterans described how meeting IVAW members helped them to vocalize their antiwar positions.

Making Protest Possible

Military peace movement participants readily understood that the military forbade its workers from various forms of protest, and as discussed in chapter 1, they recognized the consequences of disobeying those rules. Since activists realized these risks, they actively sought ways to make protest possible for military individuals.

While serving on active duty themselves, Liam Madden, a Vermont Marine, and Jonathan Hutto, a Virginia sailor, cofounded the Appeal for Redress. This online petition to Congress provided a way for active duty military members to voice their opposition to the Iraq War within the confines of legal, largely nonrisky speech, since servicemembers were allowed to speak freely to senators and representatives as long as they were not in a combat zone nor in uniform and were off duty. This carefully crafted appeal was sponsored by IVAW, VFP, and MFSO and garnered over two thousand active duty servicemembers' signatures in a little over one year. The military peace movement engaged in tactics that publicized the Appeal for Redress and military resistance to the war in order to overcome the perceived risks of activism and to encourage mobilization.

The military encouraged cohesion as a way to increase military mission success and to survive harsh conditions.[8] This military insistence on conformity and cohesion led to an informal culture that discouraged people from joining peace organizations or taking part in actions that could be construed as antiwar. This likely led to the American cultural perception that peace protest and military affiliation were incompatible. In the following sections I elaborate how activists came to see that activism and the military were compatible by highlighting four main paths to activism I found in data from my interviews, Web posts, and speeches of military peace movement activists.

BECOMING MILITARY OUTSIDERS

People who eventually joined the military peace movement perceived that they were outsiders within the wider military for the following four reasons: (1) information led them to be critical of the Iraq War; (2) they redefined patriotism as requiring activism, (3) personal grievances with their treatment by the military led them to question military cohesion; and (4) personal connections to left-wing politics opened cracks for additional questioning of the military. Although I discuss these paths to mobilization separately, activists experienced combinations of these motivations, as is clear from Blake's example. These four factors, found in varying combinations in the activists' biographies, drove people to seek out social movement activism. In the military peace movement, information literacy included education, research, and other exposure to information critical of U.S. foreign policy in Iraq. The primary ideology that led military-affiliated individuals to seek out peace activism was a belief that, for this war, activism was patriotic and an extension of the military's mission. Military members also sought activism when personal injuries or perceived military/governmental injustices led them to become disillusioned with the Iraq War. Finally, some individuals were already familiar with peace activism or antiwar arguments because they or their parents had left-leaning politics. This variety of reasons for outsider status reveals the diversity within both the military and the military peace movement.

Information: Growing into an Antiwar Position

In the interviews, nearly all of the veterans and military family members described their activism as developing out of new information or as a natural part of their intellectual growth. A number of military peace movement activists learned facts through intensive research on the war; others directly faced the realities of poor policy decisions as soldiers; and some family members discovered information indirectly through their loved ones. For the military peace movement activists in this section, learning new information about the Iraq War was central to their decision to seek out peace activism. This new information led to a shared political belief that the American occupation of Iraq should end, though activists developed a wide range of positions on issues about the military and foreign policy in general.

Growing Up

Some members of VFP believed that people gained new political information as a part of growing up. During the Vietnam War, Mike Hearington signed up for the Army the day he turned seventeen. Since the war ended not long after he turned eighteen and because he had been reprimanded for fighting and other problems, the military discharged him.[9] At the time, Hearington was given a general discharge under honorable conditions, but it would take a long time for him to join the peace movement. For Hearington, being a veteran and an activist was not contradictory; he saw it as a sign of maturity. He said that Americans did not really learn to think for themselves until after twenty-five, and that was why the military could get young people to fight in its wars:

> I was a child, and of course that's what our system relies upon is that. And I think that we're motivated through movies and, of course, video games now and everything else to accept war and participation in it. Actually, my dad, as I've said, was in World War II, and my brother had already gone to Vietnam, and it was just like a family—this is what you do. You get to be eighteen, and you go into the military, and you fight Communism, or you fight, you know, whatever's going on. So it was a nonthought.

Family history with the military and the impressionability of being a teenager led Hearington to join the Army. His peace activism came from knowledge about philosophy and foreign affairs and the personal growth he achieved later in life. Activists believed that aging brought people in contact with new information that shaped their political opinions.

Similarly, some IVAW members believed that adopting an antiwar position was a part of the process of growing up. Jenn Hogg, who joined the Army National Guard at eighteen in 2001, was trying to be tough and "bought into the honor of the military." During and after her time in the military, however, she learned "newfound truths" about gender, war, and U.S. foreign policy that led her to protest the war. Likewise, Stephen Potts said, "Being a peace activist just feels like a simple growth from [military service], and not even a big one. I mean, I changed so gradually over the years." Potts's conservative upbringing encouraged him to attend the Air Force Academy, but as he matured, Stephen slowly came to believe that all wars were wrong and then became a CO. Other veterans, including many of the COs in IVAW and VFP, shared similar stories that linked military service to activism as a sign of maturity.

The War Contradicted the Rhetoric

Most military peace movement activists did not buy into the reasons for the Iraq War or were very critical of its conduct and became so because of information they received from the media, academia, or their own experiences. Many doubted that Iraq had weapons of mass destruction or that Saddam Hussein had ties to al-Qaeda. Other activists' interpretations of U.S. and international law contrasted sharply with the doctrines of preemptive war, the military's rules of engagement, and the rebuilding that appeared as an occupation. When members of the military learned things that contradicted the rosy picture prowar officials painted of Iraq and, later, Afghanistan, they felt compelled to end the war through protest. Many military peace movement activists believed that if others knew what they did, they would protest, too.

Military peace movement activists regularly described their belief that Americans were deceived at the start of the war. In hundreds of speeches, family members referenced lies being used to justify the Iraq War. Lietta Ruger, an early MFSO activist who was the mother-in-law of one and an aunt of another Iraq War veteran who each served two lengthy tours in Iraq, had a blog entitled *Dying for the Lies*. Similarly, in 2006 at a Washington, D.C., press conference for MFSO's Operation House Call, Elizabeth Frederick spoke about calls from her partner of five years, who was in Iraq: "Nearly every conversation I have with Mike reinforces the fact that this war was based on lies." She expressed frustrations with both the planning of the war and its implementation and felt that military servicemembers' "patriotism and service to this nation [were] being wasted." Family members such as Ruger and Frederick depicted feelings of pride in their loved ones' military service, but they took issue with the Iraq War because they believed it was based on faulty intelligence and continued to be perpetrated in ways that were shameful.

Vietnam veterans within VFP frequently discussed a sense of déjà vu and saw the Iraq War also as perpetrated by lies. Michael Cervantes, a Vietnam veteran and the founder of VFP's Ventura, California, chapter, avoided the military and politics after returning from combat. When Michael saw the preparations for the Iraq War, however, he sought a way to protest. He outlined his reason for protesting as follows:

> The reason why I'm doing activity now is because of the unjust nature of the war back then. I see it happening again today; [the Iraq War is] an unjust war situation even though the military is volunteer. . . . It's a similar unjust cause. There are no formal reasons to be there. We discovered that we don't have to be there because of WMDs or because of connections to 9/11. Those reasons are not there.

Cervantes connected Vietnam to Iraq through the faulty reasons for these wars and their effects on the soldiers. He believed he had an obligation to today's military that required him to protest.

Most military peace movement members learned, often firsthand, that the war was not only wrong but destructive to the U.S. military. All but one of the thirty interviewees referred to the taxing of military resources, including military personnel, as leading to their frustration with the Iraq War. Additionally, this topic of conversation was common at military peace movement events. During my participant observation in Crawford in August 2006, one Army veteran described the lack of proper equipment and training for military units who were being redeployed to Iraq. He said that the multiple deployments caused family problems for his friends and ruined morale in his old unit. Theresa Dawson drew similar conclusions from her research, which led her to believe that the war had tarnished the image and reputation of the American military:

> I feel it's an irresponsible use of military power, and I feel like it has degenerated our own standing in the world. I feel like it has brought shame upon America and our military. Our military should always be held up as a gold standard. And by that I mean we should always see them as the knights in shining armor, not the ones that go in and kick in doors and frighten children and things like that. And the things that have gone on there—it's, it's just wrong.

As a military family member who felt positively about the military, Dawson was troubled by the cost of the war on it. She came to believe that the Iraq War was "an illegal war based on false pretenses." She spent more time in her interview, however, describing her belief that the war had hurt the U.S. military's reputation than laying out a political case against the war. Activists' descriptions of the war as harmful to the military are important in understanding their belief that they could combine their military affiliation and their peace activism. If military people believed the war had damaged the military, then this belief could logically push them to seek out peace activism as a way to improve it.

Differentiating between Afghanistan and Iraq

For a few military peace movement members, their protests against the Iraq War developed from a belief that the Iraq War had led America to abandon Afghanistan and the search for al-Qaeda. In particular, many of the IVAW members who were stationed in Afghanistan from 2001 to 2008 expressed their frustrations with the lack of progress there. In speeches, letters, and Web posts, many activists called Iraq a distraction from the war on terror and the fight against al-Qaeda and its leader, Osama Bin Laden. Most activists initially supported the war in Afghanistan, though not necessarily how it was implemented.[10]

One military peace movement member had a unique, personal view of the war there. Colonel Ann Wright (Retired), a twenty-nine-year Army and Army Reserve veteran, was able to closely observe the effects of the Iraq War on Afghanistan as a member of the U.S. diplomatic corps. She helped reopen the American embassy in Kabul in December 2001 and was there until July 2002, when she saw that President Bush was shifting government resources and focus to Iraq. Wright was frustrated that both Afghanistan's economic needs and its military security were being ignored. To make matters worse, none of the information she accessed through diplomatic channels indicated why the United States was changing its focus to Iraq. Despite daily emails to members of the U.S. Foreign Service, Wright learned nothing that led her to believe the impending Iraq War was necessary. She described her colleagues as "very, very cryptic in their responses, so you knew that they couldn't talk to you about what their feelings were." While in Mongolia, where she was assigned after Afghanistan,

Wright was so stressed over the lead-up to the Iraq War that she had to be medically evacuated to Singapore after developing severe gastro-esophageal reflux disease, which produced symptoms of a coming heart attack. As her first moment of protest, in March 2003, Wright resigned from official service to the U.S. government in a letter to Secretary of State Colin Powell. Almost immediately, her gastric issues subsided. As government employees, many in the military peace movement had access to information that contradicted the government's stated reasons for the Iraq War.

Prior to 2007, many in the movement joined the military to fight in Afghanistan or accepted it when their family was involved in the Afghanistan War, but Iraq was seen as altogether different because of the preemptive strike and the faulty reasons offered for the war. Army First Lieutenant Ehren Watada refused to deploy to Iraq in June 2006 because of what he learned when he immersed himself in information on the history of Iraq and the Iraq War during the year leading up to his unit's deployment. As Watada explained in an interview with *Democracy Now* on June 8, 2006:

> When I learned that I was going to be deployed last year, I thought it was my responsibility as an officer to learn everything I could about war in general—its effects on people, its effects on the soldiers, and also specifically why we were there, what was occurring at that time, what had occurred in the past—in order to get a better understanding, as was my job. And the more I read different articles by international and constitutional law experts, and the reports coming out from government agencies and non-governmental agencies, and the reports and the revelations from independent journalists and the Iraqi people themselves and the soldiers coming home, I came to the conclusion that the war and what we're doing over there is illegal. And, being so, I felt it was my duty to morally, and also legally, refuse any orders to participate in it.

Watada had intended to be a good soldier and read widely to prepare himself and his troops for battle in Iraq. Although he initially had faith in the war's justifications—WMDs and Iraq's ties to al-Qaeda—his research led him to the belief that taking part in the Iraq War would make him a party to war crimes. Watada refused to be deployed to Iraq and offered to be sent to Afghanistan instead.

As soldiers, veterans, and military family members were exposed to information that suggested the Iraq War was problematic, some were moved to protest the war. Individual research into facts about and opinions of the war provided a gateway to information that challenged prior acceptance of U.S. foreign policy. Members of the military peace movement did not necessarily become pacifists, but most learned something about the war that led them to develop what Jane Mansbridge and Aldon Morris call an "oppositional consciousness."[11] Information, both firsthand and research based, led activists to recognize the injustices of the Iraq War that their military community faced and inspired them to seek out activism. While the majority of Americans were supporting the Iraq War in its first few years, military peace movement members accessed information that pushed them to seek others who wanted to protest the war.

Value Redefinition: American Pride

One of the primary reasons military peace movement participants sought activism was their belief that the Iraq War violated American values. A number of military peace activists perceived their peace activism, as opposed to their or their loved ones' participation in war, as patriotic. Vietnam veterans who protested against the Vietnam War viewed their peace participation as a new and transformed patriotism, as well.[12] For the majority of veterans, their activism in the military peace movement was an extension of the ideals that they had hoped to defend as members of the military. Although *patriotism* became a contested term in the Iraq War, nearly all of my interviewees believed patriotism, an adherence to American values such as democracy, or aspects of the U.S. Constitution led them to seek out activism. Military peace movement activists' ideological definitions of these terms were similar to those found in the rhetoric uttered by the mainstream peace movement at the time, which argued that peace and political dissent were patriotic.[13] Activists in the military peace movement often placed emphasis, however, on their military affiliation as a further demonstration of their own patriotism and transformed ideology.

Patriots

Members of the military peace movement frequently called themselves patriots. Postings to movement Listservs and websites, as well as speeches at protest events, referred to antiwar protestors, particularly those within the military peace movement, as patriots. In particular, most members of the military peace movement described their strong positive feelings toward the United States as part of their reason for protest. This interpretation of patriotism led to the creation of certain tactics and the names used for them. In March 2006 in Salt Lake City, a coalition that included military peace movement organizations entitled a weekend event Love America: End the Iraq War! In addition to having GSFSO and MFSO speakers at the Saturday rally, the following day, VFP organized a coordinating educational panel featuring speakers and artists from the military peace movement.

As of August 2008, over one hundred posts to the IVAW website discussed patriotism and the new meaning many of these young activists attached to it. Similarly, in letters by and media articles about MFSO and VFP, members pointed to their activism as patriotic support of the military. Holidays such as Memorial Day and Veterans Day often led to long Web posts, letters, and other musings in which activists suggested that "true American patriots" should protest the war. In 2008 an active duty Army sergeant wrote a post entitled "My Views of the Fourth of July." Sergeant Coppa rebuked Americans for turning it into an "extra day off from work," with fireworks and barbeques, and proposed that they recommit themselves to the country's founding purpose of fighting against injustice. She described her love for her country and how it led her to protest the Iraq War:

> What a low, shivering thing would I be, if I saw the truth, that America is wasting its soldiers, breaking its military, and destroying its economy, all in the name of the interests of a few, and I did not stand up! If I did not stand up for fear, or a wish to preserve my comfort, if I did not stand up for fear of reprisal, or imprisonment—how those Founding Fathers would be ashamed!

The sergeant's protest was born out of her interpretation of the war as un-American. In linking her belief in protesting the war to a holiday that celebrated the birth of the United States and to its founding fathers, the sergeant invoked a struggle that she believed had to continue in order for America to live up to its vision of itself as a country that fights injustice. While she was an active duty soldier, the sergeant did not claim that her warrior actions made her patriotic—it was her protest that answered "America's call."

Constitutional Defenders

Members of the military peace movement frequently referenced the Constitution in their work. As I describe in chapter 4, activists used the Constitution as a framework for connecting their antiwar message to the increased patriotism in America post-9/11, but for most military peace movement participants, the constitutional rhetoric was not just strategic. Many believed they were supporting the Constitution—as the military should have been—by protesting the Iraq War.

VFP labeled a 2006–7 series of antiwar events the Support and Defend the Constitution Campaign, and in several speeches, VFP and IVAW members explained that their protest actions were "supporting the Constitution." One member of IVAW, who graduated from the Air Force Academy but was discharged for protesting the war, discussed his protest as follows:

> It is not an easy thing for any military member to dissent against their own government, particularly in time of war. Yet we took an oath to defend the Constitution. Under our Constitution, no one is above the law—not even the president. I believe it is our duty as citizens and as military members to speak out publicly, within the bounds of pertinent laws and regulations, against the grave abuses of power which have been committed by Bush administration officials in the name of security and freedom. . . . If the Constitution is not upheld in these challenging times, we will not have security or liberty—only fear and terror.

This man linked his protest to a defense of the Constitution and the American system of law. He believed that the office of the president had betrayed the Constitution by intentionally providing Congress with false information, and he was concerned that America's system of checks and balances was being disregarded. Whereas he joined the military to fight terrorism in the wake of 9/11, he linked his protest to a defense of the Constitution.

A number of issues led military peace movement members to deem the Iraq War unconstitutional. In particular, its status as a preemptive war struck many military peace activists as antithetical to their reasons for being in the military. In an entry on the IVAW website, Navy Petty Officer Matthew Rhodes Winter wrote:

> What really blew my mind was the fact that they were openly talking about "preemptive" war. Well, not only did the bastards talk about it, they sent us to do it. By my way of thinking there is never a justification for preemptive war. Once you do this you can never go back to the way things were before. In my mind America was not the sort of country that attacked first . . . sort of like on the playground . . . it's okay to hit back if someone hit you first, but no matter what names they called you could never throw that first punch.

For Winter, preemptive war was un-American, and therefore, peace activism was justified. He made it clear that it was not just morally reprehensible, bully behavior but against what America stood for. Military families also became involved in peace activism because they believed preemptive war was un-American. In fact, MFSO parents were involved in multiple (unsuccessful) lawsuits that challenged the Iraq War on the grounds that preemptive war was unconstitutional. As veterans and military family members who trusted the principles set forth in the American legal system, they felt compelled to protest the war.

Military peace movement activists frequently cited not only the preemptive nature of the Iraq War but also the conduct of the war itself in their reasons for turning to protest. In an entry on the IVAW website, Iraq War veteran Jen Hogg, a former sergeant in the Army National Guard, wrote that her reasons for joining the military were the same patriotic reasons she had for being in the peace movement. She had entered the military to serve her country, but her faith in its service to American ideals was shaken:

Imagine my surprise when I learned honorable service to my country involved a pre-emptive strike against a non-threatening nation that in turn hurt the civilian population the most and led to the torture of many innocent people in mass sweeps of any male old enough to hold a weapon (or too old to hold a weapon).

Hogg became disillusioned with the war when she was asked to take part in actions in which she felt the American military should not be involved. A belief that the Iraq War was not being fought for a just cause motivated veterans and military families to protest the war.

Nearly all of the military peace movement's members shared an ideology that linked patriotism to protest. Some members of the movement—particularly, a handful of Vietnam-era veterans who had been involved in antiwar protest for several decades—believed that patriotism itself should be questioned, but the majority of activists cited American values, freedoms, and laws as instrumental in their decision to protest the war. Many military family members and veterans expressed the pain that accompanied their realization that being patriotic meant protesting the war, and activists often cried when speaking about these issues at protest actions.

Personal Grievances: Disillusionment with the Military's Treatment of Soldiers and Families

Though *grievances* could be broadly construed to include understandings of the war as unjust, in this section I outline nonideological troubles movement activists faced that caused them to seek ways to better their own situations. These grievances led some military-connected activists to become beneficiaries of the movement, who hoped to better their own situation through activism, rather than conscience constituents, who sought to better the situations of others. In order to protest, activists must understand that their personal troubles have structural or cultural bases that can be changed, which is key to the development of an oppositional consciousness.[14] Activists must recognize not only that they themselves or specific individuals face negative circumstances but that an entire group is threatened or denied something they are due, such as opportunities, rights, and respect.

The military peace movement saw veterans and military families as categories of people who were wronged by the Iraq and, later, Afghanistan wars. They believed that the Iraq War had placed too heavy a burden on them. They were particularly concerned with the multiple, rapid deployments and the strains on the VA's health system.

Many military peace movement activists endured the types of rough circumstances that burdened other military veterans and families during these wars. Many military veterans and families perceived the lack of equipment in the early years of the war, the repeated deployments in the later years, the stop-loss policy, and the use of the military's Individual Ready Reserves (IRRs) as neglect by the military and the United States. A number of people affiliated with the military turned to activism when they or their family members experienced difficulty obtaining adequate health care—particularly, mental health services—after returning from war. Also, some veterans and military family members were greatly disturbed by their own or their loved ones' war experiences, which often included civilian deaths. These situations directed many veterans and military families to seek out people who understood their predicaments and offered aid and support. For many, the horrors of war brought out a more nuanced understanding of U.S. foreign policy and of war. These experiences led some to be disillusioned by the Iraq War and/or the Afghanistan War and eventually pushed them toward peace movement activism. The majority of activists who stated personal grievances in interviews and speeches were members of military families and current veterans, though many veterans of past wars had grievances that led to their entry into activism years ago.

Posttraumatic Stress Disorder

Activists' most commonly described frustration was with the military's and the government's handling of combat-related psychological and emotional trauma. Posttraumatic stress disorder (PTSD) was particularly difficult for members of the military to acknowledge, because they were expected to be strong both physically and mentally. Within movement discussions, PTSD was frequently used as a catchall term for what one military wife called "the war crazies," meaning any form of psychological trouble that developed after combat experiences.[15] Families talked about their children and spouses as being "dead inside," "not there," "easily irritable," or "angry all the time." Iraq War veterans described nightmares, irrational fears, hypervigilance, and thoughts of or attempts at suicide. At a rally at the movement's Camp Casey III in 2006, Charlie Anderson, a Navy medic who served with the Marines during the Iraq War, explained the effect that the military's policy of redeploying soldiers with PTSD and other psychological troubles had on him:

> I was facing my second deployment. I knew that I couldn't go, because I had psychological problems. And I also knew that I couldn't say that I had psychological problems, because that was just not part of the unspoken code. And so I sped my truck up to sixty-five miles an hour on a bridge over the Chesapeake Bay, and I was preparing to drive it off and take my life rather than face that.... Luckily, at the last second I somehow came out of it.

Anderson was unaware of a way to reconcile his military obligations, his mental health needs, and his conscience. Although Anderson could recognize the war's effects on his mental state, the culture of the military kept him from initially seeking help. The military's continued deployment of soldiers who had mental health needs became a reason for his separating from the rest of the military community and becoming a military peace movement activist.

Military peace movement activists like Anderson attributed PTSD to the Iraq War, and in so doing they distinguished it from other mental illnesses. Anderson called PTSD one of a number of "psychological injuries as a result of the war." He explained:

> I did not just use the word *illness*. Posttraumatic [stress] disorder is not a mental illness. The anxiety disorders that are caused by combat are not mental illnesses. The nightmares, the flashbacks, all of those are not psychological illnesses. That was something that was done to us, and that is something that we have to live with for the rest of our lives.

Anderson's personal battles with the war's psychological effects turned him against the war in general. As he realized what had been done to him, he began to seek a way to express his frustrations with the war. Anderson fortunately received some care for his PTSD from the military health care system, but at least three other IVAW members committed suicide as a result of their combat-related disorders. Many IVAW members depicted the importance of their personal battles with PTSD as a catalyst for their activism.

When seeking help for service-related trauma, veterans and families frequently ran into various roadblocks, including difficult and confusing military and VA paperwork and regulations. Seeking treatment cost the servicemember her or his security clearance, promotions, or leadership position. In addition, servicemembers had to overcome the macho culture of the military in order to ask for treatment. These activists described themselves or their loved ones as healthy or mentally stable before the war. They blamed the military and the government for not caring for the veterans on their return to the United States. Former officer and enlisted soldier Jim Worlien linked his disappointment with the care he received for PTSD to "the anger that [boiled] within [him] over the war." By linking their experience of trauma to a problem with a policy, activists distinguished themselves from the wider military community.

The families of servicemembers who received mental and physical injuries while in Iraq claimed these war wounds were catalysts for their own activism. In the fight to improve mental health care for veterans—and to not send soldiers to "unnecessary wars" where they received mental and physical wounds—few were as prominent as Kevin and Joyce Lucey. They met with several state and national politicians and testified before the Senate Veterans' Affairs Committee. They appeared on numerous talk shows, including *Dr. Phil*; were featured in at least four documentaries; and spoke to dozens of media outlets on this issue. The Luceys did not participate in antiwar activism, however, until they experienced a tragedy they believed was brought on by the war and could have been prevented had the military taken soldiers' mental health care more seriously. The Luceys' son, Corporal Jeffrey Lucey, served with the Marines in the initial invasion of Iraq, and within months of his return, he exhibited signs of

PTSD. He started to drink heavily and had hallucinations and nightmares, and his despair led him to lash out and pull away from family and friends. In speeches, interviews, and writings, the Luceys told the story of Christmas 2003, when Jeff threw his dog tags at his sister and yelled, "Don't you know your brother's a murderer?" Jeff Lucey hanged himself with a garden hose in his parents' basement on June 22, 2004, after being denied treatment from the VA for his PTSD. The Luceys successfully sued the VA, winning monetary damages, and although the VA did not admit responsibility in the suicide, the Luceys believed that this suit would change VA policy. This lawsuit, along with another suit brought by VCS and VUFT against the VA, in which many military peace movement members took part, put these individuals squarely at odds with mainstream military communities.

The Luceys' personal tragedy turned them into peace activists, though they maintained patriotic tendencies and a respect for the military. In an open letter to MFSO members, the Luceys wrote that although their antiwar activism came out of a failure on behalf of the government, they still saw themselves as loyal Americans:

> As with Jeffrey, our love and commitment for this country and her people knows no bounds. Yet we look upon our government and ask: why have you truly failed us? Why did you truly rush into this conflict and jeopardize the safety and lives of this country's finest and then fail them? Why have you grown so arrogant, close minded and pursue failed policies? Why have you failed to applaud those who disagree and dissent for it is these people who actually are showing the world the strengths and beauty of this great nation and her constitution? Why have you tried to chill their right to question and dissent and yet at the same time voice that these are the very rights which you are trying to bestow on others? Why have you tried to convince all that those who don't support the war don't support the troops, when the facts appear to be that those who don't believe in the war actually have cared and supported for the troops more than those who have shouted such from the rooftops?

The Luceys blamed the government for what happened to their son, and the country's failure to care for its returning veterans led them to activism against the war. By their litany of questions, the Luceys demonstrated that they had a broad range of frustrations with the Iraq War. According to the Luceys, those who loved their country should mobilize to end the war, though they themselves had to be spurred to protest when the war hit home.

Forces and Contract Stipulations Rarely Used

The U.S. military faced a shortage of active duty servicemembers to meet the needs of fighting wars in both Iraq and Afghanistan. To maintain a sufficient fighting force, the military called up more units and individuals from the National Guard and Reserve forces than ever before and at a pace of deployment faster than previously experienced by those forces. The military leveraged parts of servicemembers' contracts in unprecedented ways to keep them in the military beyond the term for which most believed they had signed up, and by regularly using the stop-loss policy and the IRR, the military extended servicemembers' military obligations like never before.

Whereas members of the Reserves and National Guard were kept largely in the United States during Vietnam, these forces faced extraordinary levels of deployment during the wars in Iraq and Afghanistan. In speeches, military peace movement activists blamed this trend for the lack of servicemembers available for disaster relief in the United States. At Newark's August 25, 2007, March for Peace, Equality, Jobs, and Justice, Paula Rogovin, whose Marine son served two tours in Iraq, said:

> When Hurricane Katrina struck, many of us wondered why the National Guard wasn't there en masse to rescue people. I ask you, where was our National Guard and their equipment during Hurricane Katrina? People died needlessly. And their families and loved ones have suffered.

Not only those who served in the National Guard and the Reserve but those who were affected by the lack of troops at home opposed this dramatic change in deployed-force allocation.

Military peace movement activists pointed out that Reserve and

National Guard units were unprepared for the years of deployments required by the OPTEMPO of the wars in Iraq and Afghanistan. These forces often did not have active family support groups prior to the Iraq War, and when deployments occurred, these support organizations functioned unevenly. Additionally, as people in the Reserves and National Guard were activated, they typically lost their civilian salaries and benefits, which in many cases were higher or better than their military compensation, and no military support systems were in place to help families make up the difference.[16] Some activists in the National Guard and the Reserves reported that the war cost them their jobs or promotions. Decreases in pay sent some military peace movement families into foreclosures, debts, and bankruptcies.

Stop-loss was a rarely used element of a standard military contract that obligated servicemembers to continue to serve on active duty after reaching the end of their contracts.[17] In a conversation at a meeting following a large antiwar rally in Washington, D.C., in September 2006, a few MFSO mothers talked in a hotel lobby about stop-loss. One described it as the "straw that broke the camel's back" that pushed her into protesting the Iraq War. In March 2008, Army Specialist Casey Porter spoke to CBS's *The Early Show* during his second deployment to Iraq, which was a fifteen-month deployment that occurred after his initial contract had ended. From his base in Iraq, he explained that he had joined IVAW because he believed people should speak out when a country did something wrong to its veterans. Like many military peace movement activists, Porter and his parents sought ways to protest the Iraq War after experiencing stop-loss. These activists joined the military peace movement to right this wrong.

When protesting the wars, New Jersey MFSO member Nancy Nygard, whose husband was a Vietnam veteran, made a point of discussing stop-loss's affects on her family. Her son was affected by it twice. The first time, his active duty contract was extended while he served in Afghanistan with the Army's 3rd Brigade, 10th Mountain Division. He spent sixteen months in Afghanistan during 2006 and 2007, with eight of these months coming after his initial active duty contract. After President Obama announced a surge in Afghanistan in December 2009, her son was stop-lossed again. This time, the orders were delivered to Nygard's son by FedEx, since he had left the

Army and was living as a civilian. He had a good job, was caring for his new son and daughter, and was using his GI bill to attend college. In a speech at the 2010 VFP convention, given while her son was in Iraq, Nygard expressed her frustration with the military's ability to alter its regulations and enforce stop-loss beyond servicemembers' initial contract periods. Her descriptions of stop-loss conveyed the betrayal felt by many military peace movement veterans and families affected by this policy. They linked their experiences with stop-loss to their search for a way to protest the war.

A related issue that pushed military-affiliated individuals to seek out activism was the use of the military's IRR. In order to fill its ranks, the military called servicemembers out of the IRR to serve in Iraq and Afghanistan. After soldiers fulfilled their contracts with the military, they were placed on IRR duty for a period ranging from two to twelve years, depending on their contract and military specialty. While in the IRR, servicemembers lived as civilians, did not receive money from the military, and did not drill or otherwise perform for the military. Under their military contracts, however, soldiers in the IRR could be called to serve during a time of war or a national emergency. This was not an obligation of which many servicemembers, particularly junior enlisted personnel, were aware, and it had been little used. In September 2006, MFSO member Terry Bennett wrote to a Seattle paper about her son's deployment to Iraq while in the IRR. In the letter she expressed her frustration with its current use:

> Although it is true that IRR duty is part of the contract an enlistee signs when entering the Army, it was never intended to be used as it has been by the Bush administration. . . . Invading and occupying a country is not a national emergency, especially when there is no end plan.

Members of the peace movement often referred to stop-loss and the use of the military's IRR as the back-door draft. They believed that the United States should have instituted a widespread draft to spread out the obligations for war and that, instead, American soldiers were being abused. This critique placed these individuals in direct opposition to military policy, and they therefore sought the military peace movement in order to join others who were outside the mainstream military community.

Lack of War Preparation

Many affiliated with the military sought ways to speak out because they believed the military was not adequately equipped or prepared for the war. The military peace movement highlighted these issues before they became fodder for the 2004 U.S. presidential debates. Families frequently described their loved ones' lack of water and food rations in Iraq. Many spoke about their family members'—particularly, those pulled from the Reserves and the National Guard—lack of adequate body armor. A number of MFSO and IVAW members paid for these supplies out of their own pockets. Carla Hitz, the mother of an Army helicopter pilot, explained that her son's lack of water caused her to find her "antiwar voice." In an October 2007 speech in Salt Lake City, Hitz referred to such things as "abuse of the finest and bravest among us." These shortfalls in basic supplies led people associated with the military to believe that it was not taking care of those who risked their lives during the "rush to war," and these beliefs pushed people to seek an outlet for opposition to the war.

Military families faced other treatment from the military that they said was unacceptable. When spouses or parents were deployed, their families often scrambled to keep the family together in ways one would expect after a divorce or a death. The military promised to help them with services and groups, but MFSO members frequently described these as inadequate to meeting military families' needs. In particular, many Reserve and National Guard families lacked the support systems offered on military bases, such as classes about family and money troubles and access to cheaper goods. This situation left many family members angry and questioning the war. One woman, who signed her name as Trish, wrote a letter to MFSO that was later posted on their website. In it, she wrote that she had been the perfect military wife before her Army National Guard husband's deployment to Iraq, but afterward, she soon came to believe the military was treating her family and her husband as "expendable." Although the National Guard promised to take care of her family while her husband was deployed, she felt abandoned when she asked for help with military benefits, household repairs, and her son's hospitalization. When her husband returned, he was a different person, and her family needed counseling. Their military health care benefits ended, however, sixty days after his return, since he was in the National Guard and was expected to return to his civilian job and health care.[18] Trish's personal grievances with the military caused her to change her "political view on Iraq drastically." She went from "waving the flag" to asking people to "pray that someone [stopped] this nonsense." Many activists felt similarly pushed outside the military community and were motivated by their personal grievances to find a way to protest the war.

Death

Death was always a factor in military peace movement protest. Activists hoped to stop the deaths of their friends, family members, and colleagues and of strangers. Guilt over death motivated many IVAW activists. Some activists were driven to protest not just out of the fear of or guilt about death but because tragedy had struck home.

In 2006 a Marine from Michigan told an audience in Crawford about himself. As he explained why he came to the protest encampment, he talked about how losing friends and coworkers in Iraq compelled him to protest. He described his most recent loss as follows:

> I had to come back [to the Camp Casey protests]. On the 26th of August, I lost another friend. He was on his third tour, and the thing that is making me really upset is, now, their names are blending together now. [My girlfriend] asked what his name was, and I gave her a name, a wrong first name and a wrong last name. . . . I saw him in my dream. In his typical joking attitude, [he] said that I was fresh out of friends, that I need to make some new ones. And he was joking around, but he used to always say shit like that. Anyway, it's my duty now. It is my duty to stand up and speak, and I'll do this until this war is over.

Members of the military peace movement felt compelled to become activists often in order to make sense of deaths and to make those deaths meaningful.

Like Cindy Sheehan, some people searched for ways to protest after they lost their children or other relatives to war. John Fenton held his son's hand while he died at Walter Reed Army Medical Center of shrapnel injuries from an improvised explosive device (IED) that required multiple brain surgeries. He joined a weekly MFSO rally in Teaneck, New Jersey, and said that he wished he had started going to antiwar rallies earlier. He explained his reason for protesting as follows: "I don't want other parents to go through what I went through." Personal tragedies led some military families to seek a way to express the anger and the loss they experienced when their loved ones died. Although some believed the war was wrong, as Sheehan and Fenton did, they did not speak out until they felt the tragic consequences of the war.

Some military community members became protestors only after they experienced its effects. Without this personal connection to the war, many might have sat idly by. Personal grievances pushed them outside the traditional military community, and they sought a way to protest.

Personal History: Politically Left

Doug McAdam suggests that some people hold receptive beliefs or attitudes that predispose them to activism.[19] In this context, left-leaning politics predisposed some in the military community to antiwar activism. A number of military peace movement activists recognized that they were already different from other military-affiliated individuals, and this difference primed them for joining the military peace movement. This difference often made them feel that they were not fully accepted and, thus, outside the traditional military community. Several activists explained that they already had left-leaning politics before joining the military or having their family members in the service. Some believed that they had never fit in with the military. During quiet moments at military peace movement events, some even wondered aloud, "How did I get into the military life?" At this point, the conversation usually turned to the fact that they or their loved ones had joined for money or for other benefits or had joined because they believed the military would, as one spouse described, "do good things." Many of these veterans and military families recognized that as liberals, or as the children of liberals, they were different from many of the people they interacted with in the military.

Pre-Iraq Antiwar Activists

VFP started in 1985, and about half of the VFP activists I encountered during my participant observation had protested with this organization or with another left-leaning organization prior to the Iraq War. Several members of VFP had been members of VVAW, and in 2009 seven of the thirteen members of the VFP board had begun participating in antiwar activism during the Vietnam War. In his organizational self-description, Thomas Brinson, a VFP board member, recalled leading teach-ins about the Vietnam War before serving there with the Army. Seven of the ten VFP members I interviewed became activists against the Vietnam War after they fought in it. Some VFP activists spent time in military confinement for their refusal to deploy or for participation in protests against the Vietnam War after being drafted. These past antiwar experiences separated these activists from veterans in mainstream organizations such as the Veterans of Foreign War and the American Legion, both of which supported the Iraq War.

Other VFP activists became involved in antiwar activities much later than Vietnam but before the Iraq War. Ellen Barfield, a former VFP vice president and board member, served in the Army from 1977 to 1981 and became a self-described "full-time peace and justice activist" in 1988. She was active in the War Resisters League and the School of the Americas Watch. These paths to military peace movement activism show that this movement drew in part from participants who had been already mobilized by the antiwar movement.

Similarly, many MFSO parents were active against the Vietnam War, and some had protested subsequent wars. Some of these parents were horrified when their children joined the military. In fact, nearly half of the parents in MFSO that I spoke with described previous liberal activism. Jane Collins gave a speech in 2008 in which she explained the links between her previous activism and her membership in MFSO. Collins said that she and her husband had been peace activists since the Vietnam War and were upset when her son joined the Marines, though she did draw some comfort from the fact that the military was, at the time, acting primarily as a peace-keeping force. During the lead-up to the Iraq War, they "hit the streets hard" to protest, all the while worrying that their son would come home "damaged," like many of the Vietnam War's soldiers they had known. Collins's past as a peace protestor set her apart from many other military parents, and her worry for her son's safety set her apart from most of the peace protestors. Collins was happy when she found other military families in the peace movement, since she no longer felt "alone" as an outsider in the peace movement. The involvement of other military families in the movement was so meaningful to Collins that she wrote a book focused on these individuals.[20] Finding a group that connected participants' military identities to their activist identities encouraged their protest.

Post-Iraq Antiwar Activists

Many activists, particularly IVAW and MFSO members, were novices to protest. Some activists were freed by their differences from others in the military community to explore ideas that led them to protest. Others' fundamental differences from the military community led them to networks of people with politics that were more liberal than those typically found in the military.

A number of the military spouses in the movement believed they were a bit different from other military spouses in that they were less likely to put up with what the military and politicians threw their way. Stacey Hafley, whose Army husband came home with PTSD, did not feel that being a military spouse and being a peace activist were necessarily contradictory, but she did think that she did not fit the military spouse stereotype. In my interview with her at the 2006 VFP convention near her hometown in Missouri, Hafley said that on several issues she held views that were more liberal than those held by the military spouses she knew as an Army wife. She described how people were often surprised to see military wives protesting the war. She said, "They look at us with a kind of predetermined idea of what military wives are like. And they expect us to be, like, 'Yes, sir. No, sir'—really rigid, you know. . . . And most of us [wives in MFSO] probably don't make very good stereotypical military wives anyway." Hafley believed she protested because she was different from the military wives who had given up careers and many of their own dreams for military life. Hafley was unlikely to follow orders or to feel that it was her duty to increase troop morale, whereas other military husbands and wives toed the line in the same ways as their servicemember spouses.

A few Iraq War veterans described their activism as growing out of conflicted feelings about the military. As the grandson of a leader of the Religious Right, Stephen Potts grew up in a very religious and military-centric family. He graduated from the Air Force Academy and spent five years in active duty service. After the invasion of Afghanistan, Captain Potts began to question the role of the U.S. military in the world. He had never been comfortable with and did not enjoy being in the military or, even, going to the Air Force Academy. He felt stuck in the military, however, because getting a discharge was not easy. If Stephen had not finished school at the Academy, he would have still owed five years to the military and would have served as an enlisted member of the Air Force rather than in its officer corps. When the Iraq War ramped up in 2002, Potts decided to act on his conflicted feelings and applied for and received CO status. As a gay man in the Air Force, he had to hide his sexuality, but after he left, he came out more publicly. Like other activists, Potts's belief that he did not fit in with the military led him to seek a way to protest the Iraq War.

Some of the activists in the military peace movement had left-leaning politics that made them feel they were outside the military mainstream. These political leanings opened them to positions on the Iraq War that were outside the military's official position. Left political leanings that preceded the war were most common among VFP members and some of the parents in MFSO and the Gold Star organizations. These older members had likely experienced some of the factors that pushed them away from the military years before the Iraq War. Activists were outsiders within the wider military community, and they formed relationships with each other in the military peace movement. Rather than bonding because they or their loved ones worked together in the same military space, these activists came together, often over long distances, because they shared a political viewpoint—a sense of collectivity. Activists meshed their peace activism with their military connections rather than accept that in order to be affiliated with one community they had to give up their link to the other.

PEACE MOVEMENT OUTSIDERS

Just as the military peace movement defined itself in opposition to the rest of the military, part of defining the collective military–peace identity came through the creation of a culture of action that was separate from the rest of the peace movement. This was a product of activists' continued intentional affiliation with the military, which was a target for many antiwar activists. The military peace movement created a community in which military experiences were understood and not scorned, as they often were in other peace movement settings. A number of military peace movement activists were influenced by stereotypes of peace protestors as hippies, antimilitary, and unpatriotic. Additionally, many activists were treated poorly by some people in the wider peace movement. These stereotypes and negative firsthand interactions contributed to the military peace movement's creation of an intentional boundary between it and other peace movement organizations, resulting in a culture-of-action collective identity. This boundary making took several forms.

Degraded by Peaceniks

Activists in the military peace movement maintained distance between themselves and other antiwar organizations' protestors in part because they thought many of them had a negative opinion of the military. One woman who had deep connections to the military as a Marine mom, an Army and Marine aunt, and an Air Force and Marine sister wrote, "So many peace activists whom I've encountered through the years not only oppose war in all its forms, but they tend to be suspicious of, and negative toward, the U.S. military." One female Afghanistan veteran told me she felt "degraded by peaceniks." Military peace activists frequently expressed uneasiness with the larger peace movement because their military experiences made them feel like imposters. In our interview MFSO cofounder Nancy Lessin described getting "hate mail from the Left" when MFSO began:

We got hostile mail from people that said, "The only reason that you care about this is your loved one is there and, you know, I hope he dies, because that's what you deserve for having him join the military. Why didn't you stop him?" You know, stuff like that. You know, there's a rudeness on all sides.

This unfriendly treatment by others who considered themselves peace activists led to military peace movement activists' recognition that they shared an outsider position in relation to the larger peace movement. That is, members of the military peace movement felt uninvited into the broader antiwar movement.

Military peace activists described many participants in the general peace movement as uncomfortable with veterans or military families. Sometimes, members of the military peace movement engaged with the broader antiwar community around these issues, and this often highlighted their differences. In the summer of 2006, IVAW member Geoff Millard told me he was going to organize a seminar for the activists who were not in the military peace movement. He called it a "how to talk to a vet" session. He said this meeting was necessary because activists in the general peace movement were often well meaning but frequently asked "ignorant" questions of veterans and military families. He thought that activists needed to understand the fragile emotional and psychological state of veterans and military families. Millard thought that questions such as, "So did you kill anybody?" which was posed to veterans, or, "Why didn't you stop them from going to Iraq?" which was posed to spouses or parents, were unconscionable and needed to end. Millard believed that moderating a conversation between two different movement constituencies would help ease tensions and make a stronger coalition. I witnessed numerous examples of negative or ignorant treatment of military veterans and their family members, and in fact, I was asked, "How could you marry someone whose job it is to kill?" The stigmatization of members of the military often made it difficult for military-affiliated activists to identify with the broader antiwar movement. This marginalization, however, from the wider movement pushed together activists within this culture of action and provided fodder for bonding conversations among them. Some activists believed that others in the peace movement blamed the military or individual soldiers for aspects of the war. This led activists to be especially cautious about the types of organizations and protests they joined. These activists were drawn to the military peace movement because of how carefully participants worked to separate military individuals from those who directed the military to engage in the wars. In peace movement coalition meetings, military peace movement members continually edited statements and plans in order to ensure people would understand the difference between servicemembers and the policies of the wars. This distinction was prominently featured in movement actions such as the 2006 Santa Barbara Veterans Day parade, in which VFP and MFSO members marched behind a sign that read, "Question Leadership, Not Our Soldiers." By marching in a parade celebrating veterans and carrying U.S. and VFP flags, these activists sought to convey both their solidarity with military members and their displeasure with the Iraq War.

FIGURE 8. VFP Chapter 54 members (right to left) Bob Potter (Army Reserves, Korean War era), Ernie Moquin, Mischa Seligman (Army, World War II), Rowland "Lane" Anderson (Navy, Vietnam War), and Ron Dexter (Navy, Korean War) and an unknown man prepare to march in the 2007 Santa Barbara Veterans Day parade. Photograph by the author.

Boundaries

A number of activists described feeling a connection to the military peace movement rather than the wider peace movement because they believed their military experiences were more readily understood in this culture of action. I recorded nearly three dozen times when activists expressed relief that they did not have to explain their military connections. In his interview Iraq War veteran Geoff Millard said that VFP and IVAW were a "natural fit" for him. He was very clear about the ways in which military-affiliated individuals were different from the rest of the peace movement:

> And so there's a lot of things [that make us different]. We have a different language than everybody else. We have our own language, our own body motions, our own shared experience that really bring us closer than any other peace organizations I feel.

Millard said that military individuals were different from the rest of the peace movement because they shared a vocabulary that included terms to describe war and their own lives and a body language that was learned in the military. This idea of a separate language was important. Several military peace movement members expressed joy in finding a group in which they did not need to explain military acronyms or the military's policies that affected their lives. The intense emotional experiences of life in the military separated these activists from the wider peace movement—through language, experience, and ideology—and these experiences were important for the military peace movement's coalescence.

Activists in the military peace movement created their own submovement identity that rejected negative framing of the military. While military peace movement activities did draw participants without a direct connection to the military, identification with it separated the *us* from the *them*. VFP was the only organization I examined that included nonmilitary members, and they were designated as affiliate members and not given voting status. Although nonmilitary activists were a part of the movement, military service carried a unique perspective. A small percentage of nonveteran activists played an important role in VFP, and many, though not all, were military family members.

Many were wives of veterans from previous wars, and some were the children of veterans. These participants clearly saw themselves as part of the military peace movement, and affiliate members made clear their collective identification with VFP through clothing, verbal declarations, and meeting participation.

The boundary making I describe—through participation, materials, protest choices, and interactions—was rooted in an understanding of military peace activists' differences from other peace activists. During my interviews and fieldwork, I observed that all members expressed that "we" were those who not only participated in organizational tactics but who "got it." To get it was to link sympathy with Americans involved in the military and their families with actions to end the war, instead of criticism. The boundaries of the military–peace identity separated those who felt a connection to the military and worked to end the war from people who did not have a connection to the military in the peace movement, as well as from those with a connection to the military who supported the war in Iraq. This boundary making was important because it allowed activists to carve out a collective identity by making clear what they were not, which was often easier to define than who they were. Activists bonded over their shared outsider status, and they redefined this status as a positive aspect of their collective identity.

INSIDERS

Members of the military peace movement struggled to build a collective identity around their connection to the U.S. military and their opposition to the Iraq War. Despite feeling like outsiders in the wider military and peace communities, activists intentionally constructed a collective identity that combined both of these parts of themselves. In order to do this, activists affiliated themselves with organizations whose names implied a connection to both the military and antiwar activism. Within these organizations activists developed a collective consciousness that situated them as insiders within both communities. This insider consciousness was based on shared beliefs, which included the idea that the Iraq War was harmful to the military, military experiences turned people into peace activists, and activists should work simultaneously to end the war and to care for war veterans. Activists continually negotiated their combined military and peace activist identities as they claimed a privileged position within the peace community. As I detail in chapter 4, the military peace movement participants believed their insider identities allowed them to interact with both the military community and the general American public in ways that were positive for the peace movement. The military peace movement was a space where military individuals learned to embrace peace and where peace activists came to terms with their military identities. That is, activists used these military identities to create a unique culture of action within the peace movement that asserted a special vantage point for themselves as insiders in these diverse communities.

Embracing Both Peace and the Military

Activists in the military peace movement built a collective consciousness by asserting that opposing the war and supporting the troops were not incongruent. This consciousness incorporated respect for servicemembers into a consistently antiwar agenda. This happened in part by framing antiwar activism as protroop. Activists argued that an end to the Iraq War was part of a focus on the needs of the military community. In order to combine military and peace activist identities, participants defined the war as a problem for which those in the military were not culprits but rather some of its many victims. The military peace movement recognized the costs of war borne by military members and incorporated into their antiwar stance calls for improved veterans' and military families' care and benefits. By developing a collective consciousness that intertwined a critique of the Iraq War and a positive stance on military experience, the military peace movement facilitated some activists' incorporation of these two distinct aspects of their identity.

Membership requirements for the military peace movement demonstrated that activists saw themselves as both war opponents and connected to the military, as insiders in both spaces. All of the military peace organizations restricted membership to those who had a connection to the military and who agreed to the organizations' peace goals, which included an immediate end to the Iraq War or broader statements on working to end multiple wars. All used democratic voting to come to agreements on their goals for peace, and although activists were not asked to take an oath of allegiance to the movement's peace goals, IVAW and VFP did require potential members to verify their veteran status.[21] IVAW began to require this paperwork to check on the claims of those who represented the organization after their embarrassment from an association with an activist who drew significant attention by claiming to have witnessed war crimes in Iraq but who had not even completed basic training. Military affiliation was central enough to the groups' identity that participation was forbidden without it. Organizational leaders described this background-check process as critical to maintaining the organizations' legitimacy—to representing the voices of true military veterans. Although activists saw themselves as outsiders within the wider military community, they policed their own boundaries in ways that intentionally set themselves up as military insiders within the peace movement.

Peace Is Good for the Military

The military peace movement identity allowed participants to combine two important parts of their lives, and this marriage manifested in how activists talked about the movement. Some of the activists referred to their organizations as prosoldier or promilitary. A number of times, military peace movement activists claimed promilitary, antiwar status by highlighting their sending of equipment and care packages to servicemembers stationed in Iraq. Two activists in the movement, Army spouse Tammara Rosenleaf and Iraq War veteran Charlie Anderson, began Bake Sales for Body Armor. Anderson explained to a crowd near Slidell, Louisiana, in March 2006 that when he served as a Navy hospital corpsman who assisted Marines in the initial invasion of Iraq, he was not provided front and back inserts for his interceptor vest. Similarly, Rosenleaf's husband, who deployed to Iraq in 2005, was issued chest and back protection that was incorrectly sized, and he lacked armored side and deltoid plates. In response, Anderson and Rosenleaf spearheaded a grassroots endeavor from 2005 to 2007 that connected individual American soldiers in need with progressive groups who raised funds to buy armor through actual bake sales, as well as Internet fundraising drives. In a dozen states military peace movement organizations were key organizers of bake sales that not only helped the group supply more than thirty soldiers with gear but also directed media attention to what activists described as "inadequate preparation in the rush to war." Using tactics such as these allowed activists to demonstrate solidarity with the military while simultaneously publicizing a problematic element of the Iraq War. Through these projects activists developed an oppositional consciousness that directed questions about troop support away from activists and toward politicians.

Whereas a number of organizations in the anti–Iraq War movement were pacifist and some sought to dismantle the U.S. military, military peace movement members came together to fight against the Iraq War not because they were antimilitary but because they believed the war was detrimental to the military.[22] This belief made them outsiders among the mainstream military and peace activist communities, and it enabled activists to incorporate both military and peace activist aspects of their collective identity. In over two dozen speeches, pamphlets, and Web posts, IVAW referred to ending the war as "the best way to care for our brothers and sisters in the military." An IVAW strategy pamphlet stated:

> We are the troops, we know that there is no military solution in Iraq, and we know that the policies of our government are hurting the troops, destroying the military and violating the Iraqi people.

Activists believed their military service not only set them apart from others in the peace movement but also was a key component of their search for peace.

In addition to demonstrating a connection between the military and peace activism, many activists framed their antiwar activism as positive for the military. Some military peace movement participants referred to themselves as GI or soldiers' rights activists, as Gulf War veteran Dennis Kyne did in his interview. Activists' interests in the rights of people in the military led them to bring information on servicemembers' rights to Killeen, Texas, as part of an antiwar initiative in July and August 2006. Killeen was home to Fort Hood, the

FIGURE 9. Elliott Adams, who served as a U.S. Army infantry paratrooper in Vietnam, Japan, and Korea, hands out a wallet-sized card on GI rights and a postcard about local screenings of the documentary film *Sir, No Sir* (Displaced Films and BBC 2005), which is about Vietnam soldiers' protest of that war. He handed them to cars, such as the one in the foreground, that had military servicemembers and families leaving the main gate of Fort Hood in Killeen, Texas. Military police on foot and in cars (*in background*) monitor the actions of this VFP president during the summer of 2006. The number on his sleeve refers to the number of U.S. casualties in Iraq on that day. Photograph by the author.

largest U.S. Army base. Many soldiers stationed there had been deployed to Iraq, some multiple times. Activists posted fliers on cars, pasted stickers to bathroom stalls in places military members frequented, and offered free food to soldiers who attended screenings of the documentary *Sir! No Sir!* This film chronicled U.S. soldiers' resistance to the Vietnam War, and activists expressed hope that the film would, in the words of one Vietnam veteran, "inspire these guys and girls to recognize the importance of not simply following orders." Activists believed that by explaining to military members their options besides deployment, they helped both these individuals and the antiwar cause. As this example shows, activists developed tactics that framed their antiwar activism as positive for the military.

War Experience Leads One to Seek Peace

Materials and speeches in the military peace movement often used a version of the following General Douglas MacArthur quote: "On the contrary, the soldier, above all other people, prays for peace, for he must suffer and bear the deepest wounds and scars of war." All VFP pamphlets published during the Iraq War included the organization's statement of purpose, which began, "We, having dutifully served our nation, do hereby affirm our greater responsibility to serve the cause of world peace." This statement suggested that peace activism was merely an extension of public service that activists began during their time in the military.

Younger veterans shared the belief that peace activism was an extension of military duty. In a Web post Sergeant Selena Coppa detailed how each of the Army's core values (loyalty, duty, respect, selfless service, honor, integrity, and personal courage) was fulfilled by her participation in IVAW. She first listed the full Army value statement in bold and then added her take on this value:

> **Selfless Service: Put the welfare of the Nation, the Army, and your subordinates before your own.** Being a member of IVAW is hard. It is hard to stand up, to devote effort and time to an organization committed to what is right, when your leadership so firmly believes that it is wrong. It's hard to face the intimidation and harassment that many

members of the active duty military face when they begin to speak out on what they feel. It's hard to stand up and tell your higher ups that they are committing crimes. But the welfare of the Nation, our continued survival as an honorable country, and the continued survival of the Army depends on some of us standing up, and saying, "Sir, no Sir!" That we will not participate in illegal acts, and we will report them when and where we see them. We will not train our soldiers to commit them, and will train our soldiers to follow the honorable path. And the honorable path now, the hard service, means standing up and speaking the truth, so that legislators can begin to realize it, and bring us home.

Coppa explained that although it was difficult, the military community had to do the right thing, which she described as joining the antiwar movement. She suggested that they had to do so in order to bring honor back to the military and the United States. These Web posts reflected many conversations I overhead in the military peace movement. People developed a military–peace identity in part because they believed their anti–Iraq War activism reflected the military's core values.

Care Work as Central to Insider–Outsider Identity

Military peace movement members and organizations described their goals and purposes as distinct from the goals of other parts of the peace movement because they focused simultaneously on the needs of the military community and the "illegality of the Iraq War." These goals demonstrated that the military peace movement's collective identity was built on insider–outsider status. By insisting on goals that encompassed both traditional peace movement outcomes and care for troops, the military peace movement claimed a stake in both communities, but activists recognized that these dual goals were seen as contradictory by many mainstream members of the military and the peace movement. All military peace movement organizations stated goals of ending the Iraq War alongside goals of improving the lives of military families and veterans. IVAW leadership described the organization as having three points of unity that focused the organization's work on achieving not only complete U.S. withdrawal from Iraq and reparations for Iraqis but also "full benefits, adequate healthcare (including mental health), and other support for returning service-men and women." MFSO also referred to this in its mission, which can be found in its members' speeches, its recruitment brochures, its members' editorials, and its protest signs, such as, "Support Our Troops, Bring Them Home Now, *and* Take Care of Them When They Get Here!" The "and" in that statement was often italicized in the or-ganization's materials, showing that care for returning veterans was a focus. These goals distinguished the military peace movement and demonstrated their placement in two very different cultures.

Activists not only participated in fundraising, information, and ser-vice efforts for veterans' issues such as mental and physical health care but also connected these issues to the war. During an MFSO conference call in the fall of 2008, one member remarked that MFSO's message dif-fered from prowar groups' because they believed that Iraq War veterans "shouldn't have gone to war and gotten PTSD in the first place." An-other activist suggested that in order to prevent more cases of PTSD, we had to "make sure we only [used] soldiers [in war] when absolutely nec-essary." Military peace movement activists shared the belief that ending the Iraq War and caring for military veterans were linked, thus allowing them to combine these seemingly disparate identities.

In October 2010, IVAW launched a long-term campaign, called Op-eration Recovery, that endeavored to bring attention to the repeated deployment of "traumatized troops on psychotropic medications." The other military peace movement organizations were also involved in the press conferences, letter-writing campaigns, and other tactics aimed at calling attention to this issue. An Oregon MFSO chapter's newsletter described this fight against sending servicemembers with PTSD, traumatic brain injury (TBI), and military sexual trauma to war as a battle over the "right to heal for all servicemembers." Activists targeted Fort Hood, which had made the news for a rash of military suicides in 2010. IVAW created a fact sheet that outlined the lack of care, particularly psychological care, provided and available to mili-tary members, especially at Fort Hood. They used this issue to build solidarity with the wider military community by handing out hun-dreds of purple ribbons to Fort Hood soldiers, which they claimed symbolized their "solidarity with the tens of thousands of soldiers who [were] suffering from un-treated trauma because of the wars in Iraq and Afghanistan." When activists tried to meet with the base com-mander in May 2011, they were escorted off base by security guards who expressed sympathy with and interest in their protest when the IVAW activists identified as veterans suffering from PTSD.

In 2011, MFSO also focused its attention on the need for military families to heal. They offered the first of what they hoped to be an an-nual Native American healing retreat in the Black Hills of South Da-kota. This retreat, involving "a traditional Sioux healing ceremony," was open to all veterans and military families but was advertised spe-cifically within MFSO, GSFSO, and IVAW circles, with the intention of reaching people who saw care work as an important element of their antiwar military identity.

Activists could have reconciled their war protest and military con-nections by choosing to exist in the military community and not iden-tifying as peace activists or by becoming peace activists and ignoring

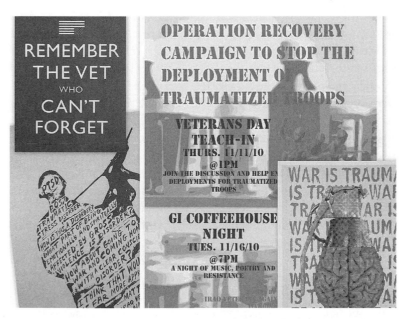

FIGURE 10. IVAW members created art meant to help them heal and that they hoped could speak to the public about the traumas of war. These images were fashioned by the Justseeds Artists' Cooperative, which included members of IVAW, and these were turned into posters for the Operation Recovery/War Is Trauma campaign.

their military connections. Military peace movement activists, however, claimed insider identities within both communities. This culture-of-action collective identity was built on a shared consciousness that military peace movement activists did not have to remain merely outsiders but rather shared a unique position as insiders in both the military and the peace movement. This unique position allowed them to see how military problems and psychological troubles resulted from the Iraq War.

CONCLUSION

Military peace movement members were outsiders in both the military and the peace movement because they tried to be connected to both. The movement created, however, a collective identity in which they could take pride and reconcile these seemingly contradictory identities. Activists' collective consciousness separated support and honor for the troops, which activists demonstrated in their rhetoric, from agreement with the policies of the wars. Activists constructed an identity that integrated their connection to the military community and their antiwar sentiments. As activists took on the combined military and peace activist identities, they challenged narrow conceptions of both constituencies. Instead of seeing these two identities as contradictory, activists did personal and collective identity work to rewrite the meaning of the military and antiwar activism so that these two conceptions could be seen as complementary.

The pathways to activism taken by military peace movement participants reflect four social-psychological motivations for activism that mobilize people who would seem unlikely to join a particular movement. First, activists must be exposed to information that challenges the status quo or dominant understandings of the situation. This information must also provide them with a way to understand that their (or the world's) troubles are not due to individual flaws but to problems in the social structure. Second, involvement in activism must speak to activists' core values and refine what it means to live up to that value by requiring action to change the situation. Third, many individuals must experience hardship firsthand before they are compelled to overcome the risks of activism. Fourth, networks must

Overall Motivations	Specific Use in Military Peace Movement	Motivating Emotions
Information literacy	Learn about atrocities or the lack of WMDs or al-Qeada connection in Iraq	Anger, betrayal
Value redefinition	Patriotism is not obedience to orders and policy makers but protest	Righteous anger
Personal experience of grievance/hardship	Lack of preparation for Iraq War, back-door draft, lack of mental health care and other services for veterans, guardsmen, and active duty families	Sadness, fear, guilt, anger
Networks	Connections to Left politics of feminism, liberals, and GLBTQ issues or movement itself	Comfort, love, group pride

FIGURE 11. Social Psychological Motivations for Unlikely Activists.

provide comfort, as well as connections to politics or world views that are contrary to what activists would otherwise experience.

While a number of factors cause people to seek out social movement activism as a way to express their political viewpoints, not all people elect to join or remain members of activist organizations. Social movement organizations must convince people that it is worthwhile to take part in social movement activism, and part of this involves developing a community where a participant feels that they are part of a collective working toward an admirable end. Social movement scholars refer to this sense of belonging, community, or we-ness among participants as collective identity. Although activists share various qualities, they do not automatically have a collective identity. Rather, a collective identity develops out of numerous interactions within a social movement.[23] Military peace movement activists built such a community by recognizing and highlighting their unique insider–outsider status.

The military peace movement was a distinct culture of action, or submovement, inside the broader peace movement.[24] Social movement scholars recognize the existence of a layer in between organizations and movements when they describe them as having branches.[25] Cultures of action vary by their definitions of problems, emotional norms, privileged identities, strategies, and tactics. Examining the culture-of-action level of identity allows scholars to understand the importance of divisions and connections between organizations in movements. Activists within a movement interact with members of various organizations, and they frequently develop strong bonds with people beyond their own organizations, but not with all members of a wider movement. An exploration of the culture-of-action level of collective identity can better explain the totality of relationships that facilitate mobilization, sustain participation, and transform activists' lives. In this chapter and the following, I demonstrate the development and importance of the culture-of-action level of collective identity.

By focusing my analysis of collective-identity formation at this level, I expand the layers of collective identity that social movement scholars have used. William Gamson suggests that collective identity has three embedded layers: solidary (or reference group), movement, and organizational.[26] The military peace movement's collective identity was distinct from their identification with individual organizations and separate from a broader peace movement identity. It also diverged from activists' identification with the military, which closely resembled the solidary level. The culture-of-action layer of collective identity allows social movement scholars to understand how activists bond within multiorganization subsections or sectors of a wider movement, not just a single organization.

Although the military peace movement saw itself as distinct from the wider military and peace movement community, it was a part of both. Activists believed that this combined identity was important for the movement's ability to effect change. Movement cultures of action are likely to have distinct targets. The military peace movement believed it was particularly suited to targeting both the military community and the general public, especially Americans who considered themselves patriotic. In chapters 4 and 5, I describe how activists displayed their integrated identity to the public through various strategies and tactics. These chapters show the importance of the strategic use of this combined identity. First, though, I continue a discussion of the interconnectedness of the organizations in this culture of action and the positive emotional consequences of movement solidarity.

3

Building a Family and Transforming Activists' Emotions

The Walkin' to New Orleans Veterans and Survivors March for Peace and Justice, which lasted from March 13 to 19, 2006, was one of many political activities that brought members of the military peace movement into close contact and where they ate and lived together for extended periods of time. The march was requested by a VFP chapter in Mobile, Alabama. The theme of the march was, "Every bomb dropped in Iraq explodes along the Gulf Coast," which is a rewording of Dr. Martin Luther King Jr.'s statement, from his autobiography, "Yet bombs in Vietnam also exploded at home."[1] The activists hoped to create a link between the lack of progress in that area's recovery in the six months following Hurricane Katrina and the spiraling costs of the Iraq War. The march was organized largely by three Army combat veterans of the Vietnam War: David Cline, Elliott Adams, and Stan Goff. Goff served in the Army Special Forces (the Rangers and Delta Force) in South and Central America, Somalia, and Haiti and was the father of an Iraq War veteran. VFP invited the other military peace movement organizations and local groups organizing for Hurricane Katrina survivors' rights to join them in the march. Although the tactic garnered some national and much local media coverage, the action is better understood as a bonding activity wherein activists shared physical exhaustion, extensive political conversations, and close, primitive living quarters for approximately one week. This sharing aided activists' healing from war-induced anger, fear, and guilt by encouraging reciprocal emotions of love between activists and focusing their anger on the causes of war.

During one evening's program with local community members, activists spoke of the horrors of war, racism, and misplaced government priorities to an audience at Mt. Pilgrim Missionary Baptist Church in

FIGURE 12. On March 16, 2006, IVAW members sit on rubble in Biloxi, Mississippi. The majority of their march from Mobile, Alabama, to New Orleans saw little recovery from Hurricane Katrina, which had destroyed most of that coastline in August 2005. Photograph by the author.

Long Beach, Mississippi.[2] The emotional speeches covered activists' personal reasons for seeking an end to the Iraq War. A Vietnam veteran elaborated on his role in that war and the resulting shame he and others felt for taking part in an unjustified war, and through tears a mother described the "mind-numbing fear and sadness" brought on by her son's deployment. A male Army medic and Iraq War veteran choked up as he described the death of a friend in Iraq, and he stared at the floor as he held his head in his hands as he described his involvement in Iraqis' deaths. The activists focused their anger on governmental and military leaders for dragging them or their loved ones into the war. A number of military peace movement activists in the audience cried on each other's shoulders while holding onto one another as activists told emotional stories. These actions demonstrated how activists sought to replace the emotions of war, which could have left them feeling powerless, with emotions such as directed anger and love for the group.

Over the next few days, activists revealed intensely personal details of their lives, discussing abuse, medical conditions, politics, travels, romantic relationships, and emotions. These conversations were a space to share their joys and sorrows. They shared food, alcohol, and other drugs and a camp-like space that was primitive but made livable thanks in part to their military experience. Participants were very communal and also very protective of each other, rotating watch duties for the night's encampment and other jobs necessary to make the week safe. Activists carefully arranged themselves in the camps in order to protect one another and offered to act as lookouts for those who wanted to bathe in makeshift military-style outdoor showers. They created a sense of community by sharing their daily routines. In addition to learning about each other and bonding over shared personal and political interests, activists faced a daily multiple-mile march through a devastated countryside and primitive camping conditions in new locations every night. This shared experience provided them with a sense of accomplishment. They even made a T-shirt to commemorate the march, which was given to all military peace movement participants in attendance.

When we marched, I was herded into a group of MFSO activists who were marching with Gold Star family members in the middle of a 100-to-500-person crowd whose numbers increased as we came closer to New Orleans. These military families marched behind IVAW and sometimes behind and sometimes ahead of VFP; the activists from other organizations marched behind us. Even Gold Star mother Cindy Sheehan, who was then at the height of her celebrity within the peace movement and in the media, marched behind IVAW. This positioning kept the military peace movement organizations together as a family and showed that IVAW was being emphasized by the other organizations. It demonstrated how this culture of action perceived itself as bounded and revealed its internal structure.

During the long marches, particularly as the group reached crowded areas, the activists chanted in ways that underlined their combined military–antiwar identities, as well as pointed out each group individually. Before the Iraq War began, VFP had used some version of these chants, which were called out as if they were a traditional military cadence. Two verses highlight their experiences as veterans:

Hey, hey, Uncle Sam,
We remember Vietnam.
We don't want this Iraq War.
Bring our troops back to our shores.

If they tell you to go,
There is one thing you should know:
They wave the flag when you attack;
When you're home, they turn their back.

These verses allude to the negative experiences of soldiers in Vietnam and the betrayal veterans felt when they returned home. The verses point to veterans' past war experiences and their poor treatment as the reasons they sought an end to the Iraq War.

VFP president David Cline wrote the following verse for MFSO, which was used during the march:

Military families speakin' out,
We know what we're talking about.
Sons and daughters, husbands, wives,
Bring our loved ones home alive.

This verse draws on MFSO's familial connection to give it emotional resonance, whereas the veterans' verses point to their direct experiences.[3] Gold Star families were given a similarly emotional verse to chant:

Gold Star Families for Peace,
Hoping that our pain will ease.
Our loved ones had to die in vain,
Speaking truth to the pain.

Like MFSO's verse, the Gold Star verse points to their familial connection to the war, and it draws on emotional language to support their activism.

IVAW chanted various cadence verses, such as the following:

Iraq Vets Against the War,
We know what we're fighting for.
Our friends had to bleed and die,
And we're left to wonder why.

These words point to both their experience of the Iraq War and the heartache it caused. This verse was originally VFP's, the IVAW vets replacing "veterans" with "Iraq vets" in the first line. This lyric change underlined the close connection between these two groups. All of these verses were chanted together, along with verses that pointed out problems activists saw with the war. Taken together, they fleshed out the family of organizations within the military peace movement. No other organizations in the march were given cadence verses, which demonstrated that the military peace movement saw itself as distinct from the larger peace and justice movement.

Each night, following the day's march, media interviews, and ceremonies, the participants came together in various bonding rituals. Most nights, activists performed music that ranged from gospel spirituals to Vietnam veterans' folk songs, such as "Touch a Name on the Wall," to rap and folk rock by IVAW activists. On Saturday, March 18, they created a stage in the Vietnamese immigrant community of East New Orleans. There, Josh Dawson, an Iraq War veteran, outlined a new initiative to encourage creative outlets for the sadness, fear, and anger created by war. He said that this Veterans Artists Collective provided him with "another way to express the intense emotions" he had due to his war experiences. He read poetry that captured his struggle to control his rage and overcome his guilt.[4] Joe Hatcher and Garrett Reppenhagen read several poems about their experiences in the Iraq War that were meant to elicit anger at the policies of war. VFP and IVAW members demonstrated solidarity when David Cline, Ward Reilly, Josh Dawson, and Ethan Crowell played music together. GSFP cofounder Bill Mitchell, also a Vietnam-era veteran, read a poem about his son who died in Iraq. IVAW member Stephen Potts read a hilarious piece that compared servicemembers not speaking against wars they knew to be wrong to holding in a fart.

One song, by former Navy medic Charlie Anderson, who was

stationed with the Marines in Iraq, is entitled "Price We've Had to Pay." This song describes Anderson's experience with posttraumatic stress disorder from his service in Iraq, which made him feel like "that crazy vet" in a bar who doesn't let a fellow patron change the TV channel from a tribute to a fallen soldier "brother." This image suggests a loneliness that veterans felt as Americans ignored the war and its veterans but offered hollow expressions of support for the troops. His lyrics include the following: "They tied yellow ribbons to a lamp-post and went out shopping again. But out there in the desert, there's blood running through the sand. My boys are taking cover any way they know how. But around here does anybody care about the price we've had to pay?" His song describes veterans' emotional journey home and their feelings of powerlessness. By singing songs or reading pieces that publicized their experiences, activists transformed these emotions into resistance.

These cultural rituals brought out expressions of love from and for fellow activists. As I quietly cried and wrote down the lyrics to Anderson's song, Geoff Millard recognized my emotional state and came over to rub my shoulders. After the song all members of IVAW gathered into a massive group hug, and Millard said he needed to "join the IVAW lovefest." This group hug demonstrated how activists actively sought to replace the negative emotions expressed in Anderson's song with demonstrations of loving emotions. Expressions of care were an important part of helping activists heal from the war and of maintaining movement cohesion.

This extended ethnographic example illuminates the family structure of this culture and how tactics that were aimed at broad political change also affected internal-movement dynamics. Activists from all organizations suggested that this march, like the time spent at Camp Casey in Crawford, was a pivotal moment for bringing the movement organizations closer together and helping activists form a connection to the movement. For these individuals the politics of war had tremendous personal and emotional consequences. These tactics brought activists, many of whom had few other military peace movement activists in their local communities, into close contact, which promoted healing. This healing began with a public presentation of their emotions of powerlessness, in which they named war, rather than themselves, as the cause of their problems. Activists were able to overcome that powerlessness through mutual support, which promoted empowerment and group pride, and through a shared consciousness, which directed their anger externally.

This chapter describes the military peace movement's collective identity by outlining how activists built a strong emotional attachment that crossed organizational boundaries. Military peace movement activists provided intense emotional support for one another. As I describe in chapter 2, movement activists built an identity as veterans and military family members who were also peace activists, which rendered them as both insiders and outsiders. Veterans, military family members, and servicemembers formed a family-like structure of organizations that valued and privileged activists' insider–outsider position. Together, these organizations created a movement collective identity based on emotional, financial, cognitive, and, in some cases, biological ties. The military connections of these organizations drew them together into a culture of action built on collective identities as insider–outsiders within the peace and military communities. The strength of a culture-of-action identity can be seen by examining the family-like structure of the militarily peace movement's collective identity, which mediated activists' emotions.

Activists had come to think of themselves as a family, and this helped to solidify bonds between the organizations. Through these bonds military peace movement activists transformed *emotions of powerlessness* into *emotions of resistance*. Veterans and military families who opposed the Iraq War often experienced guilt and anger over their participation in war or their inability to stop the participation of others, loneliness as military and peace movement outsiders, and fear over the war's consequences for friends and family. These are the emotions of powerlessness, and they can restrict activism and make it difficult for people to engage in it unless a movement actively confronts them and reaffirms stigmatized identities and supports traumatized individuals.[5] The military peace movement's family-like structure and resulting affection between activists facilitated movement continuation. The construction of a movement family identity altered activists' emotions so that they expressed group pride, love for and protectiveness of fellow activists, and anger directed at structures and authorities. Drawing on my work with Verta Taylor, I call these emotions of resistance.[6] The activists engaged in significant emotion work, and interactions among the participants functioned as a therapy that helped them channel the negative emotions of war into the more productive emotions of resistance.

THE MILITARY PEACE MOVEMENT FAMILY

During interviews and in my participant observations, many activists described intense emotional and personal commitments to the military peace movement that solidified their sense of a collective identity. Activists came together to challenge the war, discuss the latest war news, and meet with other activists with whom they felt a connection. Members described making friends through the movement and demonstrated their bonds through physical and social intimacy, such as touching, hugging, and spending time together outside movement activities. Activists characterized other participants as family, and as an activist family the movement provided more than a political community. Their bonds were intensely personal. Although a family, each organization had different roles, and important differences existed between and within organizations.

A Tight-Knit Family

All of the activists I interviewed described the military peace movement organization as tightly connected, although their personal participation colored how connected they were to other members in this culture of action. This culture-of-action identity encouraged solidarity between members of different organizations, and these family bonds affected the ability of the military peace movement to achieve its goals. The connections between the organizations were visible in activist interviews, movement materials, and embodied connections. Additionally, military peace movement families operated through face-to-face interactions at both the national and the local levels.

National Families

Activists that were able to attend national events regularly described the commonalities they shared with military peace movement organizations, praised individuals within the culture of action, and explained movement connections in familial terms. MFSO activist Theresa Dawson described the movement as connected through activists' shared experiences. She called the culture of action comprising VFP, IVAW, MFSO, and the Gold Star organizations a "big military family" where "the team effort is really what counts." This quote reveals a common theme among military peace movement activists: they believed the family of organizations made a greater impact than could their individual organizations. Activists described the importance of individual ties among actors in this culture of action rather than of official organizational alliances.

The importance of the culture-of-action level of collective identity was revealed in my interview with Colonel Ann Wright (Retired). Although I asked about her connections to other activists within her organization, VFP, she volunteered information on the connections among all parts of the military peace movement. She described not only events where activists from these different organizations collaborated but also the welcoming she received from other military peace movement organizations. She explained the military peace movement family as follows:

> Well, we are all in this together as the little part of your history that put you in this unique position, that you're part of the military structure. Whether you are a family member, a former member of a [military] family, if your loved one's been killed, or if you're a veteran of any war, particularly the war in Iraq, we're all in it together. And the uniqueness of that and the power of it . . . all of these people speaking together.

In this quote she describes how the insider–outsider identity was important to building a culture-of-action collective identity—that although the organizations had various constituencies, their shared military experiences brought them together.

The connections among these organizations were visible in their brochures and other materials. Two different MFSO brochures included information on "working in coalition" with military peace movement organizations as an important element of their protest. The brochures listed IVAW, VFP, and VVAW as members of their coalition. The 2006 brochure also listed GSFP, but the 2007 brochure had a separate paragraph on GSFSO as a chapter of MFSO. The 2006 VFP brochure described having "joined together" with MFSO and "supported recently returned vets who formed the Iraq Veterans Against the War." A 2007 IVAW brochure described how soldiers who were denied their rights could get "support from organizations like IVAW, VFP, MFSO, or GSFP." This support was described as an important benefit of membership. All of the military peace movement organizations' websites included links to the other organizations, often highlighting them as support organizations or placing their information on the site's home page. These materials demonstrate the close-knit relationship among these organizations.

Some activists were related to members of other organizations within the military peace movement. The husband of MFSO chapter leader and former board member Stacy Hafley was an Iraq War veteran and a member of IVAW. Despite having a literal family connection to IVAW, in her interview she gushed about her personal and her organization's relationship to VFP, which she described as "wonderful—these people are like my family, you know." Other IVAW members also shared biological relationships with members in MFSO, and these ties were frequently pointed to as a reason loving connections spread to unrelated members of the movement, as when mothers such as Tina Richards became mother figures for a number of veterans within IVAW. These literal familial links among the organizations strengthened the fictive family connections within this culture of action; activists drew on existing bonds and enhanced them by developing solidarity with fictional kin.

Several individuals within the movement were members of multiple military peace movement organizations. In 2007, members of IVAW were granted free dual memberships in VFP for one year. Many IVAW members chose to join VFP because they felt connected to the members of that organization and because VFP had broader peace goals. Since IVAW's focus was initially exclusively on the Iraq War, membership in VFP allowed Iraq veterans the freedom to protest other aspects of U.S. foreign policy. Since many of those who joined the U.S. volunteer forces came from military families, a number of MFSO and Gold Star activists were unsurprisingly veterans themselves.[7] Former VFP executive director Michael McPhearson (2005–10) was both a Gulf War veteran and the father of an Iraq War veteran. At a number of forums, McPhearson spoke specifically as an MFSO member rather than as a veteran or representative of VFP. Additionally, some nonveteran military and Gold Star family members joined VFP as associate members, typically for the same reasons as did IVAW members. The multiple membership overlaps demonstrate the strong connections between the organizations and the porous boundaries within this culture of action.

Since 2004, the VFP convention has provided space for IVAW and MFSO meetings or conventions to run concurrently. At national protests the activists typically shared a space from which to hand out materials, meet with the media, collect donations, and sell goods such as T-shirts and buttons. Activists coordinated marching together in large-scale protests by emailing the location of veteran and military family meet-up locations. Nearly all of the events sponsored by each organization included speakers' lists that drew from several of the military peace movement organizations, and activists from these organizations frequently listened closely to each other's sad, fearful, and angry experiences of the war. A December 10, 2006, event in Santa Barbara included the following speakers: VFP member Ann Wright, IVAW member Geoff Millard, Gold Star parents Carlos and Mélida Arredondo, and MFSO father Tim Kahlor. This mixed group of speakers allowed for interactions among the organizations, brought in speakers from across the country, and further demonstrated the close relationships that bound participants in this culture of action.

Local Families

A number of activists described important regional or city-based families of VFP, IVAW, MFSO, and Gold Star activists, whereas others had movement families comprising activists involved in national organizing and events. When a local chapter of a military peace movement organization engaged in marches, sit-ins at politicians' offices, or tabling at events, corresponding local chapters of the other organizations typically offered help through cosponsoring, manpower, and donations. My long-term participant observation in Santa Barbara and at national events allowed me to personally experience as well as to observe both local and national connections. In Santa Barbara activists described their fellow military peace movement activists as their "closest friends," their "church" and their "new family." The group welcomed me with open arms because, as they explained, I was a military family member and thus one of "us." Activists invited me to join weekly lunches and happy hours with the group, where they continued the bonding conversations about politics, personal lives, and the peace movement begun at official meetings and events. I was also invited to join some of the activists for holidays, including Christmas, and when my husband returned from his first deployment, these activists' welcomed him home with a party at a VFP member's home. Not only activists who operated on the national stage believed that the members of these organizations were connected, but local-level activists recognized members of this culture of action as part of their family by passing out the other organizations' information and welcoming the other organizations' members as equals.

An IVAW member described a similar familial relationship with activists in Los Angeles. Navy veteran Maricela Guzman felt a close connection to people in the local VFP chapter that she described as love. Guzman's constant interactions with veterans of another era on a local level allowed her to bond across organizational boundaries. These bonds were strained at the national level, however, when some VFP activists assumed she was a military family member rather than a veteran, because she was a woman. Although Guzman recognized MFSO activists as her activist family members, she wanted her veteran status acknowledged, and she was frustrated with this gendered assumption. Although Guzman had difficulty being recognized for her particular type of experience with war, she was still accepted into the military peace movement and identified with it as an important part of her own identity. The collective identity forged at the culture-of-action level did not override organizational collective identity or individual identities.

Rather, this layer interacted with the others in dynamic ways that likely bonded some activists more closely than others.

At national and local events, military peace movement organizations operated shared spaces and resources in ways that emphasized their cohesion. When IVAW decided to reach out to active duty military members through bus tours to military bases beginning in 2007, they contacted MFSO and VFP for logistical and financial support. The bus was driven by a VFP member and staffed by a group of IVAW members. As the bus came into town, it was met by people from all of the organizations within this culture of action, who arranged the details necessary to put on press conferences, reached out to local military personnel and their families, and provided food and housing for the bus occupants.

On both a national and a local level, activists developed a military peace movement family. This family of choice rested on a shared understanding of activists' identities as insider–outsiders, as described in chapter 2. Although activists maintained distinct organizational collective identities, they embraced commonalities across these boundaries. Though these relationships varied in scope, type, and locale, activists described this culture of action as a family. Activists in the military peace movement often shared physical space and multiple days in close quarters, which also led to close-knit cross-organizational relationships. The organizations often played different roles in the movement, however, and this could cause tensions.

Family Roles

Activists described the military peace movement as a family in which each of the organizations played a unique role. While it was not unusual for movement participants to describe their connections to other activists in familial terms, the familial bond was unique because it was constructed across organizations and encompassed an entire culture of action.

The Benefits of an Established Organization

As described in chapter 1, VFP was founded before the other organizations in this family.[8] At the start of the Iraq War, VFP was the most established organization in this family, which put it in the position of having resources upon which the other organizations could draw. VFP helped IVAW and MFSO develop as organizations and recruit members through financial and institutional support. One of IVAW's founders, Tim Goodrich, described in his interview a continuing close relationship with VFP and suggested that this organization played a central role in IVAW's birth:

> Vets for Peace was the fiscal sponsor of IVAW. So we obtained our 501(c)(3) nonprofit status through them. And they are actually involved, too. Many of the members of VFP helped us, kind of guide us along the way, help us with knowing what to do.

VFP provided initial start-up funds to IVAW and continued to contribute to the organization such that VFP leaders also described it as the "fiscal sponsor" of IVAW. As Tim pointed out, that money was not the only resource provided by VFP. The past organizing experience of VFP and its members helped guide the formation of IVAW by establishing organizational tax and regulation documents, providing office space, and offering staff to work for the organization. Additionally, VFP resources were used to provide MFSO and Gold Star activists with what one VFP activist called "a forum" to "support" them by arranging speaking events and providing logistical assistance. In emails, fliers, meetings, and informal conversations, a number of IVAW members referred to VFP as the "parent organization of IVAW." The long history of VFP made it what one MFSO spouse from Texas called "the daddy [organization] of us all." VFP's greater financial security, especially at the start of the Iraq War, with longer donor lists and grant-writing experience, was instrumental to MFSO's development of various campaigns. These factors sometimes lent a patriarchal quality to the military peace movement family, at least in the initial years.

During their attempts to prevent the Iraq War, VFP and MFSO marched together in national and local protests. Speaking during an assembly at the 2007 VFP convention in St. Louis, MFSO cofounders Nancy Lessin and Charlie Richardson explained, "At that first march VFP president David Cline asked us to march by their side, and we have never left." Lessin and Richardson repeated that line in numerous speeches to underscore the relationship between MFSO and VFP, which began during the prewar march in Washington, D.C., in January 2003. By claiming a position next to VFP, MFSO saw itself in an equal partnership. In her interview Lessin described the importance of MFSO's affiliation with VFP:

> These were, you know, these were people who understood 'cause they had families when they were over there [in war]. And there was just, there was a comfort in that military families/veterans community that just was, that connection was there, and it has been there. And there was something that happened to me actually personally that kind of sparked that, and it was back to that first big national march that we were in. In October of 2002 in Washington, D.C., I was standing with my poster, "Our son is a Marine, don't send him to war for oil." And there was a man probably my age, and he was wearing part of a military uniform, and it was clear that he was a Vietnam veteran, and he was coming to join this march. He came up to me. He hugged me, and he said, "I wish my mom had been doing this when I was in Vietnam." And then he walked on. And it was like, "Ahhh" [exaggerated sigh], okay. This is the right thing to be doing. So I think within sort of the larger peace movement there's been a place that we've been most comfortable with military, ex-military, and families.

Not only did VFP invite MFSO into a working relationship but this relationship was built on the recognition that these two organizations were part of a larger family. The connection between the two organizations mediated the fears created by activists' outsider status and allowed them to be comfortable in their combination of military experience and peace activism. The fact that the majority of early MFSO activists were parents of servicemembers and from the same generation as VFP activists also aided this partnership.

In May 2003, MFSO founders joined VFP for a series of press conferences and actions entitled Operation Dire Distress. According to a report by VFP's then executive director, Korean War veteran Woody Powell, this tactic led to the VFP office fielding calls from "from mothers and fathers of youngsters serving in Iraq—or who were slated to serve soon." VFP passed them to MFSO. On a national level the two organizations developed close ties, collaborating on strategy and tactics via frequently scheduled calls among board members and staff. The relationship solidified in the fall of 2003 when MFSO asked VFP to partner on a national initiative to increase the visibility of antiwar military families in the Iraq War debate, which they titled the Bring Them Home Now! Campaign. The MFSO and VFP partnership continued because activists occupied complementary positions in relation to the war: the veterans had direct work experience that made them insiders on war, and military families' insider position on the war came via their connection to veterans.

Gendered Family Ties

For activists in MFSO and the Gold Star organizations, their familial relations were the most important aspect of their activist identities. On a number of occasions, IVAW activists acknowledged MFSO and Gold Star activists as the "moms" of the group. During a speech following the 2006 march to New Orleans, Iraq War veteran Geoff Millard described the protectiveness he felt toward MFSO and GSFP/GSFSO activists. He depicted himself as a "mama's boy," and he warned prowar activists to treat the "moms of our partner organizations" well. He threatened to defend them, saying, "You don't mess with my mommas." Other IVAW activists called specific activists within MFSO and GSFSO "my activist mom" or an "IVAW mom." Similarly, some MFSO and GSFSO members referred to themselves as "mom of the Army" or "MFSO dad" or "mom to IVAW members." The most common example was the title the media and some within the movement used for Cindy Sheehan, "Peace Mom."[9] A number of open letters by military families, which MFSO posted on its website, were signed by or titled with a reference to a military branch or another aspect of military service and the familial connection to that service, such as "Seabee wife," "Mom of a Marine Stationed in Iraq," or "Army dad." MFSO and GSFSO activists used their familial relationship to someone in the military to assert a unique vantage point from which to observe, experience, and critique aspects of the Iraq War. Rich Moniak wrote a piece entitled "A Father's Story: Donald Rumsfeld and the Families of the 172nd Stryker Brigade," in which he described family reactions, including his own, to meeting with Secretary Rumsfeld, who extended their deployed family members' time in Iraq from one year to sixteen months just a few days before they were scheduled to return home. MFSO materials such as these highlighted activists' reliance on their experiences as family members to inform their views of the war, and their family position was an essential aspect of their identity as activists.

Although many active fathers were in MFSO, women were more active in MFSO than men, overall. This uneven participation likely reflected gendered aspects of family relationships and the military: many activist mothers were single parents, and most U.S. civilian military spouses were women. Culturally, women also were expected to act in a nurturing fashion that, in this case, meant taking care of servicemembers and fighting for their families. Mothers were disproportionately featured in the media's coverage of the movement, as well, likely reflecting gendered roles for social movement actors.[10]

VFP's and IVAW's memberships overwhelmingly comprised men. Both organizations drew on members' past work experiences in the military as the basis for their military peace movement identity, and since that occupation was primarily male, these demographics were not surprising.[11] Activists' descriptions of themselves in public speeches and private conversations listed the activists' military rank, branch of service, and often their military occupation specialties, referred to in military parlance as MOS. This work-based identity re flected men's gendered roles in American society.

Generational Divide

There was a significant generational divide in the movement, especially between VFP and IVAW members. At times, this divide facilitated emotional connections similar to those between parents and children, but it also led to disagreements within this culture of action.

VFP activists often described themselves as advisors to IVAW members and accentuated their age difference. Mike Hearington described in his interview the military peace movement organizations as family and pointed out generational divisions between VFP and IVAW that led to cultural and even linguistic differences. He explained, "I'm fifty-three, and they're twenty, in their early twenties. . . . I'm like Daddy!" Some MFSO activists referred to VFP as the patriarch of the military peace movement family because of their history with war and their conversion to peace activism.

A number of VFP, Gold Star, and MFSO activists, such as Army mom Theresa Dawson, suggested that IVAW activists were like their "kids." Several military spouses and military veterans who were not much older than the average IVAW member portrayed IVAW as "really young," in the words of one Gulf War veteran. Former Army Drill Sergeant Dennis Kyne explained that IVAW was "an infant" in need of "guidance and nurturance." Kyne was referring to the organization's recent development, not the members' ages, when he described IVAW as the movement's child. Other activists in MFSO, the Gold Star organizations, and VFP believed they were the ones to provide the direction and support that this youthful organization needed. Most organizations focused on providing help for veterans of the current wars who suffered from PTSD or who refused deployments to Iraq. Cindy Sheehan described the land she bought in Crawford as a "refuge for suffering soldiers and those who wish to make a stand against this war." As these organizations shared information on health care, they attempted to take care of these new veterans. The other organizations' care work for and attempts to provide guidance to IVAW highlight the differences in both war and protest experiences between these organizations.

IVAW founders frequently described finding each other through the efforts of VFP and MFSO, and leaders of MFSO and VFP expressed pride in encouraging the formation of IVAW. Through 2013, IVAW appointed members of VFP, MFSO, and/or VVAW to their advisory board. At its founding, MFSO and VFP provided necessary mentorship to IVAW not only because the organization's members were young but because their formative years were spent in an institution that did not value dissent. The "parental" organizations' mentorship helped IVAW establish a structure, interact with the press, and develop tactics and strategies. IVAW activists often attributed their ability to organize more quickly than had veterans during Vietnam to this mentoring. In a speech in March 2008, Garrett Reppenhagen mentioned that IVAW put together its Winter Soldier tactic after only five years of war, whereas Vietnam veterans took nearly ten. These Winter Soldier tactics involved panel presentations where service-members publicized problematic aspects of the wars. Although the Iraq War's Winter Soldier testimonies did not include information on military-caused massacres, as did the proceedings by Vietnam veterans, these recent veterans did describe how American foreign policy and military actions contributed to excessive civilian casualties, brutality against prisoners, and numerous problems for veterans and their families. Reppenhagen credited Vietnam veterans' "mentorship and their leadership and some of their guidance" for the faster pace of the anti–Iraq War movement. Winter Soldier panels held by Iraq and Afghanistan veterans focused on policy as the root cause of soldier's negative war-induced emotions; the focus on policy resulted from the adoption of the sophisticated arguments crafted by the military peace movement.

As the number of Iraq veterans in the antiwar movement grew, VFP and MFSO participants sought ways to move IVAW into the spotlight. Some members explained that this meant that VFP and, to a lesser extent, MFSO and the Gold Star organizations had to step out of the spotlight and allow media and public attention to focus on IVAW members. Carl Rising-Moore said, "The heart of the movement right now as far as I'm concerned is IVAW." Since IVAW was the movement's emotional center, other organizations worked to secure it a place at the front of marches and gave it prominent billing during events. Some VFP activists, such as Michael Cervantes, insisted that MFSO, GSFP, and IVAW were more important than VFP because of these organizations' immediate connection to the current war. As such, a number of VFP activists suggested that VFP should operate behind the scenes.

MFSO materials and activists highlighted IVAW. MFSO's members were to be featured in a documentary by Patricia Faulkrod that began filming in 2003. During filming, MFSO activists said that their family connection to the war provided them with knowledge of the "ground truth," or the real story about the Iraq War, which included the lack of food, water, and supplies, the war's lacking mission, the deaths, and the war guilt. According to Nancy Lessin, MFSO members told the filmmaker, "We're marking this space [in the peace movement], and the space is going to be filled by our loved ones and

FIGURE 13. Members of IVAW, including Maricela Guzman (*far left with bag, Navy*), Jeff Key (*holding IVAW sign on the left, Marines*), and Jabbar Magruder (*back to the camera on the right, Army National Guard*) lead an antiwar march in Los Angeles in January 27, 2007. Photograph by the author.

other troops themselves, the returned Iraq veterans, who will themselves firsthand be able to tell this nation the ground truth of this war." As Iraq veterans began to speak out and form IVAW, MFSO activists encouraged the filmmaker to speak directly to these soldiers. When the documentary *Ground Truth* came out in 2006, it featured primarily IVAW activists, and despite most interviews with military families being cut from the film, MFSO heavily promoted it with public screenings and house parties.

At times, IVAW activists insisted on their primacy among the other organizations, and this caused tension in the military peace movement family. Some IVAW members grumbled about sharing the front of an antiwar march in Los Angeles in 2008 with GSFP. One twentysomething male in IVAW said, "They invaded our space. It's our experiences people need to hear." Similarly, at the June 2010 U.S. Social Forum in Detroit, Iraq veterans said that the other military peace movement organizations needed to "get in line" with IVAW's "organizing ideas." They wanted the other organizations to "stop pushing" other strategies and tactics, so that IVAW could take the lead.

Most IVAW activists were younger than the members of the other organizations, and this age gap produced differences in styles and preferences for certain tactics and strategies. Some VFP and MFSO activists described IVAW tactics as "in your face" or even "reckless," whereas a few IVAW activists called the other organizations' ideas and tactics "tired." Like families who fight over music styles, IVAW activists complained that events organized by the other organizations involved what one twenty-four-year-old Iraq veteran from Colorado called "folk crap." Whereas the graying white-male veteran guitarists who played music reminiscent of the 1970s at various gatherings frequently praised IVAW, the young activists blamed these tastes and choices for the lack of youth participation in antiwar events. A female IVAW member explained:

> It's not *our* music; people our age don't want to come out and listen to them rehash their glory days. It just seems like a bunch of old hippies gettin' together, not like something that speaks to us.

Age mattered in how activists viewed members of the other organizations and often caused friction. Rather than using music typically associated with the peace movement, such as the songs of Joan Baez, IVAW activists partnered with the Hip Hop Caucus and with punk and alternative bands such as Rage Against the Machine, Anti-Flag, Bouncing Souls, Michael Franti, and the Flobots to raise awareness through music.

Although the other organizations' parental role was important in establishing IVAW, by 2006 many IVAW activists expressed the need for IVAW to claim control of itself. Although IVAW activists felt that VFP and the other organizations meant well, they needed to manage their own staff, space, and structures. IVAW members were adults, and many had lived experiences through war that aged them beyond their years, which made it difficult for IVAW to accept a subordinate position. Although IVAW activists were generally inexperienced as social movement participants, they did not appreciate their preferences and leadership being dismissed due to their youth.

Activists in the military peace movement viewed themselves as a family, and like families, the members fulfilled different roles within the movement's structure. As a family, the movement frequently interacted, sharing tactics, money, and even members. Like all families, however, these organizations were not monolithic, and disagreements occurred. Activists were also tied emotionally to one another. When a former VFP president died after a long battle with illness, he was remembered by MFSO cofounders in a written eulogy, sent to all members of MFSO and GSFSO, titled "A Death in the Family." The familial connection among military peace movement activists allowed them to channel the negative emotions brought on by their military experiences into social movement activism.

FACING AND CHANNELING THE EMOTIONS OF WAR

The familial atmosphere of the military peace movement transformed activists' *emotions of powerlessness* into *emotions of resistance*. Their emotions of powerlessness included guilt, shame, anger, fear, and loneliness. Activists' war experiences left them feeling guilty over their participation in war, fearful of what would happen to friends and family in the military, ashamed of their country, lonely because of their outsider status, and angry about the war and its personal and political consequences. Participation in the military peace movement produced emotions of resistance, which as Verta Taylor and I argue, include "righteous anger, moral outrage, and love."[12] I add group pride to this list, as it is an important element for overcoming shame and stigmatization. As activists engage with others in their organization and across their culture of action, they develop bonds that enable activism. Although anger exists in both sets of emotions, it becomes an emotion of resistance when it is channeled and focused. Activists perceived their engagement with the military peace movement as therapy that helped them both cope with the traumas brought on by war and promote the movement's goals.

Family Therapy

One thing that made the military peace movement unique within the larger peace movement was that it operated as both a support systems and a site for government-focused movement activism. Activists in the military peace movement coped with the consequences of activism in addition to handling PTSD and/or physical war-related injuries, taking care of family who suffered from psychological and/or physical war wounds, facing the constant fears of their or their loved ones' deployments, and grieving for friends and family members who had died. Interactions within the military peace movement sustained activists, helping them to heal from the negative emotions of war, and this emotion work facilitated social movement activism.

Military peace movement participants sought organizations that allowed them to combine their military experience with their activism, because they believed that these organizations would understand the pain and difficulties brought on by their military connections better than could the wider peace movement. An MFSO recruitment pamphlet referred to this in a quote from Larry Syverson, a father of four sons who served in the military and who was chairman of MFSO's board of directors:

> The year I had two sons serving in Iraq was a living hell. I don't know how I would have survived that year without MFSO. Only another military family truly knows the mind-numbing anxiety of having a loved one on the ground in Iraq—in a war that you know is wrong.

This quote highlights not only the support that military peace movement organizations provided but also how this support validated activists' emotions and allowed them to work through these emotions in order to remain productive. Military peace movement organizations brought together people whose emotionally charged military experiences were rarely understood or validated in the wider peace movement and whose blaming of the war for their pain was rejected by the broader military community. Although outsiders in those broader spaces, activists in the military peace movement bonded over emotions such as fear and anger, and their activism played an important role in coping with the stress of war.

In interviews, casual conversations, and public speeches and writings, activists frequently discussed how close-knit relationships with other activists helped them overcome the negative emotions brought on by war. A few activists even described being "saved" by other activists and, on the flip side, referred to "taking care" of each other. In fact, in one interview a military wife told me that the most important thing MFSO did for her was connect her to IVAW members who "made it home" and were "still good people." They offered the hope that her husband could also come through the war physically, emotionally, and psychologically. In numerous conversations with this MFSO activist, she shared that her connection to a male IVAW member who was not her husband kept her from "going completely fucking nuts while [her husband] was deployed." She explained that while her husband was deployed, she "lost it." She was so distraught over the war that doctors insisted on bed rest, various psychotropic medications, and even hospitalization. She described fears of her husband's death and possible war injuries or that he would be a part of something "unforgivable" and explained that these emotions kept her from finishing her education or working.

She believed the IVAW member was a "lifeline," because he gave her hope that her husband and their friends could physically and psychologically survive the war. Similarly, this IVAW member recounted being suicidal before becoming an activist, and he explained that "more than partial credit" for his life belonged to the connection he made with the military peace movement activists who brought him "back from the edge." These activists were frequently seen sharing the same space, hugging, holding hands, and demonstrating their care for each other. Additionally, the MFSO member said that the two talked on the phone daily during difficult times when not at activist events. These two activists not only emotionally supported each other but also helped each other find mental health care and other support necessary to deal with his combat-related PTSD and her war-related depression and anxiety, which activists frequently referred to as secondary PTSD. Although these activists were particularly close, their dyadic care relationship across organizations was not unique in this movement.

Activists provided not only love and support for one another but also tangible resources for overcoming stressful situations. On February 6, 2009, MFSO member Tim Kahlor told a crowd at a day-long testimonial in Washington, D.C., that he credited Kevin and Joyce Lucey with saving his son's life. Kahlor's son served two tours in Iraq with the Army, and he was "blown up four times." These war experiences left Ryan Kahlor with TBI, compressed vertebrae, PTSD, and depression. Tim Kahlor told the crowd that, thanks to the Luceys, he knew the signs of PTSD and that he, as a father, had to push the military and veterans' services on behalf of his son. As mentioned in chapter 2, the Luceys' only son committed suicide because his war-induced PTSD was not properly treated, and they were two prominent activists who worked tirelessly on war-related suicide. Kahlor explained that before meeting the Luceys he assumed the military would take "proper care of Ryan," but after learning what happened to Jeff Lucey, Kahlor spent countless hours talking to members of the military and political leaders in order to place Ryan in treatment facilities. Although the military intended to continue to deploy Ryan, Kahlor was able to secure his son a place in the Army Wounded Warriors Program and make him ineligible, at least for the immediate future, for redeployment. The Luceys helped guide Tim through the complicated VA system and provided emotional support for this trying time. In the hope of continuing to pass on that support to other families, Kahlor attracted attention to what the movement called "invisible wounds of war," such as psychological problems and internal injuries like TBIs. In October 2010, Kahlor was a featured speaker for a military families conference in Long Beach, California, where he focused on ways military families could advocate for their servicemember.

Military peace movement organizations used online tools and in-person meetings in order to plan political tactics and provide support to members. GSFP operated an Internet-based chat group where families of servicemembers who died as a result of the Iraq War could talk to one another about their loss and find comfort. Activists in this group sent each other messages on days that were particularly hard, such as birthdays, Mother's Day and Father's Day, and the anniversaries of deaths. Activists not only talked about loved ones who had died but also worked on a shared understanding that directed their anger toward the politicians who had initiated or perpetuated the Iraq War. During a meeting to discuss the implementation of online support groups, a deployed Army officer's spouse described the importance of organizational support:

> Some people need this just to get out of bed. Hell, I know that there were days when [my husband] was deployed that I was so depressed I couldn't even function. People need to help each other with this stuff so they can someday get to the point of speaking out.

FIGURE 14. On February 7, 2009, Tim Kahlor (*left*) and Kevin Lucey (*right*) march in an MFSO/GSFSO protest in Washington, D.C., meant to tell recently inaugurated President Obama about the "Change We Need: Bring Them Home Now!" Photograph by the author.

These activists relied on the emotional support of other activists in order to live their daily lives and to gain the strength to become activists. Activism offered an alternative to depression and allowed them to manage their pain in ways that promoted social-change goals.

When activists did not feel emotionally supported, they often demobilized. The wife of a Reservist told of a parent in MFSO who belittled her concern for her spouse:

> [An MFSO Mom] had the nerve to tell me that my pain wasn't as great as hers because I only married my soldier but she gave birth to hers! What the fuck?! My husband tells me things about war his mother will never hear. When he left, I had to take care of all the kids' stuff, the house, bills, everything, but her life didn't change one damn bit. When he came home, I had to deal with his PTSD anger, his

frustrations with [readjusting to] the kids, the mood swings. . . . Sure, we both worry, but it's our [military spouses'] lives that get screwed up, not theirs [military parents]!

The type of frustration expressed by this Army wife led some spouses to feel unsupported by MFSO, and this tension caused problems for the organization. Some politically active spouses left over it, and later, one spouse called this group "exiles from MFSO." Although the organization's board and staff wanted these individuals to be active members, its emotion culture favored motherly concern for children, which alienated those who were not in that role.

Tactical Therapy

Military peace movement tactics frequently involved speeches in which activists expressed both emotions of powerlessness and emotions of resistance. During the Winter Soldier protest events from 2008 to 2009, which took place in approximately twenty cities, IVAW speakers told of intense feelings of guilt over their war actions, their disconnect from American civilians, and their anger at politicians and military leaders. Michael Totten described his horrifying treatment of Iraqis while working with the Army Military Police in Karbala, and he asked for forgiveness as he denounced the continuing war and occupation. After speaking in Washington, D.C., he ripped up his citation for the Bronze Star for Valor, which he received for his service in Iraq. Participation in the military peace movement reframed activists' protest, rather than their participation in war, as something to be proud of. By sharing stories of the actions and inactions for which they were ashamed and then describing military policies that led to these incidents, activists shifted the blame from themselves to government policy. In doing so, they moved from paralyzing emotions of shame and guilt to emotions of moral outrage.

Tactics such as Winter Solider were therapeutic for activists because they offered a way to publicly display the negative emotions of the war while attempting to end it. Many activists said that speaking out was a way to heal. In discussing Winter Soldier, Camilo Mejía wrote:

If our military experience at war has taken from us our humanity, having been able to testify at Winter Soldier renewed in many of us the hope of finding a new life in resistance.[13]

Mejía explained that taking part in antiwar activism and sharing the details of their military service was beneficial to both the antiwar movement and the individual activists. While trying to change public opinion, the activists changed themselves. Activists found others who were sympathetic to their traumatizing experiences and the problems that developed from them, and these tactics channeled activists' anger about those experiences toward the war.

Participants in this culture of action described being wracked by fear and guilt that rendered them powerless until they interacted with others in the military peace movement. Cloy Richards described his involvement in the military peace movement as "the best therapy in the world." Richards needed this therapy because his experiences as a Marine corporal who took part in the initial invasion and fought in Fallujah a year later made him suicidal as he struggled with PTSD and what he called survivor's guilt over the deaths of many of his military friends. War experiences left many veterans feeling despair and anger. Some, like Richards, internalized these emotions, mistreating their bodies through alcohol, drugs, cutting; driving recklessly; and/or attempting suicide, whereas others vented their emotions through fights with strangers or those close to them. These activists credited the military peace movement family for changing their lives for the better. Richards explained, "I've only been involved in the peace movement for six and half to seven months, but working in the peace movement, working toward ending the war in Iraq, has been the best therapy for me." Peace activism helped them channel these emotions and become healthier mentally.

The movement directed their anger away from themselves and those around them by shaping it into righteous anger aimed at the architects of the Iraq War. Richards described the importance of activism for veterans:

I mean, there's no way that couldn't change you. You go from having no faith, especially from being a war vet, you go from having no

faith in humanity, no faith in society whatsoever, and then you're surrounded by all these great people, and it just empowers you so much.
It can take you back from the brink of suicide, I can tell you personally. It can turn your life around 180 degrees.

The personal connections in the military peace movement transformed activists' negative emotions and encouraged activism. Partici
pation in the military peace movement healed this despondency and
taught activists to express emotions of empowerment.

Generational Connections

The intergenerational connections among the organizations were
important in helping some younger vets heal from war. Vietnam-era
veteran Carl Rising-Moore believed that reaching out to new vets was
important "because that's the most telling thing they can do: be involved with doing this work for peace and justice." Rising-Moore described his own guilt and shame for taking part in military decisions
that led to Vietnamese deaths. Since he had "found peace" through
activism, he hoped to share it with Iraq War veterans. Additionally,
Rising-Moore encouraged military members to go AWOL in order to
avoid the war and, thus, the emotions of powerlessness.[14] At Camp
Casey, Rising-Moore operated a Native American–style sweat lodge,
where he encouraged Iraq War veterans to cleanse themselves of the
toxins of war and heal themselves by working for peace. Veterans of
past wars, such as Rising-Moore, offered a number of treatments for
Iraq War veterans, including weekend retreats, informal rap sessions
(a Vietnam-era phrasing for conversations about war experiences between veterans), and formal counseling, that allowed veterans to overcome the emotions that war instilled. Simultaneously, these veterans
spoke from experience about activism offering an emotional balm by
building emotions of resistance within participants.

Some of the VFP activists that I interviewed were behind efforts
to help younger veterans handle their war experiences without alcohol or drugs. VFP had seen a number of activists die or face personal,
professional, and legal issues because they had "dealt with their [war]
demons" through alcohol and other addictions. As Mike Hearington

explained, VFP activists tried "not to be too preachy, but we just [wanted] to help them find healthier ways to deal with their pain." Some VFP activists brought pamphlets, books, and other information on addiction to multiday gatherings of the military peace movement, and online and in advertisements for meetings, VFP posted information about workshops meant to help veterans handle issues of addiction. Lane Anderson described why he believed these efforts were important in his interview:

> I worry because of my own experience with the Vietnam Vets Against the War that the Iraq Vets Against the War will begin to fall under the booze and drug scenario that I went through. It's the same as with my kids. They have to go through the stuff I went through before they learn. That's been one of my efforts is to try to get them to deal constructively with the combat experience—to not try to go on a road trip like we did.

Anderson was concerned that the experiences of war would cause the emotions of powerlessness and spell trouble for activists and the movement. He believed that alcohol and drugs caused VVAW to lose its effectiveness toward the end of the Vietnam War, and he wanted to help veterans channel their emotions in ways that aided the movement rather than hurt it.

Although opinions varied, these efforts were not always appreciated by IVAW activists. IVAW activists often rolled their eyes at these efforts, and one IVAW member told me, "I know they're trying to help, but man, we have to find a way to get by. The VA wants to put me on drugs that's way worse than pot, you know?" IVAW activists who believed that alcohol or nonprescription drugs were a part of their own healing process gravitated toward other VFP and MFSO activists who were known to share alcohol or drugs with the younger generation. Whether imbibing or not, however, both groups offered counsel to younger veterans on reintegration to civilian life, peace activism, and handling the emotions brought on by their war experiences.

In public speeches and private conversations, activists described their guilt as part of the horror of war, their fears of losing friends and family members, and their anger over how the war had changed their lives. Fellow activists not only listened to but also physically and verbally comforted each other. Additionally, some activists helped each other locate and access mental health services and other resources to help them cope. The family network of organizations channeled activists' emotions, so that they could become more effective and attract others to their beliefs about the war. The military peace movement developed many antiwar tactics that helped activists heal from their military experiences and use their emotional stories to connect with audiences, as demonstrated in the week-long march to New Orleans in 2006.

CONCLUSION

Both cognitive and emotional processes bound the members of the military peace movement by creating a collective identity at the culture-of-action level. By situating organizations within their cultures of action, or their families, we can better understand movement development and maintenance of collective identities, tactical and strategic choices, and successes and failures. This conceptualization demonstrates the links between the organizations, as well as their internal divisions. Movements manage negative emotions through the establishment of networks, mass meetings, and rituals that facilitate identification with a collective. The extended time of activist events, such as multiday protest gatherings such as the Veterans and Survivors March or the various Camp Casey protests, assist that bonding and, thus, the emotional transformation of activists. Participants in a variety of movements perceive themselves as a family because of the time they spend together, their shared perceptions of the world, and the affective bonds that form among them. The familial connection is especially important to people whose activism and existence in a stigmatized category (e.g., gay, racial minority, diseased) alienates them from their communities or families, as was the case for many military peace movement activists.

There was considerable overlap between the organizations in the military peace movement, and for some, being a member of this culture of action was more significant than being a member of any one organization. There were, however, limits to the emotional and the familial connections within the military peace movement. Cleavages developed based on one's age, which war one had experienced, the types of experience one had with war, the nature of one's family connection to the war (e.g., parent versus spouse), and one's political ideology (particularly an association with socialist or communist organizations). IVAW activists were the most likely to see themselves as distinct from those in other organizations, because they faced the greatest risk for protesting, as discussed in chapter 1, and because their experiences with the movement focuses, the Iraq and Afghanistan wars, were the most direct. IVAW activists were significantly younger than the majority of MFSO, GSFSO, and VFP activists, and this led to tensions over differing styles and the value of past activist experience versus direct experiences of the Iraq War. These rifts likely contributed to a lack of culture-of-action-level collective identity for some members of IVAW. In addition, as the organizations grew, especially when an area had enough members to fill an MFSO or an IVAW chapter, activists sometimes gravitated exclusively to their organization rather than to the wider culture of action. These tensions hindered movement progress by making it at times difficult for organizations to share resources.

Although these schisms existed, nearly all of the activists I interacted with in my six years of research, including those activists who strongly advocated distinguishing their organization from the others, told me that they felt "more connected" or "closer" to people in other military peace movement organizations than to the broader peace movement. Although differences by generation and specific identity constructions can divide a culture of action, they can also create dynamic movement roles that facilitate its overall goals. For example, the military peace movement's "parents" helped their IVAW "children" to overcome the guilt and anger brought on by their recent war experiences by supporting their transition home and providing formal and informal counsel. IVAW members gave back to their metaphoric parents in VFP, MFSO, and the Gold Star organizations by allaying fears these individuals had and by providing the intergenerational connections for which they longed. These different roles can also allow a culture of action to flourish by expanding the amount of work that can be accomplished and reaching diverse audiences.

By sharing time, space, and a collective consciousness, activists develop strong positive affective bonds between activists, or "reciprocal emotions."[15] As activists take pleasure in protest and experience love between participants, the desire to stay or to become further involved in activism develops.[16] These reciprocal emotions foster solidarity and mobilize actors, leading to the creation of an activist collective identity.[17] This identity involves an oppositional consciousness that locates a person within a structural category and provides a framework of injustice that allows them to overcome negative emotions.[18] In other words, when individuals experience trauma or inequality, they can either internalize their situation or develop an activist collective identity that acknowledges how their situation is derived from the group's position in the social hierarchy.

The dramatic military histories of many of the members necessitated that the military peace movement develop a substantial therapeutic element to its culture. Movement participation helped activists overcome the guilt and anger brought on by their war experiences by supporting reintegration and providing formal and informal counsel. Military peace movement activists moved from emotions of powerlessness to emotions of resistance by learning to channel the anger of war externally. Activists moved from suicidal and self-destructive thoughts and behaviors brought on by the guilt, fear, and shame of war to recognizing governmental and policy causes of their pain. This emotional consciousness was a necessary component of successful activism and an important outcome of the movement for these individuals.

This emotional transformation can be understood as an outcome and a goal of social movement. Both stigma and trauma produce negative emotions of powerlessness, but activism offers opportunities to overcome these emotions and replace them with positive emotions of resistance. The emotional benefits of movement participation can include pride and moral outrage, whereby actors assert their dignity and worth.[19] Actors in the military peace movement were empowered by movement organizations and leaders who realized the importance of emotions and encouraged systems of support for the expression of those emotions. The movement facilitated this empowerment through online and face-to-face support groups, educational workshops, and informal conversations among activists. Scholars have written about the importance of identity change as an outcome of social movement participation, but more research is needed to fully understand how emotional change, which is closely tied to psychological health, can also be an outcome.[20] In chapter 4 I turn from examining how activism in the military peace movement affected participants to demonstrating how identity shaped the strategies in which this movement engaged as they worked to change society.

4

Managing and Deploying the
Insider–Outsider Identity

During a series of events over Mother's Day weekend in 2006, military peace movement organizations arranged public events, strategy seminars, and legislative meetings in conjunction with the American Friends Service Committee and September 11th Families for a Peaceful Tomorrow. The weekend of events was called Silence of the Dead, Voices of the Living: A Witness to End the War in Iraq. On Saturday May 13, veterans and military families led a silent march around the dirt path in the center of the National Mall in Washington, D.C., and to the U.S. Capitol. Iraq Veterans led the march, and Gold Star activists Sue Niederer and Summer Lipford led the military families' contingent. Activists embraced and some cried as they marched.[1]

Many of these peace activists carried signs that demonstrated their intimate connections to the wars. About one-third of the Gold Star families and most of the military families carried signs with pictures of their deployed, deceased, or soon-to-be-deployed loved ones in uniform. On one sign, Jack Amoureux placed a picture of his brother's family next to the plea "DON'T SEND MY BROTHER BACK!" written in uppercase black letters. Next to Jack was a woman from MFSO's Georgia chapter who held two signs: one a black preprinted sign with large red letters that read, "Bring My Daughter Home!" and the other a handmade poster with a stop sign, an MFSO email address, and the words "Stop the Illegal Iraq War!" While these two family members fought for their servicemembers' lives, Gold Star family members publicly displayed their mourning over their servicemembers' deaths. With one hand, Carlos Arredondo pulled a wagon made to look like a coffin draped with the American flag while with his other he held a sign with a picture of Lance Corporal Alex Arredondo in his Marine dress uniform lying in his coffin after being killed in Iraq. Joyce Lucey, whose son killed himself as a result of his combat-induced mental

FIGURE 15. On May 13, 2006, members of Veterans for Peace, Military Families Speak Out, Gold Star Families for Peace/Speak Out, and Iraq Veterans Against the War hold a silent march on the National Mall as part of the series of events Silence of the Dead, Voices of the Living: A Witness to End the War in Iraq. Photographs by author.

illness, held a sign that in large, bold lettering read, "The Human Cost of War," and that in smaller writing read, "in loving memory of Corporal Jeffrey Lucey," with the dates of his life. Joyce's sign included three large photographs of Jeff: one as a child holding a baseball bat, one in high school, and one in his Marine uniform. Another photo sign held by a Gold Star activist from South Carolina simply read, "We Mourn." Using these signs, the activists highlighted the negative consequences of war, which they claimed were experienced only by American military families, veterans, and Iraqis.

During this Mother's Day weekend, activists marched and spoke in strategically chosen clothing that they used to signal to outside observers, including government officials and the media, that this protest was not your average civilian peace protest. Dozens of Vietnam veterans wore components of their Army green uniforms; a handful of older men dressed in jackets from their military dress uniforms; and about twenty-five Iraq and Afghanistan war veterans wore their desert camouflage jackets. Most Gold Star parents dressed in T-shirts with photos of their dead servicemembers, usually in military uniforms and with some holding weaponry or sitting in military vehicles. The messages conveyed through this dress were not subtle. The back of one man's shirt placed blame squarely on the government rather than the Iraqis for the deaths of American soldiers. It declared, "Bush Killed My Nephew." Many more veterans and military families wore T-shirts, hats, or pins that declared their affiliation with a military peace movement organization, and they used words and symbols to proclaim their combined military and peace activist identities. The words on the front of the MFSO T-shirt, "Military Families Speak Out," encircled a peace sign entwined with a yellow ribbon, and the back of the shirt read, "Support our Troops: Bring Them Home Now." This movement catchphrase married support of the military to the work to end the wars. In this and many other acts, military peace movement activists used their clothing to highlight their military identities and enhance their claims against the war.

That weekend, activists displayed the art exhibit *Eyes Wide Open*, which has toured the country in various forms since 2004.[2] This iteration of the exhibit featured a grid of black and desert-tan combat boots, each pair representing one of the 2,437 U.S. servicemembers who had died in Iraq as of that Friday. At the center of the display peace activists created a spiral path of civilian shoes, representing Iraqi civilian deaths, and large cloth panels displaying pictures of prewar everyday Iraqi life and images of Iraqi experiences of grief from the war.[3] The boots and accompanying personalization offered an important way for activists to demonstrate their military connections during their peace protest activities.

FIGURE 16. On Mother's Day, May 14, 2006, Alfred (Al) Zappala carries the
boots symbolizing his foster son, National Guard Sergeant Sherwood Baker, who
was killed in Baghdad, into a memorial display covering the National Mall in
Washington, D.C. Photograph by the author.

On Mother's Day Sunday, various spokespeople from the military peace movement organizations and a handful of other sponsoring organizations took part in the Dedication of the Boots ceremony. Iraqis, war veterans, and Gold Star families were given the opportunity to talk about their loved ones' deaths. Along with descriptions of friends and relatives who had fallen victim to the Iraq War, all of these speeches called for an end to the war. When each group or individual finished speaking about a dead servicemember, they took a pair of boots, often actual pairs worn by their children, spouses, or friends in war, and walked through the crowd to place the boots among the others on the mall. At one poignant moment, activists placed boots on the mall to honor the death of a longtime MFSO activist's son who had died over the weekend. Ten days before military peace movement activists gathered in Washington, D.C., Marine Sergeant Alessandro Carbonaro was hit by an IED during his second deployment to Iraq. Normally, Gilda Carbonaro would have been in Washington, D.C., for the protest, but she was with her son and other family members when Alessandro died from his wounds in a U.S. military hospital in Germany. The placement of boots symbolizing Alessandro's death signaled the continuing and devastating consequences of war for the military community. All of these gestures were, together, stunningly powerful. As I examine further in chapter 5, cemetery-style tactics were often used to instill grief in observers.

During the Sunday dedication, a man in the National Guard from Michigan spoke from the stage, flanked by his parents and his wife. They were there to dedicate the boots of his cousin, who was like a brother to him. He said, "I am a veteran of this war, and I'm still in service today. . . . Look at this field, Congress! Look at these boots, Senators! This is your down payment, Mr. President, my Commander in Chief. What has it bought you?" Through these words this young man called attention to his own military service as a way to garner attention from those who made decisions about the war. Many members of the movement regularly referred to their antiwar activities as an extension of the public service that they provided as members of the military community. Through their rhetoric and military symbols, such as the boots, activists hoped to connect their audience emotionally to the war. A male Afghanistan War veteran explained to me that the military peace movement was there to make the war "something real, not simply something thousands of miles away or just a video game or movie on the TV."

During the rally, Richard Perle, whom many antiwar activists referred to as an architect of the Iraq War, went to the National Mall and stood about fifty yards from the dedication ceremony.[4] Many veterans and military family members quickly moved to surround him. A veteran in a black IVAW T-shirt shouted, "Did you send us to Iraq for a lie or a mistake?" As Perle attempted to answer by describing the intelligence about WMDs, veterans interrupted, saying, "So it was a mistake." He said no and attempted to explain, but they interrupted again and said, "So it was a lie." This went on in a circle several times. One male Iraq veteran whose desert camouflage jacket was decorated with antiwar buttons—including ones reading, "Classrooms not Combat," and, "Iraq Veterans Against the War"—gestured to the exhibit's boots. He told Perle that their blood was on his hands. Stacy Bannerman, the wife of a soldier in the Washington National Guard, used her organization's name, Military Families Speak Out, as she tried to draw Perle's attention to the growing dissatisfaction with the war in the military community and the troubles it created, including divorce and abuse. Karen Meredith tugged at her T-shirt's picture of her son, Army Lieutenant Ken Ballard, who was killed in action in Iraq. She asked, "Look into my eyes, and tell me why my only child came home in a flag-covered box?" When Perle described the democratization of Iraq, Meredith interrupted and pointed to her shirt asking, "Was it worth it?" These activists used their clothing, gestures, symbols, and words to highlight their military identities and distinguish themselves as worthy of answers about the Iraq War. With cameras rolling, Perle had difficulty ignoring this set of antiwar activists as they used their military identities to make claims about the war.

Throughout the series of weekend activities, activists routinely strategized new ways to make their combined military and peace activist identities visible to the broader public. At meetings away from the public eye, activists intentionally discussed, crafted, and argued about identity-deployment strategies.[5] In other face-to-face meetings, as well as over the phone and through email and other Internet mediums, they encouraged each other to highlight their identities as members of the military community in their antiwar activities and statements. This chapter examines the primary identity strategies used by military peace movement activists. Extending Mary Bernstein's conceptualizations of the ways activists intentionally use their identities, I propose three new categories of identity deployment: *novelty, authority,* and *oppositional.*[6] First, the novelty of the supposedly contradictory military–peace identities of activists attracted attention. Second, military veterans and families used their firsthand experiences of the wars and their consequences to demonstrate their credibility when protesting. Third, their identity strategies allowed military peace movement activists to claim that patriotism and troop support belonged to the peace movement rather than those who supported, instituted, and continued the wars. They publicized their insider–outsider identities in order to challenge prowar conceptualizations that portrayed Iraq War protestors as unpatriotic and unsupportive of American troops.[7]

By highlighting military-affiliated activists, the peace movement drew attention to the wars and sought to reach those who were not already in agreement with the movement. Although activists largely agreed that stressing their insider–outsider identities was important, many debated how these identities should be shown publicly. Internal fights in the movement over the Afghanistan War, patriotism, socialism, and other issues were at their roots contests over the group's collective identity and its deployment.

USING IDENTITY STRATEGIES

The military peace movement developed identity strategies for a number of purposes. First, the activists believed that their unique insider–outsider identities could grab the attention of the media, the public, and the government elites. Second, they strategically publicized this insider–outsider identity in order to suggest that speakers had legitimacy. By showcasing their identities, activists portrayed themselves as knowledgeable about the war. Third, activists demonstrated their military connections because their existence in the peace movement could counter prowar claims that troop support and patriotism belonged exclusively to those who championed the wars. Their identities directly challenged the idea that war proponents were the only ones patriotic and supportive of the troops. I call this an oppositional identity strategy.[8] Finally, military peace movement activists saw their insider–outsider identities as particularly suited to reaching those who had not been converted to the antiwar cause. Activists drew attention to their intimate connection to the military by deploying their identity through strategies of organizational affiliation, rhetoric, clothing, movement, and symbols.[9]

Novel Identities

In the hope of supporting the peace movement, military activists sought to capitalize on the novelty afforded by consolidating two identities that were widely seen as incongruent. In communications to their members, the boards and administrators of the organizations explained that it was crucial for members to identify themselves as insider–outsiders. By explaining the consolidation of their military and their antiwar activist identities in nearly every public setting, activists hoped to educate Americans about the reality of the wars and military life. Leaders often appealed to members that the country needed to hear from them. In an MFSO communication to its members from February 2007, the organization encouraged activists to "let them know that you are a military family and a member of Military Families Speak Out" before demanding that Congress vote no on appropriations bills that would further fund the Iraq War. The organizations' leadership encouraged members to highlight their insider identities as they critiqued war policies.

In official documents the movement's leadership crafted messages that began by highlighting activists' military credentials. The following quote from Linda and Phil Waste of Shellman Bluff, Georgia, included in a 2009 MFSO press release, exemplifies this tendency:

We have lived in terror for over eight years now. Three of our sons and three grandchildren have served in the Army in Iraq and/or Afghanistan. Our family has endured multiple deployments, extended deployments, stop loss, and the unconscionable practice of pressured reenlistment while in country. At present we have a grandson in Iraq and a granddaughter in Afghanistan. We believe all our sons suffer from some degree of PTSD, one more severe than the others. Our granddaughter is on all kinds of medication for PTSD, and yet is in Afghanistan on her 3rd deployment! We worked hard to get President Obama elected and sent money out of our retirement to support his election. His many words of "hope" did indeed give us "hope," however, his deeds dashed our hopes on the rocks of more death and destruction of continued wars. The only sane solution is to bring the troops home now!

Activists regularly combined their antiwar activist identities and their military identities in an attempt to use their insider–outsider positioning to generate attention from the media and the public.

Activists publicized these personal narratives in speeches and in online media. In a 2006 speech before a march in Salem, Oregon, longtime MFSO board member Adele Kubein detailed the policy-based critiques of the Iraq War. Interspersed among concerns over the planning of the war, the reduced quality of life in Iraq since the war, and the many deaths of Iraqis and American troops, Kubein contributed personal details. She described the injury of her daughter in Iraq and the experiences of other military members and families:

> The terrible costs of war are seemingly unending. National Guard and Reserve troops, who never chose to be instruments of destruction, went to Iraq as my daughter did, with the implanted belief that they would be welcomed as liberators, to bring freedom, peace, and prosperity to Iraq. Personally, I have seen the effects of this lie as my daughter struggles to control her anger, fear, and depression as she learns to live with disability.

Kubein provided these personal details in order to draw in her listeners and direct their attention toward her unique identity as a military mom and an antiwar protester. While Kubein could have highlighted her education or work experience, which would have lent credibility to her opinions, she instead pointed to her daughter because of the novelty of being both part of a military family and an outspoken critic of the war. Military peace movement rhetoric frequently combined personal experiences with the wider peace movements' framings of the wars in Iraq and Afghanistan. By highlighting their insider–outsider identities as they provided academic critiques of the war, activists attempted to attract greater attention to antiwar arguments.

Veterans included shocking and sorrowful details of war in their speeches as a way to help people understand how someone could be both military affiliated and a peace protestor. On the stage at Camp Casey, military family members and veterans stood up night after night to tell their stories, which they believed were not well understood by the American public. A Texan mother of an Army soldier clarified that unless their voices were heard, the public would "just assume the military [supported] this war." In their testimonials activists explained why this was not the case. On August 17, 2006, Cloy Richards read a journal entry at Camp Casey called "Why I Fight" because he wanted people to know "what it's like being in the military or being a military family member":

> Because I can't forget, no matter how hard I try, that they told me we were taking out and advancing on Iraqi military forces. When we checked out the bodies, we found nothing but women and children and elderly, who were desperately trying to flee their homes before we attacked their city in the morning.
>
> Because of my little brother, Jacob, [whom] it was my job to protect, joined the California National Guard to get some college money and work one weekend a month and two weeks a year, was sent to Iraq for a year. And since he's been home for the past six months, he refuses to talk to anyone in the family or any of his childhood friends. He can only be around the one friend who had made it home alive with him from Iraq. For the first time, he actually decided to talk to me for the six months he's been home. It was only to call me and tell me he's getting orders to go to Afghanistan, and how he can't sleep because all he thinks about when he lays down his head is picking up the pieces of his two best friends and the limbs that were left over after they were struck by a car bomber.
>
> Because of every single one of the brave men, the Marines, these tough, coldhearted warriors, they're just trained to kill and not even think about it, that I served with in Iraq. Every single one of them I've

served with I've talked to, and they've broken down crying in front of me, guys who wouldn't cry in a combat zone when their best friend was killed because they were that hard—break down crying in front of me. And they told me about all they can do now is bounce from job to job, drink, do drugs, and sit at home contemplating suicide to end the pain.

Because I'm tired of bouncing from job to job, drinking and doing drugs, and sitting at home contemplating suicide to end the pain.

Because last night, even though I hadn't gotten an hour or two of sleep in two days, I only slept two hours before I woke up shaking in tears and decided to make this list.

Because every time I see a child, I think of the children I've slaughtered.

Because every time I see a young soldier, I think of thousands that Bush has slaughtered.

Because every time I look in the mirror, I see a casualty of war.

Because I got a lot of lives to save to make up for all I've taken and because it's right.

That's why I fight.

Through his litany of reasons for protesting the Iraq War, he portrayed dissent as necessary for the troops. These emotionally charged and personal speeches drew attention to and supported the peace movement's arguments to end the wars, because they described the realities of war in concrete rather than theoretical, philosophical, or data-driven ways. These activists used their firsthand experiences to motivate others and mobilize new audiences.

Family members read letters from their relatives serving in combat as a way to advertise arguments against the war. At the 2010 VFP national convention, Nancy Nygard read a letter from her son, who was stationed in Afghanistan at the time:

After we dropped off our load at a little spot outside Tallil, we pulled to the side in a friendly area and waited for the rest of our guys to catch up. . . . That's when the kids came up. I always liked talking to the local kids in Afghanistan. . . . These poor children have known nothing but death and destruction in their young lives and even if after we leave,

FIGURE 17. Cloy Richards (*center*), a Marine who served an eight-month tour followed by a seven-month tour in Iraq, reads his journal entry during a speak-out by members of Iraq Veterans Against the War. Also speaking are Henry Collins, a Marine who served in Iraq from August of 2004 to May of 2005 (*left*) and Geoff Millard, of the New York Army National Guard, who served thirteen months in Iraq from October 2004 to October 2005 (*right*). Photograph by the author.

their country turns to peace, they will forever be scarred from the horrors they have seen. . . . Seeing little girls the age of my little daughter running alongside our convoy, their clothes dirty and their feet bare, offering anything, even themselves, for just a bottle of water, breaks my heart. Back on the base, eating ice cream, pizza, and buffalo wings, just makes the whole experience of war more disgusting. As these people starve to death, partly because of us, we eat like kings.

Nygard used her son's words to drive home points about war's futility, and she described her son's compassion as a way to demonstrate that the problem was in the mission not in the military members' actions. Details like this often drew media and bystander attention to movement tactics.

Identities for Authority

Military peace movement activists critiqued the Iraq War from a unique vantage point as military insiders. Throughout their activism, they drew attention to their experience with the military because they believed it lent the movement authority on issues of war.

Activists crafted personal narratives to illuminate what they called the ground truth about the Iraq and Afghanistan wars. They used this term to refer to their experience-based knowledge of the wars. This phrase showed up in numerous places, including appeals for funding on the MFSO website, which read, "Please make a one-time or monthly contribution so that we can continue to bring the ground truth of these wars to elected officials and the general public!" As mentioned in chapter 3, *Ground Truth* was also the title of a documentary on soldiers who went to Iraq and then developed a critique of the war, many of whom were members of IVAW. Activists believed that they had an impact in the debate on the Iraq War because public demonstrations of their identities claimed expertise about the war.

Activists identified with organizations whose members were veterans or military family members. When these activists publicly declared their membership identity verbally or through buttons, T-shirts, and other merchandise, they made an important strategic choice to use their insider–outsider identities. Similarly, when coalitions listed organizations with military affiliations on sponsorship and speaker lists for peace events, statements, and campaigns, they hoped to convey that individuals with sufficient knowledge of the war were involved with that particular antiwar tactic or strategy. They did so because as Korean War–era veteran Bob Potter described, when activists told people about their military affiliation, "it seemed to impress" civilians.

These efforts to highlight military affiliation went beyond talk; the military was also purposely embodied. Military peace movement activists often moved in ways that indicated their insider–outsider identities, and several activists expressed the belief that doing so would legitimize their antiwar protest. During numerous peace marches, VFP and IVAW members led cadence calls that resembled those from the 2006 march along the Gulf Coast described in chapter 3. These cadences were chanted at a typical military-marching tempo, as if the activists were a military cadre in training or war—sometimes, activists' march tempo would require them to stop so that they could fall back in with slower-paced peace marchers. Typically, the first several verses were chanted by a leader, and then the group repeated them. In the final verse the leader called, and the group responded with a different, predetermined response. The following cadence was used by the military peace movement:

CALL: Vets for peace are here to say,
RESPONSE: Vets for peace are here to say,
CALL: Bring our brothers home today![10]
RESPONSE: Bring our brothers home today!
CALL: War will mean that soldiers die!
RESPONSE: War will mean that soldiers die!
CALL: War will mean that mothers cry!
RESPONSE: War will mean that mothers cry!
CALL: Am I right or wrong?
RESPONSE: You're right!
CALL: Are we weak or strong?
RESPONSE: You're strong!
CALL: Sound off!
RESPONSE: One, two!
CALL: Sound off!
RESPONSE: Three, four!
CALL: Bring it on down!
RESPONSE: One, two, three, four! One, two, no war!

Military cadence verses typically end with, "One, two! / Three, four!" During marches, nonmilitary members of the peace movement who knew a cadence would sometimes repeat the lines said by the leader, but after "Bring it on down!" they often chanted a confused response, and only the military peace movement members would respond correctly. These cadences provided a way for the audience to recognize who had experiential legitimacy as veterans and military families, since other antiwar protest chants do not sound like military cadences. As the cadences in chapter 3 demonstrate, each verse invited attention to the activists' insider–outsider identities in an attempt to provide the peace movement with credibility. Instead of typical protest chants, these call-and-response cadences, along with the style of activists' marching movements and their flag waving, highlighted their connection to the military.

Beyond their way of marching, the veterans intentionally moved in other ways that called attention to their insider–outsider identities. During the VFP national convention on August 18, 2007, IVAW members confronted an Army recruitment booth at the Missouri Black Expo in the nearby St. Louis convention center. The recruiters, which included people in the military and military contractors, were using a Humvee with expensive wheel rims and a video-simulated war game to recruit the convention's job seekers, largely black teenagers and young adults. As the members of IVAW milled around the Army exhibit, a woman suddenly yelled, "Fall in!" and two men repeated her. The activists assembled themselves so that Jabbar Magruder, an Army National Guard sergeant in his midtwenties, stood in the front of the rows of former servicemembers, resembling a drill sergeant standing in front of a company formation of new or junior military recruits.

The IVAW members stood at attention in five rows of twelve, with their backs stiff, their hands pointed down at their sides, their chins up, and their eyes staring straight ahead. They all wore matching black T-shirts with white block lettering that had the full name of their organization and its website's address. Three times, Magruder asked, "Iraq Veterans Against the War, what have you learned?" Each time, the in-unison military-style response was the same: "War is not a game!" This action resembled a platoon of military members shouting, "Sir! Yes, sir!" in response to a question from a military leader. Then, Magruder yelled, "Fall out!" and the IVAW members went back to milling around the expo like the other civilians, with many passing out flyers. People applauded and whooped as the group came out of formation, and bystanders debated the merits of that protest, the war, and the military in general.

Sparked by that confrontation, the *St. Louis Post-Dispatch* and the national independent media interviewed two National Guard members who served in Iraq: Kelly Dougherty, the IVAW executive director at the time, who had been a medic and military police officer, and Camillo Mejía, who after spending six months in Iraq in 2003 went AWOL while on leave due to his objections to the war. Doughtery and Mejía described the action as part of IVAW's involvement in counterrecruitment, which Mejía explained as "truth telling":

> You want to join the military—this is what could happen to you. This is what's happened to our members. This is what the contract means. This is what stop-loss is. This is also what conscientious objection is.

Mejía and Doughtery described these protests as necessary to countering the military recruiters' deception and to providing "objective information" to young potential recruits and their parents about the realities of war and military service and the lack of care for veterans when they returned home. While activists could have simply shouted and/or handed out flyers, these individuals used a military-style formation to highlight their own service. By drawing attention to their identities as military members, they wanted passersby to know that this protest against the military was coming from people with authority on the war and, thus, was credible.

Similarly, in a tactical repertoire called Operation First Casualty, members of IVAW performed a form of guerrilla street theater that evoked the military. On July 4, 2007, in Denver, ten IVAW members wore their military camouflage uniforms and moved as if on anti-insurgency patrols. The activists held their arms as if holding and aiming M16 or M4 carbines that soldiers carried in Iraq. At various times, Garrett Reppenhagen, the designated squad leader for this tactic, would hold up his fist, and the other activists would drop to a crouched position. They simulated IED attacks, with everyone hitting the deck (lying flat on the ground) and certain people acting injured and requiring the attention of the designated medic. They approached approximately ten VFP, MFSO, and other peace movement members who were playing the part of Iraqis. Those acting as Iraqis shouted at the soldiers, "Go home," or, "I didn't do it," or, "I'm innocent. Don't hurt me." Those playing the part of soldiers pushed them to the ground and zip-tied their hands behind their backs. As they did so, some Iraqis would resist, and the soldiers would shout, "Don't make me shoot you!" The soldiers consulted with each other and then placed bags over some Iraqis' heads, who were then led away while the others were released.

Afterward, activists gave speeches opposing the war. One former Army staff sergeant who served in Iraq from February 2004 to 2005 said that the tactics soldiers used in the street theater and in the Iraq War itself were antithetical to winning the hearts and minds of the Iraqi people; he even described them as "terrorizing the Iraqi population." Another Army veteran of the Iraq War explained the tactic's name:

> We as veterans know that the first casualty of war is the truth. The purpose of this operation is to awaken the emotions of Colorado citizens and to give them a firsthand look at the real truths of the war in Iraq, not that which the media portrays. Our hope is that Operation First Casualty will give American people the passion and devotion to do what they can to end the illegal war in Iraq so that the next Fourth of July we can enjoy barbeques, fireworks, and camping without this dark cloud over our heads.

He said that although these actions brought up difficult memories for the soldiers, they believed Americans needed to see the war with their own eyes and experience a bit of the chaos that had been created in Iraq by the war. He called upon his own and the other soldiers' military experiences in order to explain the necessity for peace activism. Activists repeated these actions in many U.S. cities, and as a part of their protests at the 2008 Democratic National Convention in Denver, they performed a larger version that included over thirty "soldiers" and many more "Iraqis." During the second performance of Operation First Casualty in Denver, they were able to attract some of the DNC delegates and a few celebrities. By performing in these ways, the activists called attention to their military identities in a peace protest tactic that they hoped would bring "the war home to the streets of America," as said by an older female activist. Their past war experiences lent the tactic the credibility necessary to making it an emotionally impactful form of street theater.

In numerous ways, military veterans and families emphasized their insider–outsider identities in order to suggest that they alone had legitimacy in the debates over the wars in Iraq and Afghanistan. These activists tended to believe that even within the movement, some members had more legitimacy than others. They regularly suggested that those participants whose experiences were closest to the battlefield had the most legitimacy. In VVAW's fall 2007 newsletter, Ward Reilly wrote:

> Iraq Veterans Against the War are the most legitimate voice of the antiwar movement, period. [They are] young men and women that have been to Iraq or Afghanistan, and know the truth about what is happening there—brave, beautiful, and mad. Intelligent, damaged, and spit out by a lying administration. Sickened by what they know to be the real story of Iraq, that being that the US military is being used as an oppressive police and occupation force, to protect the mercenary oil-army of the Neocons, at the cost of our soldiers' sanity. IVAW has served.... IVAW is ready to make a stand. They are organized, willing, and able to lead the anti-war movement to victory. We can only help them as much as possible, and hope that they can win this fight for peace and justice.... I encourage every so-called leader, of every organization against the war, to seek them out. Send them money. Bring their members to your people and to your actions. Watch, listen, and learn about how we can stop the war pigs, by allowing IVAW into their rightful and hard earned position, as leaders of the anti-war movement. They lead with the truth, and they are all on-message. We need these Iraq and Afghanistan vets speaking in Congress now. We need them on 60 Minutes now.[11]

Although parents, partners and spouses, siblings, and friends could convey the problems of the Iraq War, soldiers who had been there, especially those damaged by what they had seen and done, were seen as having the most valuable position from which to critique the wars. Some participants in the military peace movement and in other segments of the larger peace movement critiqued this hierarchy, but

IVAW activists' direct experiences were particularly useful for countering the rhetoric that favored the wars.

Countering the Opposition's Claims

These activists regularly referenced their military identities not only because their experiences lent the movement authority but also because it was useful in challenging prowar claims. As I have written elsewhere, "Discourses that stress patriotism and a need to 'support the troops' were introduced in political speeches in the lead-up to the Iraq War and have been repeated in the media coverage as the war continues."[12] One finds so many references to patriotism because the 9/11 terrorist attacks were perceived as an attack on fundamental American ideals and the American way of life. The treatment of Vietnam War veterans shaped the view of how servicemembers should be treated during the Iraq and Afghanistan wars, and thus "troop support" was also a popular phrase at the time. Governmental and conservative elites called upon these events when they "defined patriotism to mean unquestioning loyalty to the policies of the government and defined 'supporting the troops' as backing the mission" of these wars.[13] Despite extensive antiwar activism in the lead-up to the Iraq War, this elite's framing of protest as unpatriotic and antitroop successfully stifled antiwar activism until mid-2005, when the military peace movement garnered media attention through the protests outside President Bush's Crawford ranch.[14] The broader antiwar movement benefited from the novelty of the insider–outsider identities deployed by military peace movement activists. Since one would expect members of the military community to support a war—particularly, one in which they or their families were fighting—military peace movement members employed an oppositional identity that directly countered the arguments of their opponents.[15] In this case, they aided the antiwar movement's arguments that peace and protest were patriotic and that troops needed the support that would come only by ending the wars and taking care of soldiers' physical and psychological wounds. Activists engaged in oppositional-identity strategies when they used rhetorical techniques to highlight their own identities and make claims that patriotism and troop support belonged to those opposing the wars.

Protest Is Supporting the Troops

Antiwar activists regularly framed their protest as supportive of the troops, using their insider–outsider identities.[16] In 2007 when the national coalition United for Peace and Justice (UFPJ) encouraged newly elected Democratic lawmakers to cut funding for the war despite prowar criticism that doing so would harm servicemembers, they turned to VFP, MFSO, and IVAW to spearhead the campaign. UFPJ recruited and funded the travel expenses of military peace movement members who attended their January 27 march in Washington, D.C.; their military-focused events in the base town of Fayetteville, North Carolina, that March; and their subsequent veteran and military family speaking tour. The various UFPJ organizations used an emotionally charged rhetorical strategy that focused activities around the slogan "Funding the War Is Killing Our Troops." This language framed congressional approval of the Iraq War's budget as the murder of American servicemembers. Military peace movement activists' identity deployment was essential to making this framing palatable.

MFSO talking points at this time encouraged members to use their insider–outsider identities to explain how the war hurt troops. These talking points were sent to members in an email with the following encouragement: "Your personal story as a military family is very important. Your personal story and situation can help to expose the true human toll of the war." The document persuaded members to use two key phrases:

> "As a Military Family"—Be sure to identify yourself as a military family when you speak at an event or to the press, and describe your connection to the military.

> "As a Member of Military Families Speak Out"—If you can identify yourself as a member of Military Families Speak Out, it lets the press and the public know that your voice represents a larger number of military families who are against the war. It also lets military families not yet connected with MFSO know they are not alone and that there is an organization they can connect with.

These internal documents show that military peace movement organizations believed that they provided UFPJ's strategy with legitimacy, because their identities conferred experience and intimacy with the "troops."

Using a similar tactic, in July 2007 IVAW began its Tri-folded Flag Campaign, in which activists publicly presented legislators with a folded flag reminiscent of what military honor guards gave to families during a veteran's funeral. They also distributed to UFPJ members a computer file with an image of a flag that could be printed and instructions for flag folding. It was intended to be mailed to Congress members. When properly folded, the words "Funding the war is killing our troops" appeared in the flag's sea of blue stars. In a campaign press release, former Marine Adam Kokesh used his military knowledge to defend the defunding strategy:

> As a proud combat veteran who believes in a strong US military and national defense, I find the Iraq war most offensive. Resources that could be allocated to a multitude of other projects to enhance our security are instead being diverted into the futile occupation of Iraq. The brave men and women who have sworn an oath to defend the Constitution deserve better than to risk their lives in a misadventure that is detrimental to our security and our Constitution. Further funding of this quagmire will only result in more needless deaths.

The references that activists made to their service connections, such as Kokesh highlighting that he was a combat veteran and a Marine, suggested that they were first and foremost one of the troops that people were expected to support. Kokesh drew upon his knowledge of the military and war spending to argue for a reorganization of defense funding away from the Iraq War and toward things he saw as befitting the service that military members provided. Activists in the military peace movement used emotional rhetoric to challenge prowar frames that protest harmed the military and framed support as necessitating bringing troops home and caring for veterans.

Blogs and websites were important locations for activists to outline their experiences with war and their desires for peace. In these online forums, they frequently engaged with the popular frames of patriotism and troop support. One veteran who served for twenty years on active duty in the Navy and in the Army Reserves wrote of his misgivings about the Iraq War in his personal blog while deployed in Iraq in 2004 and 2005 and, later, of his reentry experience on popular antiwar blogs such as *Daily Kos*. In 2008, under the alias "teachervet," he critiqued the following popular image of troop support: "Screw the yellow ribbons. Screw all the 'support our troops' crap. Screw the parades and flags. Why can't we commit to honor our vets by taking care of them?"[17] Activists regularly spoke out against the yellow ribbon as a show of support and pointed to the serious needs veterans had in transitioning from war to home in order to demonstrate that antiwar activism could be a form of troop support. In a post from 2006, teachervet wrote:

> Shortly after I went back to work, I began having serious anxiety attacks. Getting out the door in the morning got harder and harder. I had trouble serious trouble being in crowds. Loud noises sent my heart rate through the roof, and I heard explosions in my sleep. I knew I was angry while I was still in Iraq, but I found I could barely contain myself on some occasions now that I was home.[18]

This IVAW member regularly wrote about his experiences with combat trauma, and in this entry he positively described his activism while deriding support for the war, using words such as "ignorant" and "blind." Like the defunding activities, this kind of writing by veterans and military families attempted to educate civilians about how protest supported the troops.

Protest Is Patriotic

Military peace movement activists not only asserted that protest supported the military but claimed that protest made the country better. They saw their activism as an outgrowth of the patriotism expected of those who served the nation as military servicemembers and of their families. At a 2004 rally in Augusta, Maine, Richard Clements said that his military affiliation was an element of his patriotism:

I am here today to say that I am a proud father of an Army soldier and a patriotic American. I do not wrap myself in the flag and shout, "My country, right or wrong!" That is not true patriotism. Patriotism is to rise up and change your country when change is necessary. Now is that time. Change is of the ultimate importance. Many of the people in attendance today are working actively for peace. For those of you who just came to the march, I encourage you to not stop there. Join one of the many peace organizations represented here today. Become a political activist. Speak out!

After highlighting his insider–outsider identity, Clements framed activism as patriotic for those without a military affiliation. Using his insider–outsider identity, he insulated himself against criticism and then framed patriotism as necessitating critique of government policies.

In their self-descriptions many military peace movement members used a form of the word *patriot*. A Los Angeles IVAW member's website began, "I am a United States Marine Corps combat veteran. I am a proud American and a patriot. I love my country, democracy and the vision of our founding fathers." Theresa Dawson, whose son served with the Ohio National Guard and whose daughter served in the Army Reserves, enacted a character called the Prissy Patriot. During the 2006 peace movement activities in Washington, D.C., called Camp Democracy, she dressed in a pastel-pink business suit during her visits to Congress members' offices. Dawson discussed her military children as she handed out a business card emblazoned with the U.S. flag that had a safety pin with two small, pink cotton balls attached. She asked members of Congress and encouraged others to ask Congress members to have the "patriotic balls" to end the war in Iraq. By deploying a military identity, Dawson strategically emphasized her devotion to her country in the hope of countering the stigma that antiwar ideas and actions were unpatriotic. Dawson also played with gendered assumptions about war and peace by embellishing her feminine, nurturing role as a military mom and by contradicting the notion that troop withdrawal was weak, "unmanly" behavior.

Military veterans challenged prowar framings of patriotism by using various tactics, and as they did so, they purposefully highlighted their insider–outsider identities. On the tenth anniversary of 9/11, five members of VFP's Greater Seattle chapter leafleted seven hundred cars in downtown Seattle with cards reading, "Patriot Day Greetings from Veterans for Peace." The cards explained that September 11 had been congressionally designated Patriot Day and quoted a Representative Ron Paul speech that laid out a case for protest being patriotic. The card began and ended by calling attention to the participants' status as veterans, spelling out "Veterans for Peace" and using an image of the damaged Twin Towers and VFP's logo. Military peace movement activists regularly railed against what they called "blind patriotism" and sought to use the belief that military members' service was the highest form of patriotism to their advantage in the contest over patriotism's connection to the wars.

As Adam Kokesh's earlier quote demonstrates, activists invoked the U.S. Constitution as a way to frame their protest activities as patriotic. VFP wrote extensively about the constitutionality of the Iraq War and military members' duty to the Constitution in a 2008 letter distributed to generals. The letter dealt with the case of Army Lieutenant Ehren Watada, who refused to deploy to Iraq because he believed the war was unconstitutional:

> The test of patriotism, for generals as well as civilians, is fidelity to our Constitution, not abject submission to a desperate clique of individuals mired in the corruption of empire. We realize that, as a general whose decisions affect thousands of lives, you are in a very difficult position. You face the same dilemma that 1st Lt. Ehren Watada confronted when he learned about the systematic atrocities in the field and the duplicity of the administration. No doubt you feel a strong obligation to your Commander in Chief, and ordinarily expect to carry out his orders. But legal and illegal orders are profoundly different. When the requirements of law conflict with the policies of command, it is the law, not those who abuse their power, that must be followed.

Throughout the letter VFP activists connected their interpretation of antiwar activities, including servicemembers' refusal of orders to fight in Iraq, to the oath that military members swore to the Constitution. To enhance the patriotic framing of their argument, the activists referenced other patriotic symbols such as the Founding Fathers, U.S. Supreme Court decisions, UN documents, and U.S. treaties.

Activists invoked the constitutional duties of government officials and of the military, as well. On March 1, 2006, IVAW and MFSO members met with Senator John Kerry in order to urge him to lead the call to end the Iraq War. Although many of the activists linked their request to Kerry's past antiwar activism, in one letter parents from Needham, Massachusetts, framed their request using the politician's oath to the Constitution. These parents, whose daughter was serving in Iraq, wrote:

> As constituents and the proud parents of an Army soldier, we urgently request that you stand up to address this issue by working in Congress to bring our troops home now. We sincerely believe that such action would be in keeping with your oath of office to defend the Constitution of the United States. Thank you for making this issue your first priority as our Senator.

By referencing this symbol of America, activists intended to demonstrate that an antiwar position was patriotic. Military peace movement participants highlighted their military identities in nearly all protest activities because they knew that many associated military service with patriotism. They hoped that by stressing the patriotism of their antiwar protests, they could reach people who did not support the peace movement yet.

Reaching the Unconverted

The movement's collective identity was based on a shared consciousness, or set of common beliefs, that the Iraq War was damaging to the U.S. military and that military peace movement activists were the most successful at communicating this to those on the fence or who tried to disregard protest. Military peace movement participants considered their insider–outsider identities crucial to making antiwar arguments palatable to people who were otherwise indifferent to peace activism. They believed that the positive feelings that conservative Americans had toward the military could be capitalized on to make them susceptible to antiwar arguments. Activists deployed military identities to target three main audiences they hoped to convert to an antiwar ideology: civilian nonactivists, other members of the military, and government officials.

Civilians

Military peace movement activists believed that their identity strategies were particularly well suited to reaching civilians who had not yet been converted to antiwar beliefs. Vietnam veteran Lane Anderson said that he joined VFP while protesting the Gulf War because the organization was valuable in the same way VVAW had been:

> I think I could have been easily a demonstrator against the war in Vietnam without being a veteran, but again, I felt like I was having more of an effect as a veteran. So I showed my colors and encouraged everybody else. Most recently, there's a Navy commander [in VFP] that I'm trying to get in uniform, and she's still not in uniform, but I try to convince people if they have military credentials, show them [at peace events], even if they don't feel it's necessary. It's more effective.

For Anderson military peace movement activists' effectiveness came from highlighting their military identities. He wanted everyone in the movement, including Commander Leah Bolger (Retired), who was the VFP president in 2012, to wear clothing that indicated their military credentials, particularly those who had long and distinguished records. He believed that "to reach out to the unconverted, there's nobody better than a veteran in a time of war." Like many in the military peace movement, Anderson felt that insider–outsider identities were useful in reaching people on the other side or who were neutral on this issue.

On March 8, 2009, at the northwest regional VFP conference, Army veteran and high-level CIA officer Ray McGovern suggested that people listened to him not because of his distinguished career in the CIA, including regularly briefing the White House, but because he was a military veteran. Another VFP member described this speech as encouraging veterans to use their "unique and essential voice" in their attempts to gain civilians' attention. Similarly, former VFP executive director Michael McPhearson said that these activists provided a "bridge to a more conservative America" that might believe all peace activists were hippies.[19] As McPhearson pointed out, military peace movement activists could engage those with whom they were not already politically aligned not only because there was a general respect for veterans in America but also because veterans were assumed to be more similar to mainstream or even conservative Americans than were supposedly left-leaning peace activists.

Veterans were not the only ones to draw on their insider–outsider status to reach the unconverted. During a series of speeches made by activists during the aforementioned 2006 Silence of the Dead, Voices of the Living event in Washington, D.C., an activist whose long-term boyfriend had served in Iraq with the Army utilized her combined military–peace activist identity to highlight the long-term consequences of the war:

> I carried this picture with me every day my soldier was gone. I still carry this tattered picture because the person who came home to me is not the same person in this picture. . . . The first time he told me the man I fell in love with had died in Iraq and wouldn't ever be coming home, I felt sick, and I cried. I cried as he apologized to me for not being the same. I cried as he apologized and told me he wouldn't blame me if I wanted to leave him and find someone else. He shouldn't be the one apologizing. I am so thankful he came home alive, and yet so angry. I'm angry because he's not the same, and he doesn't laugh the way he used to, or sleep through the night, or walk down the street without looking around him for insurgents, thinking he's still on patrol. I'm angry that all of our shouting and marching and speaking out wasn't enough to keep him from losing a part of his soul or to bring these soldiers [as she gestured to the boots] home before they passed. I am left to wonder if anyone who is in a position to end [the Iraq War] can hear my anger, my desperation, my despair. Can they hear me? Can they hear us? I hope so, but I'm going to keep speaking out until I know they've heard me, until the troops are brought home.

This young woman cried as she spoke, and the military families on stage shed their own tears as they nodded in agreement and placed

their hands on her back and shoulders in gestures of support and solidarity. In telling her experience as a military family member, this
activist used rhetoric to encourage an emotional reaction she hoped
would move people to work to end the Iraq War. This public display of
emotion was used to explain to a large audience how military peace activists could combine these seemingly disparate identities. The claim
made over and over again was that "bad wars" turned military families
into peace activists. Military peace movement activists hoped to use
this emotional rhetoric and display to form a connection to those who
were not already opposed to the war and who did not regularly see the
devastating effects of war on people.

The Military Community

In addition to civilians, military peace movement activists sought to
influence members of the military. In 2007, IVAW executive director Kelly Dougherty announced a renewed strategic focus to "organize veterans and active duty soldiers to withdraw their consent for
the war." Since many military members had negative impressions of
peace activists, military peace movement identities were useful in getting antiwar positions into the consciousness of this community.

Career public servant Ann Wright began speaking out against the
Iraq War as one of the diplomats who helped open the American embassy in Afghanistan after 9/11 and who then resigned in protest after
the Iraq War began. As the war continued, she shifted her public presentation of identity:

> I almost moved from speaking as a diplomat to speaking as an Army
> veteran because that has more credence these days. . . . In these times
> an Army colonel does have a certain cache. That's why I'm wearing the
> [camouflage] jacket now. I didn't even start that until this summer,
> because I did more of the diplomatic stuff. Several veterans kept say-
> ing, "You know, you oughta find yourself an old [military] jacket, you
> know." We all wear these jackets. This summer when I was in Wash-
> ington, I went over to the Fort Meyers clothing sales. I wasn't about
> to buy a new one, and I couldn't find my old ones. I didn't know where
> they went. So I went over to Fort Meyers in Washington, and I got a

couple of jackets and started getting some [military patches and insignia] on them, and it does make an impression on people when you are standing there as a retired colonel in the Army.

Wright's choice to wear the military jacket and identify herself as a person with a lengthy military career was intended to garner legitimacy that would be readily understood by people in the military. During a hunger strike in front of the White House, she made sure that she rather than activists unaffiliated with the military interacted with active duty military members and families who came by the protest. She said that by using her insider–outsider identity she was able to have lengthy and sometimes meaningful conversations rather than "hateful shouting matches."

This alliance building was not always easy. In the November 11, 2007, Boston Veterans Day parade, the American Legion, who organized the event, forbade VFP from marching with their peace signs and their peace-worded cadences. In response, the members of the Smedley Butler Brigade, as the Boston VFP chapter was called, marched with other peace groups after the street sweepers at the end of the parade.[20] A contingent of about thirty veterans, mostly white, over forty, and male, led this peace counterprotest while wearing VFP and military clothing. They waved upside-down American flags and white flags with a black VFP logo (a dove coming out of a military helmet). Many held signs that read, "Upside-down flag means distress not disrespect." Activists carried the flag this way because they believed that in one activists' words, "engaging in this illegal war" had put the country and its military in a "state of distress." They offered an explanation of the upside-down flags because they knew that carrying a flag this way was often understood as disrespectful, and they wanted to educate the audience about their use of the flag. As military veterans, they believed people would respond more positively toward them than toward other peace activists carrying these flags and signs, since veterans' patriotism was "above reproach."

As VFP marched through the streets of Boston, a balding white man on the sidewalk who appeared to be in his sixties entered the VFP contingent, yelling, "You don't blame the soldiers! You say, 'Fuck Bush!'" Vietnam veterans yelled back, "We don't blame the soldiers," and a few approached him to talk to him. As they did, the man began crying, and he leaned his head on a VFP member's shoulder as the member put his arm around him and said, "You all right?" Another VFP member approached and put a hand on this individual's back and said, "Hey, brother, we are not here to hurt you. I was a paratrooper in Vietnam, and I lost a lot of friends over there. I know what the cost of war is." The man explained that he was in the Marines for six years as he wiped his eyes. The second VFP man continued, "We are your brothers [gesturing to their military clothing, which indicated their group identity], and we just have strong feelings against this war. It's an unjust war, and . . . ." The man from the sidelines interrupted with a tight voice and tears, saying, "I know it is! It's the president [whose fault it is and who should be protested], not nobody else." By emphasizing their insider–outsider identities, the activists were able to make their antiwar message palatable to this angry veteran. Through their style of marching and their treatment of this man as a military comrade, the VFP activists demonstrated their military identities and used them to calm counterprotesters and draw attention to their message.[21]

IVAW's 2007–12 strategic focus on removing military support for the Iraq and, later, Afghanistan wars had three main parts: (1) convincing people not to join the military while the wars continued, (2) getting people in the service to protest the wars, and (3) convincing servicemembers not to renew their military contracts. The movement referred to the first part as Truth in Recruiting, or *counterrecruitment,* and it involved speaking events at schools and other places aimed at enlistment-aged groups where veterans and Gold Star activists told harrowing stories of combat. Other tactics included protests aimed at recruiting centers and recruiters, as well as fun events such as concerts and movies. The second part included minimizing the risk for servicemembers who wished to express dissatisfaction with the war, as exemplified by the Appeal for Redress discussed in chapter 2, and building communities or chapters near military bases. Additionally, it involved direct help for and publicizing the stories of those who refused to follow orders to deploy to the wars. The third part of this strategy, called *counterretention,* entailed publicizing options for nonmilitary futures and helping military members transition out of the service. In support of this strategy, the military peace movement opened coffee shops near large bases where military members could build extramilitary solidarity and learn about career opportunities, training, and veterans' benefits. While IVAW never achieved its goal of creating a manpower problem for fighting the wars, it did succeed in mobilizing many current servicemembers to join the movement.

Military peace movement activists highlighted their military credentials when talking with other members of the military community. Since that community could be highly insular, they believed their own experiences could give them access to this group. Similarly, activists believed that their experience-based credibility could gain them access to government officials.

Government Officials

Military peace movement activists believed that government officials would listen to them because of the sacrifices they had made through their own or their family members' service to the country. Many believed that their representatives owed them because those officials sent the military into harm's way. During the 2006 Mother's Day events, activists drew on their military identities in attempts to arrange official meetings and government attendance at the events. An MFSO activist from Chicago sent invitations to her Congress members via email and the post office that highlighted her status as the mother of an Army soldier serving in Afghanistan. She hand-delivered letters explaining the heartbreak of the Iraq War to the offices of the then senator Barack Obama and Senator Richard Durbin from herself and from other Chicago-area people whose children were serving in the military.

That same weekend, a Michigan National Guard soldier, his family, and a few other activists met with senators Debbie Stabenow and Carl Levin, as well as Representative Sander Levin. Military experience was purposefully front and center in these meetings. In their meeting with Senator Levin, they shared the pain of losing a family member to the war. The Michigan Guardsman's family described their experience with what they called a "lack of family support" before, after, and during deployments, particularly for members of the Reserves and National Guard. They described the troubling experiences they had witnessed with reentry counseling postdeployment. Other MFSO activists then described secondary PTSD through stories of their experiences as military family members, as well as those of their friends and their friends' children who experienced psychological distress from the war. The MFSO coordinator for the District of Columbia area said that her boyfriend, an Army military policeman, was exposed to various chemicals because his base was put on top of a former Iraqi toxic waste dump, and she expressed frustration over the lack of testing and treatment provided when he and his unit returned to the United States. These conversations were not easy, and during the discussion of the toxic base, the National Guard soldier left the room, his body visibly stiff with anger.

The Congress members, even if they disagreed on the war, typically thanked military peace movement activists for coming, and in most of the meetings I attended, they acknowledged learning something about the military community's hardships during these wars. The wife of the Michigan Guardsman described these meetings as exhausting, but she was pleased that their military connections had gotten their voices heard. She wrote:

> When we finally left, I had a sense of catharsis, knowing that even if it made no difference [to the Congress members' positions on the war] ... I had at least had the chance to drive home exactly what they were doing to military families and personnel. I decided that my new mantra would be "if I can't change their minds, I'm going to make them feel guilty for holding the positions that they do." It seemed to work in Carl Levin's case.

Here and in many other venues, activists used their positions as military family members to get their foot in the door of government officials' offices. Once there, they drew on their personal accounts as military servicemembers and military family members in an attempt to connect emotions of grief and fear to the Iraq War. They occasionally changed minds, as they eventually did with Senator Kerry, but more often they simply enlightened government leaders to the variety of opinions and needs of veterans and military families.

NAVIGATING IDENTITY STRATEGIES

Although activists regularly used their military peace movement identities to support their claims, identity strategies were occasionally controversial within the movement. Since these strategies defined the activists themselves, some fights over identity-deployment tactics were especially bitter. Activists carefully negotiated the merits of putting forth a patriotic image, particularly during a time of war, and whether it was useful to affiliate with more radical elements of the peace movement, such as socialist organizations, antimilitary activists, and pacifists. Tensions regularly erupted between those activists whose military identity was stronger than their peace activist identity and those with the opposite identity salience ranking. Which group controlled the official identity prescriptions for members depended on several factors, including the organization's leadership at the time, the moment's specific political context, and the length of time that the wars had been raging. These internal debates sometimes led individuals to leave the movement or a specific organization.

Movement members were constantly discussing what it meant to be both connected to the military and involved in peace activism. Oftentimes, activists carefully parsed words. MFSO/GSFSO and IVAW saw themselves as antiwar, not peace, organizations because their organizational missions described opposition to particular military actions, not to all military actions. The word *peace* was used neither on the IVAW website page that listed its mission and goals nor on the page that discussed why the organization was against the wars. Although their organizational names suggest VFP and GSFSP were peace organizations, their official documents made it clear that some wars were seen as acceptable by their membership. In fact, VFP did not oppose the war in Afghanistan until 2008, and until the Iraq War ended, the organization's home page rarely referenced Afghanistan. Part of the distinction between *antiwar* and *peace* for these organizations was a careful and strategic separation of these organizations from organizations opposed to all military actions. In the 2009 frequently asked questions section on MFSO's website, the organization carefully delineated itself from pacifists and those who were antimilitary. They described their membership as follows:

Our members have diverse opinions about war and political beliefs. However, we all have in common a determination to support our loved ones in the military. We stand united in opposition, not to war in general, but to the wars in Iraq and Afghanistan, on the basis that they are unjust wars which the U.S. waged based on lies.

Like the organizations themselves, activists within them had diverse self-identities in relation to peace. Whereas some military community members chose to identify as peace activists, the majority of my interviewees used "antiwar activist" to describe themselves. Several of the informal interviews I held with parents and spouses of military members, as well as veterans of Afghanistan and other wars, included similar distinctions between war and peace. Other terms and identities abounded; in a 2013 email with the author, Navy Korean War veteran Ron Dexter explained:

I hesitate to use the term "antiwar." I prefer "less wars," "cost of war," "peace is better than war," "support the troops and vets but not the leaders that send them into unnecessary wars." We need a strong military because there are people that want to hurt us, but we don't need wars like Iraq, Afghanistan, or Iran.

A number of debates within the movement highlighted the contentious and fluid nature of collective identity construction. The movement's controversies over Afghanistan, patriotism, and socialism demonstrated ways in which the collective identity of this culture of action had to be managed. Many of these debates were about finding a balance between using the best strategies to reach their audience and staying true to members' ideals.

Afghanistan

Opposing multiple wars and military actions pushed these organizations closer to a broader peace movement identity and away from a narrow identity focused on opposing only a single war. The most contentious debate within the military peace movement came when the organizations broadened their missions to oppose the Afghanistan War. While veterans of the Afghanistan War were welcomed into VFP and IVAW and their families into MFSO, GSFSO, and GSFP, the military peace movement was initially united in their opposition only to the Iraq War. From 2002 to 2008, their memberships varied in their support for the post-9/11 war in Afghanistan. Some believed that the war in Afghanistan was justified by the Taliban's support for al-Qaeda, since they were responsible for the 9/11 terrorist attacks. Other activists believed that the United States had wrongly attacked a state and killed innocent, uninvolved civilians, when it was a non–state actor's behavior it sought to punish and rectify.

Attempts to add opposition to the Afghanistan War to the organizations' missions intensified until a series of votes were conducted by each organization in 2008 and 2009.[22] At the 2008 VFP convention in Minneapolis, a proposal to oppose the Afghanistan War was adopted by a majority vote. Although a few individuals were vocal supporters of that war, VFP's broad peace mission and the war's length made that vote relatively smooth. In contrast, the process for MFSO (which included GSFSO) and IVAW was longer and more contentious. These two organizations engaged in lengthy communications that allowed members to engage with experts on both sides of the issue. Both organizations received a majority vote for opposition to Afghanistan, but the IVAW majority's margin was too slim to add opposition to the war to their mission statement.

Several members of both organizations threatened to leave over these processes and organizational decisions, and some did. In fact, the Michigan National Guard soldier and his wife, who are discussed throughout this chapter, left MFSO over this vote because they believed the war in Afghanistan was justified. Alternatively, an entire MFSO chapter in Oregon threatened to leave when the vote did not happen as quickly as they would have liked. In 2012 IVAW continued to debate whether veterans of Afghanistan who oppose that war should be in their own organization rather than in an IVAW chapter and whether the organization's call for reparations for civilians applied to Afghanistan as well. By 2013, IVAW had a mission statement that focused on ending "militarism." These debates over which wars to oppose and whether to organize based on which wars members fought in or had their family member fight in were at their root debates over the best ways to combine both desires for peace and military connections. Activists fought over whether extending opposition to Afghanistan limited their distinctiveness and the credibility they derived from their military connections.

Patriotism

The military peace movement had serious internal debates about the organizations' relationship with patriotism. While activists often used their military credentials to suggest they were patriots, doing so meant encouraging positive associations with patriotism rather than questioning nationalism. A number of sessions at the national conventions debated patriotism's proper role in the movement, and this issue was regularly discussed in movement meetings. Some members fought in online media and social-networking sites over this issue, and a few resigned and made their resignation letters public.

This problem was particularly volatile in IVAW after 2007. Several politically conservative members who strongly valued patriotism left IVAW after the organization did not move quickly to terminate the memberships of people such as Texas Army National Guard soldier Carl Webb, who encouraged soldiers in Iraq and Afghanistan to sabotage military equipment—some saying that in doing so, he offered a justification for killing U.S. servicemembers. Other members claimed patriotism was simply "nationalism in disguise." In person, emails, and Web forums, IVAW members critiqued each other for their type of military service and discharge. While numerous activists proudly wore premade shirts or carried signs that read, "Honor the warrior, not the war," others countered with their own homemade versions that said things like, "Soldiers are not heroes." Some combat veterans and those still on active duty commonly critiqued IVAW members who had not faced combat—particularly, war resisters for "abandoning their brothers and sisters." Other members of IVAW—particularly, war resisters—critiqued active duty servicemembers for willingly staying in the military during an "illegal war." Each side claimed that individuals who disagreed with them needed to find another organization to join. These fights centered on military members' different notions of patriotism and military duty. Those with more radical or left-leaning politics suggested that patriotism supported the expansion of the U.S. "military empire." This contrasted sharply with the positive use of patriotism discussed earlier.

This fight was reminiscent of the 2005–6 debates and votes in IVAW and MFSO over whether these organizations (as opposed to individual members) supported war resisters, who refused to deploy or went AWOL rather than fight in the wars.[23] While both organizations were coming to official positions that supported war resisters, some members redirected their energies into VFP, which had always supported military members who refused to fight. Others left the military peace movement because they did not agree with people in the military refusing orders or thought supporting those who did hurt the organization's image.

These conflicts were fundamentally a fight over what types of antiwar activism were compatible with patriotism. They were also fights over which troops were worthy of support—those who fought in wars or those who refused out of moral conviction. These debates reflected the contentious nature of identity deployment as the organizations sought to tightly control their combined military and antiwar identities.

On March 20, 2010, members of MFSO and IVAW on both sides of the debate over patriotism threatened to resign. During a protest against war in Washington, D.C., a large peace movement crowd organized by ANSWER listened to three activists from the military peace movement: former Army "poster girl" Robynn Murray, Army war resister Matthis Chiroux, and Marine mom Elaine Brower, whose son served three deployments to the wars in Afghanistan and Iraq.[24] Murray and Chiroux held an American flag as Brower lit it on fire. They had introduced themselves as members of their military peace movement organizations and wore the clothing associated with IVAW and MFSO. Several members of both organizations demanded that these individuals be reprimanded. After conversations between the boards of directors, both MFSO and IVAW sent out pacifying messages to their membership and online sites, where the incident was depicted in photographs and descriptions. In the message they affirmed that these individuals were representing their own views, not the views of the organization, and made clear that these individuals had a right to free speech but that they should consider how their actions could hurt others in their organizations. These individuals were asked to be more careful when they acted as spokespeople for the military peace movement. While these organizations had no official member-conduct prohibitions against flag burning, these actions sparked controversy because they highlighted these organizations' internal divide over patriotism. This incident forced the organizations to address this debate between those with deeply held patriotic beliefs and those who questioned American patriotism as support for an "imperialist force in Iraq and Afghanistan." The boards of these organizations were particularly concerned with the public perception of this act and how it worked against some of their identity-deployment tactics. This incident and the conversations it triggered offered a window onto the contentious negotiations surrounding when, where, and how activists should use strategies that publicized their insider–outsider identity.

Socialism and the Left

In addition to debates over which wars to oppose and negotiating how best to engage with issues of patriotism and troop support, debates existed over the role of the military peace movement in the broad spectrum of left-leaning political organizing. Some activists believed strongly in a capitalist economic system, whereas others believed that war was a "symptom of the capitalist machine," as a VFP member from Washington State was fond of saying. Fights developed over how connected to or distanced from feminist causes such as military sexual trauma organizations should be, as well as international conflicts such as that between Palestine and Israel.[25,26] Like the other internal movement conflicts, the debates about the military peace movement's place in Left politics were fights over the movement's collective identity.

Like many youth-oriented liberal-leaning organizations, IVAW struggled against a socialist take-over. Many of the same people who questioned the utility of patriotism worked with various peace organizations affiliated with communist and socialist organizations, such as the International Socialist Organization (ISO), the Revolutionary Communist Party (associated with World Can't Wait), and the

Workers World Party (associated with ANSWER). These members attempted to push IVAW politics further to the left, and some delighted in seeing conservative members leave the organization. Tensions around the attempted "take-over" of IVAW raged from 2008 to 2010. In the end, World Can't Wait created its own organization focused on militarism, and members pushing a socialist agenda in IVAW either left or minimized this effort within IVAW.

A few members who were opposed to the influence of these communist and socialist organizations left during this period, as well, and a few of their resignation letters were made public by prowar bloggers, who used them to further their framing of IVAW as a radical organization. When Selena Coppa initially resigned as secretary of the IVAW's board of directors in 2009, she posted her resignation statement critiquing the organizations' links to communist and socialist groups on her blog *Active Duty Patriot*. Some of the information in her letter was incorrect, so she was asked and agreed to take it down. This incident sparked a lively series of comments in which other IVAW members expressed their misgivings over communist and socialist influence in the organization. A former GI rights counselor and active duty infantry officer in the U.S. Army wrote:

> There is an infected vein within IVAW that pushes a socialist agenda. . . . My position has always been that some folks push the socialist agenda because of the fact that socialist organizations prey upon IVAW members and provide monetary support to these members. Speaking tours, books, travel expenses, and other perks. . . . While down in Savannah GA as a GI Rights Hotline counselor for the [IVAW] Summer [Military] Base tour, an IVAW ally put out some ISO material and I literally exploded. She left shortly after being confronted and giving me some weak excuse as to why it was appropriate. Of course, another IVAW member defended the material, unable to grasp why such material was inappropriate for an organization that is interested in growing. This is something that needs to be addressed within IVAW. I remember thinking after this incident; heck, I am going to start handing out the New Testament at IVAW functions given its important role in forming my beliefs as a conscientious

objector to war. . . . While I love to discuss my faith, I don't feel a cult-like need to shove it down people's throats.

He compared pushing socialist material at an IVAW event to evangelizing. This comment illustrates that this fight was not simply about political ideology but also over strategy. This officer was concerned that socialist materials would turn away potential recruits to IVAW and ultimately make their antiwar message less palatable. He saw his antiwar stance as separate from his other political opinions, unlike those who believed war was a "tool of rich countries and corporations," as one socialist member described it.

The military peace movement debated whether and how to maintain the impact of their legitimacy as insider–outsiders while working with the broader coalitions within the antiwar movement. Many times, military peace movement organizations attempted to control the language of coalition-led tactics in order to focus the agenda narrowly on the wars they opposed or to make space in the tactics' frame for issues of veterans' and their families' needs. At various times the organizations refused to cooperate with antiwar organizations and coalitions such as World Can't Wait and ANSWER. Even working with the popular women's peace organization CodePink, which was a big supporter of GSFP spokesperson Cindy Sheehan, was difficult for the movement due to some of their tactics aimed at military bases, recruiting centers, and servicemembers. One Southern California Army mom said, "[MFSO] doesn't do base protests, because we don't want to be seen as protesting the troops." When MFSO and other groups were in control of the messaging and the tactics, however, they did protest outside armories and recruiting stations. As I have written elsewhere, harnessing "the discourses of patriotism and troop support limited" these organizations' "ability to adopt more radical critiques of militarism and nationalism."[27] While some military peace movement activists believed in broader peace missions, the leadership was cautious about extending their organizations' message beyond these wars for strategic reasons. Although this narrow focus supported the movement's identity-deployment strategies, it sometimes left members and allies dissatisfied.

CONCLUSION

Veterans and military family members in the antiwar movement not only bonded over their shared, complicated identity as people both inside and outside the traditional military and peace movement but also used this identity to make antiwar claims. They believed that publicizing their insider–outsider identities could make a significant impact on the wider public, so they developed strategies to deploy their identities. In particular, they recognized and exploited the novelty of their combined military–antiwar identities and used the attention given to them to reframe the Iraq War as unpatriotic and bad for the troops. Throughout their participation, activists drew attention to this insider–outsider identity through their rhetoric, symbolism, behavior, organizational affiliation, and clothing.[28] Military peace movement participants drew attention to their military identities in order to gain attention, be perceived as legitimate in antiwar debates, counter their opposition's claims, and reach people who were not already sympathetic to the peace movement.

In order to reach their goals, activists in social movements make strategic decisions about which aspects of their identities to emphasize or which identity categories spokespeople should be in.[29] Mary Bernstein refers to these decisions as identity deployment—the strategic decision making about which images of a movement to promote and the enactment of these images.[30] The organizations discussed exploited their novelty by deploying participants' military and antiwar activist identities. People expect military veterans and their families to support wars, so the seeming contradiction in these activists' identities drew attention to the peace movement. The power of this novelty is indicated by the disproportionate attention paid to military peace movement organizations by the media.[31]

These military individuals likely received more press and attention from audiences than did others in the peace movement because of a cultural preference for "real people," who were portrayed as authentic actors with experience with an issue, over mere "advocates for a cause," who came to their position through knowledge, opinion, or emotion.[32] The peace movement strategically highlighted veterans because of this audience and media preference for quotes and interviews from those who had experienced the horrible conditions they protested.[33] In this way, firsthand experience can be an important aspect of gaining credibility. The military peace movement identity drew its power from activists' claims of standing, or importance because of their experience, based on their connections to the U.S. military.[34] By deploying their identities as veterans and military family members, participants asserted a privileged position from which to comment on the war.

These findings demonstrate the need for an expansion of the categories of identity deployment beyond education and critique, or some combination of the two, to an inclusion of the deployment of identities for authority.[35] This identity-deployment strategy was used by activists in the military peace movement to lend the movement credibility, legitimate critique, and encourage interest in the movement. A variety of movements deploy identities for authority, including experts and celebrities, and the role of experience-based identity in helping or hindering movement outcomes must be understood. While veterans and military families may have validated the peace movement's claims to supporting the troops, their military–peace identity deployment demonstrated the authority these activists had more broadly on issues of the Iraq War.[36] Movement messages are more likely to resonate when audiences believe that the articulators of the messages are credible authorities on an issue.

According to Mary Bernstein, many movement decisions about which aspects of an identity to highlight center around whether activists desire their movement to be perceived as mainstream or as a challenge to the mainstream.[37] By appealing to the mainstream, the military peace movement was able to use two of what Patrick Coy, Lynne Woehrle, and Gregory Maney call "discursive legacies" (cultural ways of remembering the past that influence the present) to make these claims of credibility.[38] First, in the aftermath of 9/11, patriotism was heightened in the United States.[39] The military was symbolic of patriotism, and few were seen as more patriotic than members of the military. This shielded military peace movement activists from many of the charges leveled at other antiwar protestors, who were perceived as unpatriotic.[40] Second, in wars after Vietnam Americans were sensitive to the call to support the troops, who were believed to have been mistreated after returning from Vietnam.[41] Military peace movement activists capitalized on the moral authority that their status as "troops" granted them in order to reframe what it meant to support the troops. By emphasizing their association with the military, activists were able to exploit dominant American discourses on patriotism and troop support in ways that countered prowar arguments. As I demonstrate, however, these strategies that appealed to the mainstream were controversial in military peace movement organizations and limited the movement's ability to critique the underlying and enduring causes of war and injustice.

The discursive context propels some movements to highlight identities that speak directly to the claims made by their opposition.[42] The military peace movement used an oppositional identity strategy, which involved emphasizing activists' identity aspects that would usually predispose those individuals to be part of the movement's opposition. People would tend to believe that military members were prowar, so these activists' position in the peace movement provided intrigue and led to media coverage and public interest. This positioning is not unique to the military peace movement. Similar oppositional identity strategies have been used in activism around abortion, since religious figures are assumed to be pro-life and feminists to be pro-choice.[43] Audiences often perceive these oppositional identities as contradictory, and that uniqueness generates attention and makes for great media stories.

Since they could use identity strategies to bring the movement novelty and legitimacy, as well as overturn their opposition's arguments, veterans and military families were placed at the front of marches and on speaker's lists even when their organizations were much smaller than other organizations in a local or a national campaign or a tactical coalition. Chapter 5 further delves into the use of movement identities to affect broad segments of the U.S. population, examining in particular how military peace movement identities were portrayed in antiwar war memorials.

5

Using Grief to Connect with Bystanders

In January 2007 a young man whose high-and-tight haircut and military-insignia tattoos on his bare shoulders indicated he was a Marine approached a small cluster of peace activists on a popular beach in Santa Barbara, California. He said that he had heard on the news about their memorial to the soldiers who had died in Iraq, and he wanted to visit the crosses that memorialized some of his friends. The memorial consisted of three thousand white crosses in perfectly regimented rows, many with name tags and memorabilia from past visits by other servicemembers and their families. Bob Potter, a Korean War–era Army veteran and the Santa Barbara VFP's chapter president, helped the young man locate name tags for two deceased Marines, aged twenty and twenty-two. Potter then affixed those tags to two crosses in the middle of the memorial. A female Army veteran of an earlier period brought the young man two small jars filled with fresh purple irises and white carnations. She asked how he knew these men, and when he said they had fought together in the war, she nodded her head, squeezed his shoulder, and said, "I'm sorry. They were so young." Then, on his knees and using his hands, the young Marine carefully dug holes in the sand beside the two crosses, so that the arrangements would stand up to the ocean winds. He shook his head, crumpled to the sand with his head in his hands, and silently wept.

When I approached him to offer condolences, he smiled sadly and said, "I didn't get to say good-bye. It was too crazy, and I couldn't fall apart [in Iraq], but I'll be OK." He sat there and cried for over thirty minutes, undisturbed by the dozens of tourists and locals passing the busy pier and this weekly memorial. When the Marine stood up, he saluted the crosses and came back to the table where the activists were congregated. After thanking them, he was given pamphlets on finding psychological care, on his rights in the military, and about IVAW. He took them, saying he would share the information with his

FIGURE 18. Memorial Day 2008, Arlington West in Santa Barbara. In this image the memorial is prepared for an overnight candlelight vigil, similar to the one created on the night of the author's speech from the preface. Photograph by the author.

friends. He was one of seventeen visitors that day who sought to memorialize those they cared about. He had heard about the memorial from the news and had driven to Santa Barbara for the sole purpose of taking part in the memorial.

For the tourists who did not come to town for the memorial, it raised questions. A young girl asked her mother what it was all about when they stopped on the pier to gaze at the crosses. Her mother explained the war in brief terms, and then a Vietnam veteran handed them a postcard with information about the memorial. The mother asked if they could place flowers next to a cross representing her neighbor's son. The little girl picked out some flowers as a civilian activist pointed her to a cross that already had the name of that Navy Seabee on it. The cross had been first memorialized by the deceased's commanding officer, and every Sunday after that, his name tag and corresponding memorabilia were placed on this cross, as the name tags and memorabilia brought in honor of other servicemembers were placed on their crosses. The mother and daughter took pictures of the cross and flowers, saying they would share the images with the Seabee's parents, who would appreciate that he was remembered. The mother asked about who maintained the memorial and why. Her jaw dropped at the regularity of the memorial, and she proceeded to thank each of the activists for their service to their country and what they were doing here, because people forgot about "the sacrifices and effects of the war." She took materials on the memorial and the military peace movement to share with the parents of the dead servicemember. She thought they would appreciate knowing about and perhaps joining the movement.

These visits to what activists termed Arlington West were not unusual. Each Sunday, thousands of tourists and locals were stunned to see the beach filled with three thousand crosses in flawlessly straight rows. For over six years peace activists marked the deaths of U.S. soldiers in Iraq and, later, Afghanistan with this weekly memorial reminiscent of Arlington National Cemetery. At Arlington West, members of VFP and affiliated organizations comforted those who like the Marine, had lost loved ones in the war, and they provided information on the Iraq War to passersby in order to encourage opposition to it. This memorial tactic was striking, and it garnered significant public engagement. Recognizing Arlington West's success in drawing attention to the war, other U.S. peace organizations set up similar displays of crosses, flags, headstones, and combat boots in over thirty cities. This tactic spread rapidly and provoked national media attention, including front-page spreads in the *Los Angeles Times* and *USA Today* and extended pictorial and video pieces on *USA Today*'s and the *New York Times'* websites.[1] Much of this attention highlighted the participation and leadership roles of military peace movement activists at the memorials. This tactic was important to the military peace movement because it helped activists connect with the general public by evoking grief and highlighting activists' military identities.

Whereas state-sanctioned war memorials were criticized for glorifying war, military peace movement organizations used similar imagery to confront bystanders with war casualties, to encourage public grieving, and to spur antiwar action.[2] This chapter describes how activists strategically deployed an identity in order to heighten the emotional impact of their tactic. If as movement scholar James Jasper suggests, "there is no more powerful rhetoric than that of death," then memorials may be the ultimate cultural tactic.[3] Indeed, in the military peace movement the use of memorials allowed activists to generate emotional connections with bystanders, encourage grief over the Iraq War, and parlay these emotions into antiwar sentiment and movement solidarity. The power of these memorials lay in their ability to elicit emotions in bystanders, which could then shape the collective memory of an event, a group, or a person. The activists of Arlington West and other memorials intentionally incorporated organizational clothing and signage, which deployed military peace movement identities and asserted authority about the Iraq War.

THE ANTIWAR WAR MEMORIAL TACTICAL REPERTOIRE

The Arlington-style memorial was a prominent *tactical repertoire* of the military peace movement.[4] Just as a theater company has a repertoire of plays it can perform, a social movement has a repertoire of tactics, organizational strategies, and other features on which it can draw in the pursuit of change. The military peace movement used several standard tactics, such as teach-ins, marches, and rallies, but also innovated new tactics including these memorials and the combat street-theater performance Operation First Casualty, as discussed in chapters 1 and 4.

Santa Barbara's Arlington West

In September 2003 this important instrument in the military peace movement's toolkit began to take shape in Santa Barbara. In my interviews and during my participant observation, activists related discussions had at local peace marches by Stephen Sherrill and a few of his activist friends in which they fleshed out his idea of constructing an art installation on the beach that would demonstrate the "human cost of war." Like many U.S. peace activists, including nearly all of the military peace movement participants I interviewed, these Santa Barbara residents were concerned by the rarity of war casualty images on

American television and by President George W. Bush's ban on photographs of returning coffins. On November 2, 2003, a group of ten activists erected a memorial to the American soldiers killed in the Iraq War on the busy beach front next to Stearns Wharf, a popular tourist attraction in Santa Barbara. They planted 340 unpainted wooden crosses in the beach sand, one for each U.S. soldier who had died in Iraq as of that day. Two members of Santa Barbara's VFP Chapter 54 joined Sherrill on the first day of the memorial, and VFP agreed to maintain the project as a weekly vigil.

The Arlington West memorial became a professional production with separate individuals in charge of each task, such as constructing and painting the crosses; laying out the grid for cross placement; making and organizing the name tags; greeting passersby and handing out literature about the memorial, veterans' care, and the wars; ushering individuals looking for the names of a dead loved one; keeping track of the memorabilia left by visitors; and building and maintaining the vehicles and carts necessary to store and carry the crosses. Setting up and taking down the memorial was backbreaking work that took dozens of volunteers several hours at each end. On a typical weekend, the memorial's setup started around 7:00 a.m. on Sunday, and it was completely taken down around 6:30 p.m. When I asked activists why they put so much time into this tactic, one veteran of World War II responded, "It works. See all of those people walking by? Many of them are going to cry. Some of them will read our materials. None of them will be able to forget the war today." Another said, "We show the world that we're here. There are all of these tourists from Europe, from all over, even the Middle East. They see we don't all go along with the war. Plus, we can show Americans it's okay to question Bush and these wars." Activists had a diverse range of hopes for the memorial's effectiveness, but most believed its striking visual display would move members of the public emotionally and therefore further the antiwar cause. The memorial received tremendous support from Santa Barbara–area residents. Schools, churches, and political organizations volunteered to help the veterans and military families take down and set up the memorial. Local businesses donated food to the activists and flowers for the weekly remembrance visits made by the family and the friends of the deceased.

From 2003 to 2006, veterans, military families, and others watched Arlington West grow with the war's death toll, until the crosses numbered three thousand on New Year's Day 2007. At that point, organizers continued the weekly memorial but stopped adding new crosses, owing to space and logistical constraints. A large sign proclaimed how large a similar memorial would have been for Iraqi civilian casualties: "over 12 miles long for the Iraqi dead." In 2010 and in conjunction with other shifts in the broader peace movement, activists continued to place crosses, Stars of David, and Islamic crescents in the sand but shifted to their representing American casualties in Afghanistan. Activists continually updated signs around the memorial that pointed to problems in American war policy and implementation, to veterans' struggles with benefits and the psychological injuries of war, and to Iraqi and Afghanistan civilians' deaths and war-related consequences. Arlington West occurred less frequently after the Iraq War ended and as the Afghanistan War drew to a close; by 2013 a skeleton crew of eight set up only one thousand crosses once a month rather than weekly.

The Modality of the Memorial Tactic

Between 2003 and 2007, the antiwar memorial tactic spread throughout the United States peace movement. Word traveled quickly through the media and the VFP Listservs, and soon after the first memorial, the San Diego VFP chapter erected its own Arlington West. On February 15, 2004, the Los Angeles VFP chapter placed 540 crosses in the sand next to the iconic Santa Monica Pier. By September 2004, less than a year after the first memorial, at least seven other Arlington-style memorials had emerged on the East Coast and in the Midwest and the South. In the spring of 2005, a traveling Arlington-style memorial was displayed in seven states and the District of Columbia. The tactic spread further in 2006 when members of the Santa Barbara VFP chapter presented a how-to workshop on their memorial at the VFP national convention. The VFP national office later packaged information from the workshop as a booklet and CD in a mailing to their nearly 125 chapters across the country. This led to the further adoption of the memorial tactic, and by the end of 2007, over thirty Arlington-style memorials were displayed with some regularity across the country. At least two documentaries were made about the California memorials, and one that showed veterans and military families discussing their feelings about the memorial was shown in hundreds of schools across the United States.[5]

In conservative cities such as Houston as well as more liberal enclaves such as California's Bay Area, veterans and military families set up a variety of memorials using boots, flags, tombstones, and other objects to represent soldiers killed. Many memorials incorporated "Arlington" into their names. Philadelphia's became Arlington Liberty Bell; the Olympia, Washington, memorial was Arlington Northwest; and activists named the Traverse City, Michigan, memorial Arlington Northern Michigan. Between 2004 and 2007, ten of these memorials were erected weekly or monthly to mark the increasing number of U.S. casualties in Iraq. Some of the memorials took place in the same location each time, such as Santa Barbara's and Santa Monica's popular pier locations. Activists set up memorials where the public gathered on particular holidays or for certain events, such as the 2007 Super Bowl in Miami.

The memorial tactic was an important element of the military peace movement's contestation of state policy and American apathy regarding the Iraq War. Although this chapter focuses on Arlington West in Santa Barbara, where VFP was the driving force, members of other military peace movement organizations used memorials, as well. A mother whose son died in Iraq and who was an active member of GSFSO requested help from the other organizations in constructing an Arlington-style memorial in Statesville, North Carolina. Members of these groups cut and painted nearly 3,500 crosses in just a few weekends in May 2007, and they placed the Arlington Cemetery of the South in a local park over Memorial Day weekend.

When veterans and military families gathered to protest the war, they often used Arlington-style displays as poignant backdrops to their activities. At the 2006 VFP annual convention in Seattle, an Army sergeant who had gone AWOL rather than return for a second tour in Iraq held a press conference in front of an Arlington-style memorial, where he announced his surrender to military authorities. These organizations planted crosses in Crawford each time Cindy Sheehan and other members of these organizations camped outside President Bush's ranch. At large-scale marches and other peace events, the organizations built Arlington-style memorials to "honor the fallen and end the war." The military peace movement intentionally deployed memorials as both symbols of and backdrops to antiwar activism.

The memorial tactic used powerful symbolic imagery of death to contest the Iraq War. As this style of memorial was adopted by groups across the United States, the tactic became modular (easily recognizable and employable), which was essential to its becoming a part of the movement's larger repertoire.[6] The Arlington-style memorials were made modular because VFP chapters and other organizations in the movement saw the tactic as successful, developed ways to perform it systematically, and spread it across the United States, not unlike the ways in which other movements' tactics have become institutionalized.[7] The memorials brought people together in grief, thus helping the movement's message resonate with the public and participants to construct a military peace movement collective identity.

THE EMOTIONAL APPEAL OF THE MEMORIAL

Activists focused on the human cost of war with the intention of emotionally engaging the public and turning them against the Iraq War. When the memorials began, a majority of the public favored the Iraq War, and war protestors were attacked for not supporting the troops and for being unpatriotic.[8] The memorials were important tactics for deploying a military identity in an effort to overcome these accusations. The memorials' organizers and participants intended for the cemetery imagery to pull viewers into the memorial and elicit feelings of sadness that would open them to the activists' messages. Rather than evoking anger, an emotion often used in other tactics and that could alienate bystanders, memorial activists employed grief as a *connecting emotion* that linked movement participants to their audiences.[9]

Using Shock and Grief to Connect the General Public to War

Each Sunday in Santa Barbara, hundreds of vacationers and locals enjoying the beach were taken aback by the sight of the memorial. Many visitors' relaxed, vacation-like demeanors changed quickly, and several stopped to read the signs and stare at the memorial. Numerous visitors said they were shocked by the visual representation of war casualties. It was clear from movement participants that this shock was intentional, and they hoped that bystanders would be moved by the symbols of death juxtaposed with the surrounding beautiful sandy beaches and harbor. Most bystanders read at least a few of the large signs, and over half stopped to read the detailed panels. Like many of the vacationers who were surprised by the memorial, in April 2006 a middle-aged African American man from Cleveland who had two young children with him exclaimed, "Wow! It is just all so sad. I knew that more than two thousand had died, but I had no idea what that looked like. There is just so many." This reaction exemplified the shock that led bystanders to feel sadness over and think about the war. In August 2008 when I was at the memorial, a man in his twenties stopped and absently took an information card on the memorial from me. After staring open-mouthed at the memorial for a few seconds, he said, "Before I saw this, the numbers didn't mean much." At the memorials I saw this expression repeated in numerous ways by almost one hundred passersby.

Shock may have been the initial reaction, but grief was the emotional response that really connected bystanders to the message of the tactic. Many members of the public cried when they viewed the memorial, either from the walkways surrounding it or from among the crosses. Usually, people cried quietly, releasing a few tears. When activists saw people cry, they approached them and asked if they had lost someone in the war. More often than not, those crying did not have an immediate association to people in the Iraq War, though a few said that they had lost a loved one in a different war. Although most members of the public were not personally connected to the Iraq War, the memorial succeeded in evoking an intimate emotional reaction, and many people were pulled into the memorial through these emotions. Several dozen times per day, visitors reached across the railing of the pier to hug or hold the hand of a participant in the tactic. At least once a day, groups of men and women spent up to two hours walking among the crosses, often with tears running down their cheeks. The sadness that the memorial drew out encouraged members of the public to seek a connection with the movement participants.

Connecting to individuals through grief made the antiwar message palatable, even allowing activists to engage with many individuals who supported the war. During my participant observation, I talked with and overheard many people who described the war positively, though they recognized and sometimes acknowledged the authority of the war critique offered by the memorial. In September 2007 one man in his fifties said that he liked what we had to say and hoped that the memorial was successful in getting people to oppose the war. He said that his wife supported the war but was moved by the display. After I had talked with the man for a few minutes, his wife came over. She had tears running down her cheeks, and she said, "Thank you for doing this. We need to see this." Although the woman supported the policy of the Iraq War, she engaged with and appreciated this antiwar tactic. While the memorial had its critics, it was an invaluable tactic for connecting people emotionally to the war and for allowing those who supported the war to dialogue with those who opposed it. Their shock and sadness stopped busy tourists and locals long enough to read a sign, take some literature, or write down remarks on the war in the comment book offered at the memorial.[10]

Over the course of the first year of the memorial, the antiwar politics of the memorial were intentionally toned down, but the critical sentiment and the prominence of the antiwar organizations remained. This toning down was an attempt at making the memorial accessible to a wide audience, including those who were prowar, and at building bridges that could facilitate "dialogue," as several VFP members said. All of the reactions to the shock of the memorial were not positive, however. Some people who saw the memorial expressed anger not at the war but at the activists. In its early years, a few times per day, members of the public attempted to engage memorial activists in heated arguments about the war. After 2005 most of the negative reactions became what one activist described as "hit-and-run" events, which involved a member of the public making a comment such as, "What about 9/11?" and then walking away before anyone could respond. Three military family members objected to the use of their service-members' names in the memorial, and these names were removed, though each of their crosses was sought out a number of times by other family members, friends, and comrades. Some of those opposed to the memorials wrote opinion pieces in local papers, and a few wrote emails to the organization. Although negative reactions occurred routinely—approximately once a day during 2008—the overwhelming majority of reactions were positive or, at worst, indifferent. When negative reactions did occur, activists attempted to move the dialogue in a positive direction by asserting their identities as veterans and military family members.

Connecting Peace Activism to the Military

Activists' decisions to elicit grief rather than express anger developed out of their own military experiences and their collective desire to respect others' military service. A number of activists expressed their discomfort with traditional peace protest tactics that could be construed as antitroop and felt the need to find new ways to express their antiwar position. As Lane Anderson, a Vietnam combat veteran, suggested, the memorial "just seemed like the perfect compromise" between critiquing the war and respecting the service of troops. Anderson and other activists felt that the memorial should be a way for participants to reconcile their antiwar position with their respect for the military.

One reason the memorial was such a powerful tactic was its use as a space for collective mourning. Over its first five years, more than one thousand servicemembers were memorialized by friends and family at Arlington West, many of them multiple times. Mourners ranged from a lone widow to large families, from a group of young Marines to an Army major, and from neighbors to college roommates. On an average Sunday, approximately fifteen crosses were visited, and that number jumped on holidays such as Memorial Day, when as many as thirty-five crosses were visited. Soon after the memorial was created, activists affixed name tags to the crosses for those being memorialized. Family, friends, and fellow servicemembers often left hand-written notes, pictures, dog tags, military patches, ribbons, coins, and other personal mementos when they visited their loved ones' crosses. These mementos demonstrated the intense emotional connection many of the military-connected visitors felt toward the memorial. Most of the visitors stayed next to the symbol of their loved one for several minutes, and members of the military both in uniform and in civilian

FIGURE 19. Members of VFP and MFSO set up Arlington West in October 2008. Many crosses bear mementos left by friends and family, such as those displayed on Army Lieutenant Ken Ballard's cross, which were mostly left by his mother, GSFSO cofounder Karen Meredith. Photograph by the author.

clothes cried. During memorialization, military families demonstrated their new connection to the activists by hugging or otherwise touching them. These interactions revealed how grief pulled those with military connections, who were often assumed to be the most prowar, into this antiwar tactic.

These memorializations had a secondary impact, as well. During the set up of Santa Barbara's Arlington West, activists put the name tags and memorabilia out for all of the servicemembers who had been memorialized so far. These mementos left behind by family and friends helped personalize the crosses, and these intimate touches magnified the significance of the memorial in many visitors' eyes. When members of the general public learned that many of the crosses had been visited, they often responded audibly, cried, shook their heads, or engaged in other gestures of sorrow. One breezy

November Sunday, three heterosexual couples likely in their late twenties or early thirties stopped at the memorial. As I handed them an informational card, one of the young women asked why some of the crosses had flowers. I explained that the flowers were placed by that person's friends or family who had visited that day. One young woman exclaimed, "Oh! I didn't realize that so many military people would think this was OK." One of the men in the group then pointed out some of the other visible mementos on the crosses as the others looked on and shook their heads. After a few more questions about the memorial, during which one of the women cried, the group turned to leave. Before leaving, a female in the group thanked me "for all that [I was] doing for these families and to end the war" and said, "Keep up the good work." This interaction captured not only how the memorial elicited grief but also how the public involvement of military individuals in the tactic amplified these effects. Knowing that those with loved ones who had died in the Iraq War condoned the memorial allowed the public to accept the tactic and its antiwar message. In the polarized political climate surrounding the Iraq War, particularly from 2003 to 2007, spaces where prowar and antiwar people discussed the war were few and far between.[11] Had the activists attempted to tap into the anger over the war, their tactic would have been polarizing. Instead, the memorials' ability to tap into grief facilitated connections between politically disparate individuals.

During the four years after the founding of the memorials, reactions from the public became increasingly positive, which was not surprising given that American public opinion about the Iraq War also shifted during this time. By 2008 most visitors were supportive of the installation and said, "Thank you." Some added, "This is really great," or used other adjectives such as "powerful," "impressive," or "important." Though the memorials encouraged members of the public to experience grief, most people also expressed gratitude for the tactic. At the memorial activists used the grief to make connections with passersby, strike up discussions even with those who supported the war, and perhaps engender change. Such reactions are indicative of a tactical repertoire that strikes a cultural nerve. This resonance was, however, clearly tied up with the public identities of the activists themselves.

THE IMPORTANCE OF DEPLOYING A MILITARY PEACE MOVEMENT IDENTITY

Santa Barbara's memorial intentionally identified itself as a tactic undertaken by Veterans for Peace—an organization whose name implied a connection to both the military and antiwar activism. VFP provided literature and signage that highlighted the role of the military community in the tactic. Arlington West activists wore T-shirts, sweatshirts, buttons, and hats that read, "VFP, Arlington West," "Vietnam Veterans Against the War," "Military Families Speak Out," and "Iraq Veterans Against the War." The cards handed out to the public explained that the memorial was put on by VFP and listed the websites of military peace movement organizations and veterans' services. In this way, Arlington West and other memorials established the military peace movement identity as distinct from the general peace movement identity.

FIGURE 20. Over part of the informational display encircling Arlington West, VFP member Tom Urban hands a card to a woman who showed surprise and sadness at the memorial. Photograph by the author.

At Arlington West, activists strategically deployed their military identities to heighten awareness of the memorial, encourage people to take their criticism of the war seriously, and challenge the idea that only those who were prowar cared about troops. To further illuminate my extension of the concept of identity deployment, as discussed in chapter 4, I examine how activists used a knowledge-based identity to claim credibility and clout in the issue at hand. The source of knowledge for military peace movement activists was their firsthand experience of war. In the case of Arlington West, activists asserted their military peace movement identities through their signs, clothing, leaflets, speech, and actions in order to increase the positive reception of the message, minimize dissent, heighten the emotional response of bystanders, and connect to and mobilize other military-affiliated individuals. By asserting this authority, activists hoped to increase the emotional impact of the memorial. They believed that their own military connections would not only encourage people to engage with the memorial but also personalize the war and thus heighten and lengthen the grief response. In addition to attracting attention, these intentional choices to deploy identity had a number of other outcomes.

Enhancing the Tactic's Emotional Appeal

Military peace movement activists used a variety of means—akin to those described by myself and by Mary Bernstein and Kristine Olsen—to deploy their identities, such as clothing, rhetoric, movements, and symbols.[12] Many wore clothing to highlight their identities as veterans and military families. Several veterans who participated in Arlington West wore hats that specified something about their service, identified them as disabled veterans, or demonstrated their membership in less controversial veterans groups such as Veterans of Foreign Wars (VFW) or the American Legion. Activists described these decisions to identify with mainstream and, often, conservative veterans' groups as a way to "reach out to the undecided" and to engage those who supported the war. When asked about their clothing, activists suggested that it was used to assert that memorial participants were *real* veterans who had authority in times of war. Similar identity declarations were made through the signs around the memorial and the cards activists handed to passersby, which were often printed with the full VFP statement of purpose. The statement begins, "We, having dutifully served our nation, do hereby affirm our greater responsibility to serve the cause of world peace." Activists used these strategies to clearly show that this peace tactic was undertaken by people with war experience, and in so doing, they deployed a military–peace identity to heighten the tactic's impact on bystanders.

In conversation with people who came to the memorial, many activists described their military service or that of their family members, recognizing that their military experiences lent them authenticity in the Iraq War debate. Ron Dexter's self-description was as a member of "VFW, American Legion, Korean War Vets, VUFT, GI Forum, and VFP," and he often described Don Calamar, a now-deceased VFP member, to Arlington West visitors. Calamar helped found Arlington West and earned both a Bronze Star and a Silver Star in World War II for "dragging wounded troops out of the line of fire." Activists set up a memorial within the memorial to honor Calamar and the three other Santa Barbara military peace activists who had died since the founding of Arlington West. This piece of the memorial served a second purpose: demonstrating the link between veterans of past wars and those of the current wars. Activists actively asserted their war-based expertise in discussions about the Iraq War by drawing connections to this expertise through dedications, signs, and naming, like making clear that the memorial was put on by *Veterans* for Peace. In doing so, they were deploying their identities in order to demonstrate their authority on this issue and to heighten their critique of the wars.

Evidence from discussions at Arlington West, comment book reflections, and interviews revealed that when members of the public realized the activists had a direct connection to the military, it made an impact on their own reactions and viewpoints. One windy fall afternoon at Arlington West, a Chicano man in his thirties viewed the memorial for several minutes and then commented, "We just find it really amazing that it is the veterans who are putting this together, you know?" The deployment of military identities heightened the message of the memorial because members of the public accorded weight to veterans and military families in the Iraq War discourse. Activists were aware of the power of this rhetorical strategy. Lane Anderson described this power in simple terms, stating, "To reach out to the unconverted, there's nobody better than a veteran in a time of war."

The deployment of a military identity heightened the grief that activists were trying to evoke. When visitors learned that the activists were veterans or military family members, many of those who were not crying started to cry or express similar sympathetic responses. This personal connection to the military made the protest and its antiwar message more moving and more real for visitors. In April 2007 a smartly dressed woman who appeared to be in her late sixties asked me if I had anyone in the military. When I replied affirmatively, she asked if they were in the war. I said, "My husband is aboard the [USS] Nimitz. It is in the Persian Gulf, and he's flying missions in Iraq." The woman's eyes welled up, and a tear slid down her cheek as she reached across the wooden pier railing, squeezed my hand tightly, and said, "We'll be praying for you. We pray for all of them. We just want them to come home." This and similar interactions revealed that the visibility of the military community powerfully enhanced the emotional appeal of the tactic. When members of the public saw that military families and veterans were involved in the memorials, their own grief over the war deaths was intensified by this personalization. By calling attention to their military identities, activists were able to, in their own words, "bring the war home" for civilians, who were largely disconnected from the Iraq War, and let them see and ultimately experience the grief that the war elicited. The combination of both a military and a peace identity suggested an authority on the Iraq War that influenced bystanders, even to the point of mitigating negative reactions.

Mitigating Negative Reactions

Arlington West activists believed that their military experiences lent them credibility on the issue of war, even with those who did not agree with the tactic's antiwar message. Michael Cervantes, a combat veteran from the Vietnam War, described being a veteran and talking with the public:

I think being a veteran helped the cause some because otherwise being a nonveteran you're going to get a lot more discussion going on. The public civilian is going to want to know what your reasons are [for activism], but with a veteran they're going to say, "Oh, well here's a person who really knows what the battle is about. They've probably been to a theater. They've gone through the whole thing of being trained, being sent through the airports and going overseas and joining the forces that are there." And that just pops into the public's mind. They'll be more willing to do the intellectual battle even with a nonvet Arlington West staff member, where they might not find it necessary to do that with a veteran because a veteran can speak with experience, too.

Cervantes expressed a common sentiment in the military peace movement, that the public was less likely to argue with a veteran or military family member about the war than with a person who was not affiliated with the military. In this way, movement participants used their military–peace identities to confer standing and to mollify opposing views.[13] When Arlington West participants declared their military affiliations, they deployed their military peace movement identities to bolster the reception and impact of their message even among those who were typically unfriendly to antiwar activism.

The military-affiliated activists' credibility often minimized dissent by the public. When members of the public reacted negatively to the memorial by saying, for instance, that the protestors didn't "understand the military" or that they "hated the United States," veterans or military family members were tasked with engaging them. By drawing on their military identity, these activists were able in most cases to calm visitors enough to get them to nod their heads or even agree with aspects of the military peace movement's antiwar position. Similarly, when negative editorials were written about the memorial, the group typically responded with a letter written by a veteran or a military family member that pointed to the instrumental involvement of military-affiliated activists. The local newspapers usually ran these follow-ups, and bystanders would mention being influenced to support the memorial because of the military identities of the activists.

Deploying a military identity was central to activists diffusing criticisms from bystanders at the memorial. In May 2006 one bystander, who presumably did not see the sign indicating the memorial was sponsored by VFP, yelled out, "You're all just a bunch of hypocrites using pictures of the military. They signed up for this; they want to be there fighting terrorists!" As the man walked past the memorial in a hurried pace, a veteran in his sixties approached the walkway and said, "Listen, I was Army in Vietnam, man. I'm here trying to end this for the guys and gals on the ground who deserve better. They were lied to, just like I was. This war isn't about making us safer; those kids are dying for nothing." As the activist spoke about his military identity, the bystander slowed his pace and eventually stopped and engaged the activist in a less heated discussion. As this example shows, activists' military identities facilitated connections with bystanders, even those who vocally disagreed with the intentions of the protest. Deploying a military identity was important for opening up bystanders to the emotional and the intellectual messages of the memorial.

Growing the Military Peace Movement

The identity deployment strategy used by the Arlington West activists affected the opinions of observers, engendered solidarity, and brought people into the movement. Memorial activists connected with visiting Iraq War veterans and their families through shared experiences. When recent veterans approached the memorial to remember a fallen comrade, movement activists with personal military connections often approached and connected with the visitors. Activists briefly described their own or their family member's military service in order to provide an opening for solidarity with visitors. Rod Brown was the son of a career military man and the brother of a naval officer who joined the Army Reserves at seventeen, before the Vietnam draft made that an option for people who wanted to avoid that war. He described how someone might approach a fellow servicemember at a memorial:

> First thing you say is, "Hey, I'm ex-Navy," and that kind of thing, just to let them know. I mean, it's like when a cop meets another cop, and you know, "Hey, I'm a cop in Santa Anna." You know right off the bat you've got this kind of bond thing. Firemen, same thing. It's your group; you can talk, you've got some credibility.

Brown and the other Arlington West activists used the bonds of military experiences to connect to veterans and military families. The reactions of relatives and friends of those who died in the Iraq War showed how this tactic harnessed grief and the assumed shared experiences of the military to reach out to military-affiliated individuals and generate individual and cultural change. On a number of occasions, visitors spontaneously played taps on bugles at the memorial, an act typically done to mark military mourning. A number of commanding or other senior officers left insignia for those who died under them in Iraq. One Sunday, a Marine in dress blues sat in front of an Arlington West cross and pounded a coin representing his military unit into the sand in front of the cross bearing the name of his best friend. Although he did not express antiwar opinions, he did browse the materials offered at the memorial. These examples demonstrate how visitors often treated the memorial as a military space for mourning, something that was possible only if activists made explicit their own military connections. This shared sense of mourning allowed military individuals to become comfortable with the peace movement, which was a significant accomplishment, since many military individuals saw the peace movement as their opposition.

This connection was often intimate and rooted firmly in the unique horrors of war. One sunny afternoon, a young, white Army veteran and his female partner came to Arlington West. They sat beside the crosses bearing the names of a few of his military comrades after activists helped him find their names. When he came back to the table where the activists congregated, he looked visibly upset, and he mentioned that people "wouldn't understand the horrible things [he'd] done." A Marine Vietnam combat veteran who had recently begun participating weekly in Arlington West and whose own war experiences had led to homelessness, substance abuse, and posttraumatic stress disorder, lit a cigarette, looked him the eye, and said, "Yeah, I do." The Vietnam veteran and the young Iraq veteran went a short distance away from the larger group, and the two talked, smoked, and bonded for over an hour. The woman told me about some of the ways the war had changed her partner, saying that he now engaged in various risky behaviors and that his depression "scared" her. When the young man left, he took literature on IVAW membership and about a veterans' retreat to "heal war wounds." This incident and the many like it I observed demonstrated the memorial's power to build networks by functioning as an emotional touchstone. The activists used their military connections and the memorial's reverence for the lives of soldiers to facilitate mobilization into the peace movement. The military families and service-members were always given membership brochures and often given the contact information for local activists in order to connect them to the growing movement. In these ways the memorial facilitated changes in people's views of and participation in the antiwar movement.

Recognizing their shared identity and experience, some veterans and their families went into the memorial and shook hands with the activists. One day, a middle-aged man with a military-style buzz cut who said he was a senior officer grabbed my hand, shook it, and said, "Thank you for what you are doing. People need to see this. I'm glad you are doing this, because I can't, and it is awful what they are doing to our military." This reaction—based on a shared support for the troops and an intimacy with the military—was evidence that the intentional deployment of military identity was crucial to the tactic's success. In fact, the second time an Arlington-style memorial was set up outside Marine Corps Base Camp Pendleton in Southern California, two flatbed military trucks filled with Marines drove off base to the memorial. Activists described being nervous about the arrival of such a large number of Marines, but their fear turned quickly to solidarity and grief as the Marines helped to set up the memorial and memorialized hundreds of their friends who died in battle. A three-star general visiting Camp Pendleton told the activists, "You guys are doing it right." Such comments and actions reflected the majority feeling from the wider military community that these memorials were a legitimate space for mourning, and many military veterans had positive interactions with this peace movement tactic. This constructive contact between veterans and military families with peace activists was surprising given that the military community was usually resistant to antiwar critiques. The deployment of military identities by activists encouraged solidarity, however, between veterans and military families and the antiwar movement.

Negotiating Identity and Increasing Impact

The memorial was instrumental in helping activists negotiate their military past and their current antiwar positions. As activists participated in the memorials, they were able to deploy their military peace movement identities in ways that increased the impact of the tactic. In this way, the movement showed new recruits how to authentically enhance the reception of their messages.

Rod Brown did not publicly declare himself a veteran until he participated in Arlington West, and while participating in the memorial, he joined VFP, his first veteran's organization. Every day he worked at Arlington West, Brown wore a shirt that declared his veteran status because he knew that it gave him credibility when talking about the war.

Colonel Ann Wright (Retired) said that Arlington West was the catalyst for her deployment of a military–peace identity. Before her experience with the memorial, she spoke to the press and other groups as a diplomat, but as she explained, while visiting a friend in Santa Barbara she discovered VFP:

> And then it was actually coming to right here in Santa Barbara, in probably, April or May of 2004 and seeing Arlington West. . . . Yeah, I mean, you're on the beach in Santa Barbara. There are guys and gals just like me who have been in the military who were questioning this war. And they were questioning it very obliquely through the presentation of all these crosses. And I thought, well, my goodness. This is bravery. . . . I've, kind of, almost moved from speaking as a diplomat to speaking as an Army veteran.

For Ann and for the veterans and the military families who opposed the war, Arlington West served as a gateway to the military peace movement and offered an identity that combined their military connection and their antiwar beliefs. Before Arlington West many of these veterans did not believe it was possible or productive to publicly combine these identities. Arlington West and the activists involved in it offered an alternative to the mainstream conception of military and antiwar identities as incompatible, and the tactic was a site of

FIGURE 21. GSFP cofounder Cindy Sheehan speaks at the 2006 Memorial Day gathering at Arlington West, which was part of her inspiration for the highly publicized protests in Crawford, Texas. Photograph by the author.

collective-identity negotiation where activists and the public outlined an antiwar position that respected military experiences.[14]

Some of those who memorialized their loved one were motivated by Arlington West to take part in other forms of antiwar activism. Although Cindy Sheehan was already becoming politicized, she acknowledged in several speeches that her Mother's Day 2005 visit to Arlington West "inspired" her activism. She explained that the memorial offered her an example of how she could deploy the military aspects of her identity in ways that attracted attention and made an impact on her audience. Her own protests highlighted military experience via her son's wartime death in Iraq. The memorial encouraged activism also among less famous visitors. From what I observed at the memorial and throughout the movement, at least three Iraq War veterans, over two dozen veterans of past wars, and a number of military family and Gold Star family members attributed at least part of their activism to Arlington West. These individuals were attracted to the movement not only as a way to combine their military and peace activist identities but also as a way to have a greater impact in the Iraq War debate.

Arlington West helped grow and sustain the local VFP chapter. Bob Potter, who led the VFP chapter meetings in Santa Barbara until his death in 2010, asserted, "Arlington West was what brought us together.... Very early on instead of just marching in peace marches, we had this. The crosses turned up there, and we all started being a part of it." Many activists described intense emotional and personal commitment to the memorial, which not only kept a labor-intensive tactic going for over four years but also solidified their sense of a collective identity. Members made friends at the memorial and demonstrated their bonds through physical and social intimacy by touching, hugging, and spending time together. Sunday after Sunday for over seven years, as activists explained, Arlington West participants were their "family" or their "church." The memorial was more than a protest site. For many participants, it was a political and a personal community. Activists gathered to challenge the war, discuss the latest war news, and meet other activists with whom they felt a connection. Arlington West not only influenced the public's beliefs about the war but also bonded military-affiliated individuals to the peace movement.

This unique combination of memorial and protest affected members of the public in profound ways. Activists' deployment of military–peace identities propelled the somber and quietly political memorial into becoming an effective protest tactic. The activists' connections to the military allowed them to speak from a place of authority about the Iraq War and made their message both more palatable and more effective.

CONCLUSION

The Arlington West–style memorials played a key role in getting many Americans to question the Iraq War. This was due not only to the visual impact of the memorials but also to the intentional cultivation of grief and authority by the activists themselves. Activists drew on emotional symbols of death in order to affect members of the public and encourage resonance with their message. More significant, they deployed their military identity to enhance the emotional appeal of their tactical repertoire and cultivate change in public opinion and in public policy. Military peace movement activists used grief as a connecting emotion to facilitate interactions between activists and bystanders. Activists intentionally deployed their military peace movement identity as part of a strategy to urge Americans to seek an end to the Iraq War. Moreover, activists leveraged their military identities to substantiate their authority and build solidarity with previously unmobilized members of the general public. Expanding upon Verta Taylor, Leila Rupp, and Joshua Gamson's conceptualization of tactical repertoires, this chapter demonstrates that identity deployment and emotions are critically important elements of tactics and strategies.[15] Over ten years after the start of the Iraq War, military peace movement activists were still erecting Arlington West next to the Santa Monica Pier every week and organizing the use of this tactic throughout the country because they continued to believe that it had power to highlight military–antiwar identities and elicit emotions in viewers.

Whereas most research on emotions in social movements focuses on the emotions that activists experience, this research shows that emotions can be strategically employed to improve the cultural resonance of political messages.[16] Psychologists and neurobiologists find that emotions affect how we remember, what we remember, and the impact of memories.[17] Studies about political and social issues demonstrate that emotions play an important role in shaping how people receive messages about issues.[18] Social movement actors strategize about how to make their messages emotionally appealing.[19] Although movements may make rational and factual arguments, the reception of movement messages is fundamentally shaped by activists' ability to connect emotionally with an audience.

Activists make choices about the kinds of emotions they hope to elicit in their audiences. Emotions are broadly associated with irrationality, as can be seen in early social movement literature, and anthropological research on emotions suggests that displays of anger are especially criticized as such and that Americans associate this emotion with immaturity and a lack of discipline.[20] Some movements, such as the radical culture of action involved in AIDS activism, assert "the rationality of their anger and confrontational activism," but angry tactics can discredit the movement in the eyes of some potential allies.[21] Although anger may be necessary to facilitate mobilization and angry tactics can bring attention to an issue, anger is an antisocial emotion that creates boundaries between activists, allies, potential allies, and audiences. Activists may instead choose to draw on *emotions of connection* to pull people into their tactic. This strategic choice can facilitate solidarity between activists and their audiences. Using an emotion such as grief instead of anger is an important strategic choice that can connect to people who are unreceptive to a movement's message or who are indifferent or inactive. As opposed to die-ins and other confrontational tactics, the memorial tactic highlights death and uses grief to connect a movement to a broader audience. This is a particularly important strategic choice for cultures of action that play a bridging role to mainstream or even hostile audiences. As I highlight throughout the book, the military peace movement often made connections to those not traditionally involved in peace activism, and thus its use of connecting emotions fit well with its identity and role in the larger peace movement.

This chapter demonstrates that tactical repertoires not only build collective identity within movements but also involve the strategic deployment of identity.[22] The response to a tactic is affected by the way an audience perceives those engaged in the tactic. Therefore, social movements strategize about how identities will be deployed in a tactic. Who performs a tactic and how they publicize their identities can be as important as what they do as activists. This chapter highlights several outcomes of the types of identity deployment I outline in chapter 4. First, the memorial tactic attracted significant attention because it was enacted by people with novel identities. Second, since the deployment of a military identity suggested authority on or a closeness to the deaths of troops, this identity strategy enhanced the memorial tactic's ability to generate feelings of grief. Third, military peace movement participants were able to dampen critique of this protest tactic by employing oppositional identities that undermined prowar characterizations of the movement and this tactic. Fourth, identity deployment was able to mobilize and recruit other members of the military community for peace movement activism. Finally, the memorial tactic provided a space where seasoned activists could demonstrate how to negotiate the group's complicated and supposedly contradictory collective identity and, thus, increased the impact of new activists' protest.

In the conclusion I describe how ten years of protest took its toll on the military peace movement, including the Santa Barbara memorial, which after 2008 was no longer held every week. As the American public shifted their attention from the wars overseas to the economic downturn and political campaigns of 2008, the media focused less attention on the military peace movement and these memorials. As mentioned, the memorials increasingly protested the war in Afghanistan, and the peace movement as a whole focused on both wars as President Obama drew down troop levels in Iraq while increasing troop levels in Afghanistan. In conversations with Arlington West and other peace movement activists from 2009 to 2011, they described their frustration over having "convinced the public to oppose the war" but not succeeding in "really ending the war," in the words of a Gold Star sister who had served on the board of MFSO. Rod Brown asked, "How do you get people to care when they think the war is already over? Only military families like you and the guys getting deployed know it is still going on." These sentiments illuminated the movement's general disarray in the latter years of the Iraq War and the frustrating disconnect between America's civilian population and its military.

Conclusion

One War Ends, Another War Continues

As part of the military peace movements' post-Iraq protests, nearly fifty U.S. veterans of Iraq and Afghanistan joined protests of a NATO conference in Chicago on May 20, 2012. IVAW and Gold Star family members led a march of several hundred thousand through the streets of Chicago and were the only ones to speak at the rally after the march, though they were flanked by VFP and MFSO members. Men and women in desert camouflage, black IVAW T-shirts, and the remnants of dress uniforms called cadence, including the lines, "Obama, Obama, can't you see / Oh what the NATO's done to me?" In singing this cadence, the servicemembers brought attention to the emotional and psychological injuries of war. In addition to their marching, clothing, and speeches, they focused attention on their military identities by standing in formation before the rally.

Todd Dennis, a veteran of the Navy during the Iraq and Afghanistan wars, threw some of his military medals toward McCormack Place, where NATO leaders were meeting, from the police line drawn around the area to keep protestors from these military leaders. Dennis said that the letter he received from the military accompanying these medals indicated that they were given to him for "hard work and dedication." He told the audience, "I was a hard worker because I buried my PTSD and overworked myself in the military. I am throwing these medals back and invoking my right to heal." In that statement he referenced a large part of the ongoing work in the military peace movement during the later years of the war, which focused on helping veterans and military families find the care they needed for their physical and psychological war injuries. The military peace movement regularly suggested that traumatized veterans were being abused by the U.S. military, which often redeployed servicemembers without diagnosing injuries or providing proper medical or psychological care.

Another IVAW member who threw his medals was Scott Olsen,

FIGURE 22. Members of Gold Star Families Speak Out, including Celeste Zappala (*second from left*), Gilda Carbonaro (*third from right*), Sue Niederer (*far right*), and Kevin (*second from right*) and Joyce Lucey (fifth from the right), protest at the White House on February 7, 2009, to ask for a swifter end to the Iraq and Afghanistan wars. Photograph by the author.

a Marine who served two tours in Iraq. Olsen had been critically wounded by police during the economic-focused Occupy protests in Oakland, California.[1] Olsen's presence at Occupy protests in his IVAW T-shirt and then at this NATO protest was intended to highlight that money used for the war was unavailable for programs in the United States, a similar message to the one the military peace movement made in its Gulf Coast protest, as described in chapter 3. Olsen threw back his Global War on Terrorism Service Medal, his Operation Iraqi Freedom Medal, his National Defense Medal, and his Marine Corps Good Conduct Medal. As he threw the medals, he said, "These medals once upon a time made me feel good about what I was doing; they made me feel like I was doing the right thing. I came back to reality, and I don't want these anymore." His medals made him feel guilty about his role in the Iraq War, and he said that members of the military like him were "doing the right thing" by trying to bring peace through antiwar protest rather than engaging in military action. These statements demonstrated the importance of morality to the military peace movement's consciousness. Many of the veterans who threw medals described their "shame" over involvement in the wars in Afghanistan and Iraq, and the majority of IVAW members apologized for participating in the wars. Others talked about feeling connections to the people of Iraq and Afghanistan. Each statement demonstrated the long-term consequences of the wars for those who served in them.

In published media reports before and after the event, several of these veterans described their involvement in this tactic as an important part of the process of healing from their psychological and emotional war wounds. Although this NATO protest intended to draw attention to the continuing U.S.-led war in Afghanistan and encourage officials and citizens to push for an end to the war, the tactic also played an important role in emotional transformation. Some veterans used words such as "cathartic" or spoke about this tactic as bringing closure for them. Multiple-tour Marine veteran of Iraq Vincent Emanuele said that the protest offered an opportunity "for many veterans to deal internally with what it is we have experienced overseas and to make amends with ourselves." These servicemembers were suffering from an affliction of conscience that for some manifested in actual diagnoses of PTSD and for others led to suicide, drug abuse, or a near obsession with protest, which could become another way to bury or put off their troubles. Tactics such as this protest provided tangible steps for activists to transform their emotions, as well as a supportive culture for that transformation. This NATO protest, like the majority of military peace movement protests after 2007, was focused on displaying the human costs of war. Even though more military members survived the wars in Afghanistan and Iraq than the war in Vietnam, the military peace movement was bent on showing the nation there were costs beyond the deaths of servicemembers to troops and society. The military peace movement was still deploying their insider–outsider identities to enhance tactics, attract attention to U.S. foreign policy, and mobilize other activists.

Although the U.S. military officially ended its mission in Iraq on December 15, 2011, the military peace movement continued organizing to stop the deployments of troops to foreign wars and to develop comprehensive plans for the care of those veterans and families affected by war. Despite the widely publicized troop drawdown in Iraq, the American military continued to face a heightened OPTEMPO with relatively short downtime between deployments because of American's involvement in Afghanistan and other deployments related to the broader war on terror, the Libyan civil war, and other military engagements. The movement hoped to publicize the continuation of war deployments because many Americans mistakenly believed troops' engagement in wars was in the past. Additionally, over a decade of war had taken its toll on American troops and their families in ways the movement sought to rectify.

Activists often said that Americans needed to be more aware of the trauma that military members faced. At a weekly protest in early June 2012 outside the Teaneck, New Jersey, National Guard armory, at which MFSO had been protesting since the beginning of the Iraq War, Walt Nygard took part in a vigil for the two-thousandth U.S. military casualty in Afghanistan with other MFSO and GSFSO members. Nygard was an Army veteran from Vietnam and the father of a serviceman who had served in Afghanistan and was scheduled for another deployment in 2012. He talked about his desire for recognition of the traumas of war and their connection to veteran suicides. He claimed, "The bulk of the American public doesn't know anything, and it fills me with anger and resentment. If it really meant anything to them, there would be a thousand people on this corner with us."[2] Activists felt abandoned by the American public and their government in their battles to secure adequate care for returning veterans and their families.

In the hope of drawing attention to the continued deployments and their consequences, the military peace movement focused its energy on the deployment of servicemembers who were experiencing trauma from combat or rape while in the military. MFSO and Gold Star activists spoke about the reality of veterans' suicide attempts. As one activist wrote about her cousin in a 2010 MFSO press release:

> He wasn't mentally stable enough to return to combat operations in Afghanistan but the Marines deployed him anyway. He had to go

because orders are orders. On December 26th 2009, just two weeks into combat operations in Afghanistan, he killed himself because he couldn't handle the war raging in his head.

This Gold Star activist illustrated the devastating effects of military policy that placed the burdens of the longest wartime in American history on a percentage of the country that was smaller than in any other period of its history. Suicide rates in the 2011 Army were nearly four times as high as prewar rates, and fears about negative cultural or career repercussions for seeking mental health care were voiced by servicemembers and their spouses in numerous surveys.[3] Activists hoped to publicize this information in order to bring pressure that would rectify the situation.

Some of the issues military peace activists faced pitted them directly against the military and the VA, and in doing so, they broadened the scope of the issues confronted by the mainstream peace movement. Despite increases in services and VA funding, activists gathered to publicize the myriad complaints about the military's inadequate care for its returning veterans and their families. Along with veterans' service organizations, military peace movement activists engaged in high-profile class-action lawsuits against the VA that drew attention to the unmet needs of veterans as they transitioned to civilian life.[4] Additionally, military peace movement organizations worked with service organizations to fight military policies that incorrectly categorized tens of thousands of veterans, who were actually suffering from combat-related mental health problems, as suffering from personality or adjustment disorders.[5] This categorization prohibited veterans from receiving the medical, financial, and other benefits to which they would have been entitled had they been properly diagnosed. As activists faced their own or watched their friends and families handle, or not, the psychological and emotional consequences of war, they targeted individual military bases and unit commanders, the VA, and, of course, the DoD.

Although the wars were wrapping up, the military peace movement prepared for the long war against the visible and invisible wounds of war. The movement's focus on a right to heal may have appeared like a shift from a radical demand for an immediate end to the wars to a more palatable plea to help veterans, but the movement still worked to stop the wars, which they saw as the key causes of PTSD and other injuries. They saw traumatized veterans as having normal reactions to war—particularly, wars with dubious origins and outcomes. They capitalized on Americans' positive sentiments regarding veterans in order to illuminate the negative effects of war, with the ultimate goal of encouraging politicians and citizens to pay more attention to whether wars should continue or be waged in the first place.[6] Throughout the seven years I followed the military peace movement, activists united a genuine concern for veterans and military families with an antiwar agenda by showing how war "hurt the troops." The movement held the U.S. government accountable for creating veterans' and military families' problems and for killing servicemembers because it chose to enter into what they believe were unnecessary and ill-conceived wars.

LONG WARS AND THE CIVILIAN–MILITARY DIVIDE

Whereas the military peace movement had intimate connections to war that made them beneficiaries of the peace movement, most Americans were insulated from the various consequences of the post-9/11 wars. At most only one half of one percent of Americans were serving in the military at any one time from 2001 to 2012, and only approximately five percent of Americans were immediate family members of an Iraq or Afghanistan War veteran. The U.S. antiwar movement that developed to oppose the Iraq War may have been smaller and more limited in effects than the one that opposed Vietnam because the American population was largely insulated from the war. Issue fatigue and demobilization are more likely among *conscience constituents*, who have little to gain or lose from a movement's success or failure.[7] American civilians were conscience constituents in protests against the Iraq and Afghanistan wars because they were protected from the financial and human consequences of the wars, as well as other concurrent military activities. Distance from the war developed because no draft or war taxes were enacted. Although the wars had consequences for those who fought them, the most dramatic consequences to which Americans paid attention seemed lesser than those in Vietnam, since casualty numbers in Iraq were much smaller.[8]

Although OPTEMPO and the financial costs of war remained high through 2012, polling data showed that in the Iraq War's later years, it was not a major concern for most civilians.[9] After 2007, few Americans saw the Iraq War or related issues, such as the Afghanistan War or fighting terrorism in general, as a top concern. Even more startling, around half of American civilians thought the wars in Afghanistan and Iraq had "little impact on their own lives."[10] In other words, being at war for over a decade did not significantly affect over half of Americans, a fact that is in stark contrast to the experience of the subjects of this book and other military community members.

The limited relevance of the Iraq War to most Americans' lives and political activities derived from the distance created by fighting a lengthy war with an AVF military. Only those Americans who elected to enter the military, a distinct segment of the American population, faced war consequences such as death and physical, psychological, and emotional injury.[11] During Vietnam the draft resistance movement operated in concert with the peace movement, but young Americans and their families never had to fear a draft during the Iraq War.

The lack of a draft during the Iraq and Afghanistan wars placed enormous burdens on the U.S. Armed Forces that were significantly different from those placed on servicemembers during the Vietnam War. AVF military contracts regularly required servicemembers, including those in the Reserves or the National Guard, to complete multiple deployments to Iraq or Afghanistan, unlike the single deployment required of Vietnam-era enlistees and draftees. By 2012 almost half of the military had deployed to Iraq or Afghanistan twice, and it was not unusual for a servicemember to have had five or six deployments of six months or more each. Some military members had completed twelve deployments.[12] Tours in Iraq and Afghanistan were frequently longer than deployments to Vietnam. In the Vietnam War, first deployments lasted twelve months, and these would be followed by six-month second and third deployments only if a soldier chose to volunteer for further service. During the Iraq War, Army tours extended up to twenty-two months, at their lengthiest, and regularly lasted at least one year, no matter the number of previous deployments. Vietnam-era draftees' and enlistees' terms of service in the Army and the Marines were only two years, whereas service contracts during the Iraq War obligated military members to a minimum of four years of active or of Reserve or National Guard service. After their initial military commitment, Iraq-era servicemembers faced several additional years of possible service should the military decide it needed them after the end of their contract period through policies of stop-loss and the IRR use. During the Iraq War, the military called up at least 30,000 people from this IRR force, fifteen times the number used during the Vietnam War.[13]

There were other reasons for the force used to fight in Iraq and Afghanistan being different from that used in Vietnam and for it being further distanced from the American populace. The far fewer servicemembers used to fight today's wars and their greater likelihood of surviving injuries that would have killed soldiers in the past reduced the wars' emotional impact on civilians. Additionally, the DoD hired hundreds of thousands of private military contractors who were largely invisible to Americans—most being citizens of other countries—and these contract forces were used in much higher numbers than ever before in American history.[14]

All of these factors insulated the vast majority of Americans from the consequences of the Iraq War. This separation from the immediate costs of war reduced American civilians from being beneficiary constituents of an antiwar movement, as they were in Vietnam, to being conscience constituents, whose mobilization was more difficult. Americans had to be drawn to protest through their ideology, which meant they could be easily lured away from this movement into other causes for which their own lives and livelihoods appeared to be more at stake.[15]

Scholars have used the term *civil–military divide* to focus on the challenge of reconciling a military that is not only sufficiently powerful to complete the tasks requested by civilian leadership but also subordinate enough to not overstep civilian authority. Work on this divide in political and military sociology focuses on ways in which the military holds or does not hold attitudes different from those of the civilian public or its leadership. Most research finds some expected differences in attitudes between American civilians and servicemembers over foreign policy, political affiliation, the righteousness of wars, and the use of force.[16] These dissimilarities appear to come from differences in political orientation between those who choose to enter the military and those who choose to enter the workforce or college.[17] I base my conclusions about the civilian–military divide, however, on the dramatic differences between these two groups in experience and sacrifice during extended wartime. Civilian Americans understand little of military culture or the sacrifices of military life, and few college courses examine the military.[18] Unfortunately, this lack of knowledge has resulted in a general population that is unaware of military structure and culture and a startling military–civilian gap, which the military community resents. In recent polls at least 84 percent of Iraq War–era veterans and military family members reported feeling that American civilians did not understand or appreciate their sacrifices or the resulting issues they faced.[19] American civilians largely agreed, with 71 percent reporting that they did not understand the military community's issues.[20] Due to the lack of a draft and the demographic trend of military members being more likely than civilians to have family in the military, American civilians had very little to fear from these wars. During the wars in Iraq and Afghanistan, a massive gap in sacrifice expanded between civilians and the military. This gap alienated the civilian population from their desire to see the wars end.

Military peace movement strategies attempted to overcome the sacrifice gap's resulting civilian apathy. Three main tactics were employed in an attempt to push civilians into focusing on the Iraq War. First, activists engaged in what they called "sharing our pain," or explaining the war's toll on military families by telling stories of war that were foreign to civilians. Second, they constructed memorial displays that publicized the deaths of servicemembers and drew attention to the physical and mental injuries of war. Finally, since the war took place so far from U.S. soil, activists engaged in street theater that brought mock warfare into major U.S. cities.

Mobilization into the military peace movement required that individuals look past the historical and cultural differences between the communities of peace activists and the military—located on each side of the conceptual dichotomy between peace and war. By incorporating both aspects of this dichotomy into the military peace movement, activists built a community in which emotional, political, and personal growth happened and that influenced the wider culture's interpretation of the war. Through their challenges to cultural conceptions of the Iraq War, the military peace movement provided an important complication to the dichotomy between peace and war. The movement's intentional combination of the military and peace activism challenged simplistic understandings of both communities and concepts. By straddling the divide between the military and peace activism, these activists pushed scholars and the general public to examine not just the differences but also the commonalities in desires, experiences, and beliefs between these divisions of American culture.

Overcoming the civilian–military divide is important because such a gap may have numerous negative consequences. First, it may be responsible for allowing leaders to be less answerable to their civilian population's wishes about military action. This could explain why the Iraq and Afghanistan wars persisted for years after the majority of the U.S. population opposed them. Second, such a gap may make American veterans and their families vulnerable to persistent problems, such as lacking veterans' health care, rising rates of suicide, repeated and overextended deployments, and sexual harassment and assault. Third, this gap is likely at least partially responsible for arguments that confuse support for government policies with support for military troops. If civilians have a limited sense of their own military or the consequences of war, political leaders' ideas of what is good for the military may be accepted without question. Finally, this gap is dangerous for America as it divides those with weapons from civilians and their political representatives, who ultimately decide how those weapons are used. A greater understanding of the military by wider society, particularly progressives, may make the military more permeable to arguments posed by the Left, including peace groups.

IDENTITY AND EMOTION: INSIDE AND OUTSIDE A MOVEMENT

The military peace movement attempted to bridge the civilian–military divide by pushing their audience to care about veterans and their families. To do so, they carefully managed their image and heightened the emotionality of their tactics; in other words, they used identity and emotion strategically. To do that, though, they had to first overcome significant barriers to activism, develop a collective identity that combined two seemingly contradictory aspects of themselves, and prevail over the demobilizing emotions of war. Activists overcame the unique constraints imposed by the military, and they faced heightened risks for their participation that peace activists without military connections did not face. Heightened risks of official military sanction, estrangement, and psychological trauma set the military peace movement apart from the general peace movement. These risks and the seeming contradictions of their military peace movement identity likely explain this movement's appeal to the media and their novelty to the wider public.

Identity Consolidation as Emotional Self-Help

This book contributes to the wider scholarship that examines how identity and emotion affect internal movement processes such as recruitment, mobilization, solidarity, and commitment by examining how seemingly contradictory identities can be combined in ways that improve activists' emotional states.[21] Movements function well when individuals see themselves as part of a larger collective and treat their activism as a strategy for defending their individual identities and improving their emotional health.[22] I demonstrate that activists look to social movement communities to validate their emotions and identities and that they remain in activism if they are able to use it to transform their negative emotions into productive emotions.

The military peace movement collective identity combined two seemingly contradictory identities: their intimate connection to the military and their antiwar activism. This identity consolidation and its unique risks set this segment of the peace movement apart from the wider peace movement and the military.[23] While military peace movement participants may seem a balance of contradictions, they were moved to overcome the negative perceptions of the peace movement within the military community because they viewed their activism as an extension of their service as military servicemembers and families. The demands of military life pushed families and servicemembers to search for information on the causes, implementation, and realities of the Iraq War, and activists developed an antiwar perspective in response to their search for knowledge. Their beliefs about what

America should be contrasted with what they saw or heard about the Iraq War. Negative personal experiences with the war, including the loss of lives, limbs, and sanity, also drove people to the peace movement. Some of the activists had personal history with left-leaning politics or otherwise felt like outsiders in the military already. All of these different experiences and beliefs caused members of the military community to seek a space in the peace movement to combine their military identity with their antiwar activist identity in a way that did not represent a contradiction, at least to them. Movement activists built boundaries between this culture of action and both the wider peace movement and the broader military community of servicemembers, veterans, and their families. In constructing their collective identity as different from the vast majority of the military and the peace movement, activists revealed painful divisions within these wider spaces but also took pride in their uniqueness. Not only were their war experiences painful, but these activists suffered shame and guilt precisely because they recognized that the Iraq War and, later, the Afghanistan War were wrong.

Military peace movement activists were motivated by anger that resulted from the seeming betrayal of their service or veterans' abandonment by their government. Social movement scholars find that anger over perceived injustice is an important motivator for seeking activism.[24] Experimental data from Stefan Stürmer and Bernd Simon finds that anger motivates people to seek an association with others with whom they can build a collective identity that will challenge dominant constructions of an issue.[25] Although anger can encourage people to seek social movement activism, movement experiences that allow activists to release emotions can mitigate the anger and diminish the likelihood of activism even if this catharsis does not address the ongoing causes of their disadvantaged position.[26] While events that release anger can feel good for movement participants, only if the anger is directed at the cultural or structural roots of the problem can activism make long-term positive change.

The data presented here suggests that what a movement can do best with anger is change its focal point. Rather than encouraging their members to see themselves or a shapeless system as the source of anger, movements can focus activists on particular others as culprits for their problems and provide an opportunity to make tangible changes. Thus, it is critical that a movement transform participants' emotions from self-directed shame and guilt and unfocused anger into *righteous anger*. As William Gamson describes it, righteous anger is a critical emotion in social movements because it puts "fire in the belly and iron in the soul."[27] When activists label something an injustice, they acknowledge that social change is necessary, and they become free to express productive directed anger.[28] Building on the theoretical work by Erika Summers-Effler, I demonstrate how collective identity development transforms activists' understanding of their situation so that there is external blame for negative experiences and emotions.[29]

A strong movement collective identity can provide an emotional driving force for activism. It is not mere participation but the consciousness raising that happens in activism that allows activists to define their experiences and promotes collective action.[30] The data presented throughout this book suggests that participation in social movements can transform negative *emotions of powerlessness* into positive *emotions of resistance*. Through the development of a shared consciousness, activists realize the external cause of their anger. Focusing on structural and cultural change pushes them to feel and display righteous anger, or moral outrage. Through the development of solidarity, activists exchange shame and guilt for group pride, and by fighting the cause of their injustice, they transform undirected or self-focused anger into righteous anger. Developing an emotion culture that simultaneously mobilizes and sustains activists is important for the longevity and success of a movement.[31]

Activists must be careful, however, to balance and integrate the emotional and strategic elements of protest, lest they become too overwhelmed and despairing.[32] Activism can be emotionally gratifying, which can help activists overcome the stress and risks of activism, but the moral emotions involved in it can also push them to feel compelled to work beyond their physical and emotional capacities.[33] The emotional labor performed by activists to manage and strategically use emotions can lead to a burnout that causes them to disengage, as my survey and interactions with military peace movement activists after 2010 confirmed. Activists had to intentionally take breaks from retelling their painful war experiences and opening their wounds of

war because these acts caused psychological distress and led to demobilization. This raises serious questions about the sustainability of a
movement, particularly one that does not achieve its goals quickly, as
most do not. Additionally, the end of their activism may cause some
participants to lose a sense of agency and power, causing emotions of
powerlessness to return.[34]

Using Identity and Emotion to Enhance Claims

Emotion and identity are crucial to framing movement messages and
creating tactics. Activists make strategic choices about emotion and
identity that are tailored to resonate with their various audiences. As
I demonstrate with the military peace movement, protestors often
invoke particular identities to produce a favorable emotional response in audiences that provide activists with authority over issues
and challenge their oppositions' framing of issues. Identity and emotion strategies can influence outcomes within the state, other institutions, and the culture. While the strategic deployment of identity
and emotion are usually discussed separately, these two elements are
often combined in activists' strategic choices about how to influence
audiences.[35]

Identity strategies are critical to audience reception. Some activists
can publicize aspects of their identities to capitalize on their novelty,
garner media attention, and assert authority. Seemingly contradictory identities appear to be particularly useful for grabbing attention.
Members of the military peace movement regularly attracted attention
from bystanders at protests because their presence challenged cultural
assumptions about divisions between peace activists and the military.
The novelty of this culture of action led to extensive coverage by American and foreign media in ways that were disproportionate to the organizations' size in the broader peace movement. This supports the ideas
that media and many in the nonactivist public value experience-based
knowledge, as opposed to academic or advocate knowledge.[36] Activists
who have been personally affected by an issue can utilize their identities as those with firsthand experience to make claims that are well
received, particularly in the talk-show model of modern news.[37]

Some activists' identities, such as those in the military peace movement, can challenge their opposition's arguments. I call the use of such an identity an *oppositional identity strategy*.[38] This is new terminology for an old phenomenon, and oppositional identities have competed with the hegemonic or countermovement framing of issues in many movements, including when the pro-life movement has spotlighted feminists or when clergy have stood for gay rights.[39] Military identities lent the antiwar cause credibility at a time when the general public was supportive of the troops and patriotic. Activists' combined military–antiwar identities imbued tactics such as war memorials and street theater with a greater emotional appeal and allowed the movement to reach a wider audience.

The effectiveness of social movement tactics and strategies often lies in their ability to connect emotionally with an audience.[40] Activists use value-based moral emotions to give their framing of an issue power, and they hope stories of injustice elicit sorrow, fear, and ultimately righteous anger in their audiences.[41] Military peace movement activists crafted tactics and strategies that were intended to evoke strong emotions such as grief, anger, and shock. In every military peace movement tactic and, often, in their everyday lives, participants told heart-wrenching stories about their experiences of war, intending to provoke righteous anger at the injustices of war and the holes in the care systems for veterans and military families. They hoped that by making people feel the war, they would shift public opinion and challenge governmental policies. By stimulating grief, outrage, and sympathy, they sought to motivate people to act. Recent research in the psychology of activism suggests that these emotions can increase the social movement participation of groups in privileged positions, such as American conscience constituents.[42]

Movements must be cognizant of the consequences of displaying anger in their tactics. Although angry or radical tactics can garner attention and raise issue awareness, they are likely to turn off some audiences.[43] In other words, angry protests may allow activists to blow off steam and feel better, but they may also be counterproductive to the overall goals of a movement.[44] For this reason activists in the military peace movement created tactics that deployed grief, which was an emotion that could create a connection to others. Tactics like the memorials to dead servicemembers were used to stimulate grief and bring bystanders into dialogue with activists. Organizations and cultures of action are likely to disagree over the proper role of anger, however, including whether eliciting anger or connecting emotions produces a more desirable outcome.[45] The specifics of the movement context will dictate which emotion strategies are successful, though it is likely that multiple cultures of action each deploying tactics with varying emotion strategies works best.

LESSONS FOR OBSERVING MOVEMENT CULTURE

Throughout this book I reference the cultural context in which military peace movement activism was embedded. American cultural norms and history influenced movement processes, constraints, and possibilities. Additionally, the shared attitudes, values, goals, and practices of the military, as an institution, and that of the peace movement, as a network, affected the mobilization, framing strategies, tactics, and identities of this section of the peace movement. The novelty and significance of the military peace movement cannot be understood without recognition of the cultural realities that shape individual and collective identities and emotions. My focus on the importance of aspects of culture for social movements provides three main recommendations for future social movement research.

First, social movement scholars should look beyond large-scale demonstrations and events to better understand the embodied, everyday political strategies that challenge cultural understandings of groups, policies, and practices. While media and cultural biases shape what events scholars can quantitatively examine, we need to go beyond traditional protest to examine how change happens.[46] More attention should be paid to the everyday and smaller-scale activism in which individuals engage. Following in the tradition of scholars who focus on the importance of expressive identity negotiation, I elaborate the personalized political strategies that challenge dominant understandings of groups, policies, and practices.[47] By embodying a contradiction, military peace movement activists employed oppositional and authoritative strategies—particularly, using clothing and symbols—every day, even when engaging in nonprotest activities. They emphasized their antiwar positions and their military connections in daily conversations, not just in political speeches at events. They supported one another and helped each other heal from the emotions of war when home or at work, far from protest events. Through these and other everyday personal political strategies, these activists promoted personal growth and offered challenges to the Iraq War and the peace–war dichotomy.

In wealthy modern societies, protest may be so common and ritualized that it can be easy to ignore traditional forms of street protest, and people may find it especially easy to ignore the messages of protestors with whom they disagree.[48] Personalized political strategies offer challenges, however, that go beyond the streets and other public locations of protest. By personalizing and embodying a movement message, these strategies may make protest palatable. As activism diffuses into daily lives and the forms and tactics of protest expand, scholars should pay greater attention to the everyday activism that movements encourage through handbooks and websites.[49] This everyday activism is found in strategic choices about lifestyles and one-on-one conversations, and it moves protest beyond large-scale events. These everyday forms of activism may be particularly important for introducing new ideas to those who distrust traditional protest. These everyday and smaller-scale protests can also be utilized by those who want to make a difference but who may be unwilling to face the risks of or otherwise engage in traditional protest events. Through further research on these everyday personalized political strategies, social movement scholars could address many of the shortcomings in dominant social movement research by specifying mechanisms for how movements matter and finding causality in cultural change.[50]

Second, a focus on subsections of movements, or cultures of action within movements, suggests an important meso-level of social movement research in between broad movements and organizations. I draw on Maren Klawiter's term *cultures of action* to delineate subsections within broad social movements that are divided by their framing of the problem, emotion norms, identities, and preferred tactics and by other elements of culture.[51] This concept is useful for understanding the development of a close-knit community that is distinct from a wider movement but broader than individual organizations. A focus on cultures of action can better explain mobilization and commitment to movements. The community that arises beyond organizational boundaries within a culture provides both tangible and emotional support to activists that can attract and sustain members. Future research that pays attention to the multiple cultures of action within movements will be able to further specify how social movement cultures clash or mesh in ways that promote or hinder larger movement goals. Connections between individuals and organizations inside a culture of action may best explain both individual and cultural consequences of social movement activism. Additionally, risk varies by culture of action due to tactical choices and because certain aspects of activists' identities can increase the physical, institutional, emotional, and psychological consequences of protest.

Finally, movements are constrained by their wider discursive context.[52] In order to connect to audiences, activists and organizations must exploit the familiar. Activists make intentional choices to use, change, or embrace aspects of their culture. If tactics and messages only conflict with a culture's dominant understandings of the world, activists can expect smaller mobilization and less acceptance of their messages. Mainstreaming a message to fit with cultural ideas can have its costs, as well. Strategies that use oppositional identities or that trade on connecting emotions with the hope of tapping into dominant discourses may lead to popular support, but these strategies limit a movement's critiques. Strategic choices to appeal to the middle constrain a movement's ability to challenge the structural problems at the root of their issues. Observation of other movements suggest this is likely; for example, when gay rights activists highlight the involvement of clergy in the movement, they seek to attract mainstream support, but doing so limits the movement from making broader critiques of religion's authority in social and policy issues. Additional research is necessary to understand whether and how the prominent role of the military peace movement culture of action limited the anti–Iraq War movement's ability to challenge the institutions of the government and the military. Comparative research on oppositional identity and the use of connecting-emotion strategies within other movements may expand our understanding of the costs and benefits associated with appealing to the mainstream.

CONTINUED ATTEMPTS AT HEALING AND PREVENTION

After the U.S. military left Iraq, the military peace movement focused on ending American combat operations in Afghanistan, stopping future military operations, and securing better physical, mental, and behavioral health care for veterans and their families.[53] Military peace movement activists also sought ways to tangibly help Iraqis and other victims of U.S. wars, regularly taking part in medical missions and cultural exchanges. The numbers they could mobilize for protest and their office staffs shrank, however. Many activists were, in the words of an active duty Army Iraq War veteran in his twenties, "burned out" and in need of "some peace in [their] daily life." Numerous former participants focused on other issues altogether, broadened the goals of the movement to oppose other conflicts or militarism, or altogether left activism behind. Much of the remaining activities of the military peace movement focused on fighting the war that came back home, getting military veterans and their families the resources they needed in order heal from the wounds of war. Although the wars drifted from public discourse, servicemembers and their families continued to feel their impact and required spaces for mourning and healing.

In the later years of the movement, many activists took part in artistic and writing tactics that continued to put their experiences in the public eye and offered opportunities for emotional transformation. These tactics garnered a fair amount of attention. Sara Nesson's Oscar- and Emmy-nominated documentary *Poster Girl* followed the emotional "redemptive journey" of IVAW board member Robynn Murray. Murray was featured on the cover of *Army Magazine* in August 2005 while deployed to Iraq, and the film followed her attempts to heal from PTSD. She was shown engaging in military peace movement creative tactics such as the Warrior Writers, which published three books of IVAW members' writings, and the Combat Paper Project, which transformed military uniforms into paper for those writings and other pieces of art. Healing and artistic tactics such as these attracted attention from a broad audience within the military and the veterans' community, and activists often partnered with local VA representatives and other veterans' groups. Since many in these artistic tactics' audiences likely agreed with the policies of the Iraq and Afghanistan wars, these tactics introduced new audiences to the movement's critiques while offering the military community outlets for healing.

These artistic tactics continued to broaden the audience for antiwar activism. The military peace movement hoped to put a human face on war so that Americans would have to think about specific individuals rather than nameless "troops" and what wars did to them. They believed that before committing troops to war, American politicians and citizens should see servicemembers' faces and think about how wars disrupted and pained military families. The idea was that by personalizing the pain of war, Americans would demand that troops be sent to fight only when absolutely necessary.

The only way to keep veterans and their families from experiencing the crushing consequences of war is by not sending them to battle in the first place. Though the military peace movement has attempted to bridge the civilian–military gap through their emotional and identity-focused tactics and strategies, with numerous global hot spots, hundreds of thousands of troops deployed, and continuing problems in the VA system, however, it remains to be seen whether the military peace movement will have any long-term impact on the way Americans support veterans, servicemembers, and their families.

Timeline of Major Events

Wars, Public Opinion, and Protests

Jan. 2001   President George W. Bush's first cabinet meeting dis-
            cusses toppling Saddam Hussein's government in Iraq.
Feb. 2001   Polls reveal 52 percent of Americans favor military ac-
            tion in Iraq.[1]
Sept. 2001 Terrorist attacks in the United States by fundamentalist
            Islamic organization al-Qaeda kill about 3,000 people.
Oct. 2001   U.S. and British forces bomb Afghanistan and enter
            a ground war. The United States has fewer than 2,000
            troops in Afghanistan.
Nov. 2001   American support for military action in Afghanistan
            (89 percent) and Iraq (74 percent) are at highest levels.
Dec. 2001   Bonn Conference leads to Afghan Transitional
            Authority, with Hamid Karzai appointed head, cre-
            ates International Security Assistance Force (ISAF, a
            UN-initiated peace-keeping force) in Afghanistan.
June 2002   At the United States Military Academy at West Point,
            President Bush outlines legal case for preemptive attack
            against nations seeking to harm the United States,
            focuses on Iraq.
Sept. 2002 President Bush begins encouraging U.S. Congress,
            United Nations, and international allies to consider war
            with Iraq. Secretary of Defense Donald Rumsfeld claims
            links between Iraq and al-Qaeda.[2] Polls reveal Ameri-
            cans favor war if United States has support of its allies.
Oct. 2002   Large national protest held against impending war in
            Iraq in Washington, D.C., features VFP members. Other

VFP members spearhead protests in cities across the United States.

Nov. 2002   MFSO founded. Press conference announces its formation the following January in Washington, D.C.

Feb. 2003   Secretary of State Colin Powell claims Iraq has weapons of mass destruction in UN address.[3] Army Chief of Staff Eric Shinseki says several hundred thousand troops are needed to fully secure Iraq. Millions take part in coordinated international day of protest opposing war in Iraq.

Mar. 2003   U.S.-led invasion of Iraq, with about 90,000 American troops in-country and a smaller international coalition than in Afghanistan, quickly overthrows Saddam Hussein's government. About 70 percent of Americans believe this was the right decision.

Apr. 2003   VFP spearheads Operation Dire Distress, a series of teach-ins against the war in Iraq.

May 2003   President Bush declares "Mission Accomplished" in Iraq while landing on U.S. Navy aircraft carrier. Over 60 percent of Americans believe United States made right decision in going to war with Iraq.

Aug. 2003   Violence in Iraq intensifies as various factions using low-intensity guerrilla warfare fight for power and against U.S. forces.

Oct. 2003   After NATO assumes leadership of ISAF operation in August, UN extends ISAF's mandate to all Afghanistan. Polling and media attention remains on Iraq, largely ignores Afghanistan for four years.

Nov. 2003   Arlington West in Santa Barbara, California, begins.

Mar. 2004   U.S. troop level in Iraq averages 150,000 until surge begins in 2007.

July 2004   IVAW founded at VFP convention in Boston. Americans' support for Afghanistan War begins steady decline. Now, 25 percent, compared with 9 percent at its start, think war was a mistake.

Oct. 2004   Support for Iraq War slips below 50 percent as insurgency and troop casualties increase.[4] Military peace

	movement takes part in A Trail of Mourning and Truth from Iraq to the White House, a funeral-style procession and rally in Washington, D.C.
Nov. 2004	Parliamentary and presidential elections end in Afghanistan after new constitution is drafted earlier that year. Bush reelected over Vietnam veteran Senator John Kerry.
Jan. 2005	Iraq holds first post-Hussein elections. Constitutional ratification follows in October. Support for Iraq War remains under 50 percent in the United States. GSFP is founded.
Feb. 2005	While most Americans no longer believe the war was the right decision, 55 percent want troops to stay in Iraq until country is stabilized.[5]
Mar. 2005	National protest held on third anniversary of Iraq War near Army base Fort Bragg in North Carolina features military peace movement.
May 2005	Troop level in Afghanistan is 18,000. Troop level in Iraq is 162,900.
Aug. 2005	Military peace movement begins Camp Casey protest encampment outside President Bush's Crawford, Texas, ranch, gathering intense media coverage for months and culminating in Bring Them Home Now bus tours.
Sept. 2005	Large national protest in Washington, D.C., features many military peace movement activists.
Oct. 2005	GSFSO is founded.
Nov. 2005	Vietnam veteran and Democrat hawk John Murtha calls for withdrawal of troops from Iraq.
Dec. 2005	Throughout 2005, ISAF expands operations into western and southern Afghanistan. U.S. forces double in Afghanistan.
Mar. 2006	Veterans and Survivors March from Mobile to New Orleans links Iraq War to slow pace of recovery from Hurricane Katrina.
May 2006	Military peace movement holds Silence of the Dead, Voices of the Living in Washington, D.C., featuring a large memorial and a silent march.

June 2006   MFSO members and, occasionally, other military peace
            movement participants hold Operation House Call, a
            vigil outside U.S. congressional office buildings until
            August using a boot display as a memorial to American
            servicemembers killed in Iraq.
July 2006   Deadliest twelve months in Iraq for civilians and U.S.
            troops begin. Support for war among Americans drops
            below 40 percent.
Sept. 2006 From August through September, military peace move-
            ment returns to Camp Casey and takes part in Camp
            Democracy in Washington, D.C., a series of protest
            events aimed at supporting GI resisters and encouraging
            new resisters.
Oct. 2006   Appeal for Redress campaign launched, allowing active
            duty servicemembers to reach out to their Congress
            members about their opposition to the war in Iraq with-
            out risking discharge or other punishments.
Nov. 2006   Saddam Hussein sentenced to death by Iraqi courts.
            Republicans lose majorities in House and Senate.
Mar. 2007   IVAW and VFP lead March on the Pentagon. IVAW
            launches bus tours to reach out to military base commu-
            nities. A majority of Americans (52 percent) favor troop
            withdrawal as soon as possible from Iraq.[6]
Apr. 2007   Percentage of Americans who believe Iraq War is going
            well drops to its lowest point.
June 2007   IVAW begins street theater productions of Operation
            First Casualty, and artistic ventures of Warrior Writers
            and Combat Paper Project start this year.
July 2007   Troop surge in Iraq fully under way, sending thousands
            more troops to Iraq and extending tours of duty for
            Army soldiers and Marines already there.
Oct. 2007   Troop level in Iraq peaks at 166,300. Fewer than 45 per-
            cent of Americans believe the United States did the right
            thing by going to war with Iraq.
Mar. 2008   Winter Soldier Iraq and Afghanistan testimonies
            presented in Silver Spring, Maryland, followed by

testimony to Congressional Progressive Caucus and regional Winter Soldier events.

June 2008 Troop level gradually decreases in Iraq. Fewer than 40 percent of Americans believe it was worth going to war with Iraq.

Aug. 2008 Military peace movement takes part in large Denver protests of Democratic National Convention and holds organizational annual conventions in Minneapolis in order to protest Republican National Convention. VFP adopts resolution calling for immediate withdrawal from Afghanistan. Now, 34 percent of Americans believe Afghanistan War was a mistake.

Sept. 2008 VFP begins tactic of illegally flying banners outside buildings, calling for end of Iraq War and arrests of President Bush and Vice President Cheney.

Nov. 2008 President Bush and Iraqi leadership sign Status of Forces Agreement (SOFA) for gradual withdrawal ending in December 31, 2011. The then senator Barack Obama wins presidential election against Vietnam veteran Senator John McCain on a platform that includes ending war in Iraq while escalating war in Afghanistan.

Dec. 2008 Troop level in Afghanistan gradually increases to 31,800 over 2008, the deadliest year there since invasion for U.S. troops. Over 60 percent of Americans believe Afghanistan War is going badly.[7]

Jan. 2009 IVAW adopts a resolution against Afghanistan War and begins working closely with labor movement.

Apr. 2009 MFSO, including GSFSO, vote to change mission statement to include opposition to Afghanistan War.

June 2009 In accordance with SOFA, United States withdraws from Baghdad and Iraqi cities.

Aug. 2009 Fewer than half of Americans believe Afghanistan War was worth fighting. Number remains under 50 percent.

Feb. 2010 Troop level in Afghanistan dramatically increases, but two-thirds of Americans disagree with Obama's Afghanistan surge.[8]

July 2010	Highest number of U.S. troop casualties in Afghanistan in a single month (65). U.S. force level in Afghanistan reaches and stays around 100,000.
Aug. 2010	Fewer than 50,000 "noncombat" troops remain in Iraq.
Oct. 2010	Military peace movement spearheads Operation Recovery: Stop the Deployment of Traumatized Troops, an educational campaign aimed at ending redeployment of servicemembers who suffer from PTSD and TBI.
Dec. 2010	Yearly totals of civilian and U.S. deaths in Afghanistan reach record levels. Only 34 percent of Americans believe Afghanistan War was worth fighting.
Nov. 2010	NATO sets end of operations in Afghanistan for 2014.
Dec. 2010	Iraq Parliament reconvenes nine months after elections.
Mar. 2011	Small military peace movement rally in Washington, D.C.
Aug. 2011	Violence in Iraq escalates.
Oct. 2011	VFP coordinates with others for an occupation tactic at Freedom Plaza in Washington, D.C., to link money and war issues. Since it coincides with Occupy Wall Street protests, it becomes Occupy DC and stimulates military peace movement involvement in Occupy protests across United States.
Nov. 2011	Seventy-five percent of Americans approve of withdrawing all combat troops from Iraq by end of 2011, but country is divided in half over whether the decision to use force in Iraq was right call.[9]
Dec. 2011	Last American troops leave Iraq on December 18, in accordance with SOFA.
May 2012	Anti-NATO protests held in Chicago at which IVAW members attempt to return military medals.
June 2013	Sixty-eight thousand U.S. troops remain in Afghanistan, but President Obama plans to halve that by February 2014.

Abbreviations

ANSWER	Act Now to Stop War and End Racism—U.S. antiwar coalition
AVF	all-volunteer force—a military made of enlistees rather than conscripts
Blue Star Families	immediate families of military members, sometimes used exclusively to refer to military dependents or families with a deployed servicemember
CO	conscientious objector (sometimes in military conversations, "commanding officer")
DoD	Department of Defense
DoDD	Department of Defense Directive—a broad policy document on how the military should run that is meant to turn an order from Congress, the president, or the secretary of defense into practice
GI Bill	various VA and DoD programs that cover educational expenses for military members or their dependents
Gold Star Families	people whose loved ones have died in or as a result of military service
GSFP	Gold Star Families for Peace
GSFSO	Gold Star Families Speak Out
IED	improvised explosive device
ISAF	International Security Assistance Force
ISO	International Socialist Organization
IVAW	Iraq Veterans Against the War
MFSO	Military Families Speak Out
NATO	North Atlantic Treaty Organization
NGO	nongovernmental organization

9/11	September 11, 2001, terrorist attacks in the United States in New York, Washington, D.C., and Pennsylvania
OEF	Operation Enduring Freedom—although technically broader, U.S. military mission in Afghanistan beginning in 2001
OIF	Operation Iraqi Freedom—U.S. military mission in Iraq beginning in 2003
OPTEMPO	operational tempo—pace of war/deployments
PAC	political action committee—organization that campaigns for or against a candidate, a piece of legislation, or a ballot initiative
PTSD	posttraumatic stress disorder—often used by the military community to refer to any psychological or emotional disturbances resulting from war or other upsetting experiences
TBI	traumatic brain injury—physical trauma that damages brain tissue and often impairs a person's cognitive, physical, behavioral, or psychological functioning
UCMJ	Uniform Code of Military Justice—body of criminal laws applicable to all military members serving in any location
UFPJ	United for Peace and Justice—a U.S. antiwar coalition
UN	United Nations
VCS	Veterans for Common Sense
VFP	Veterans for Peace
VMFP	Veterans and Military Families for Progress
VUFT	Veterans United for Truth
VVAW	Vietnam Veterans Against War
WMD	weapon of mass destruction

Acknowledgments

I am indebted to many colleagues and friends for their generosity of time, ideas, and support.

The participants in the military peace movement inspired me and increased my determination. I am grateful to many who generously gave their time and insights. Specifically, I thank Geoff Millard, Nancy Lessin, Charlie Richardson, Col. Ann Wright (Retired), Mike Hearington, Stephan Potts, Leah Bolger, Elliott Adams, Karen Meredith, Stacy Hafley, Annie McCabe, Keri Wheelwright, Tim Kahlor, Pat Alviso, Tammara Rosenleaf, Cloy Richards, Tina Richards, Tim Goodrich, Maricela Guzman, Al Zappala (deceased), Tina Garnanez, Melida Arredondo, Lane Anderson, Ron Dexter, Robert Potter (deceased), Michael Cervantes, Rod Brown, Carolyn Rice, Rod Edwards, Stephen Sherrill, Tom Urban, and the many volunteers at Arlington West in Santa Barbara. Not only did their heartbreaking stories motivate this book, but their kindness sustained me in many ways.

I am grateful to the people who read drafts and helped make this document better. I am particularly indebted to my academic mentor, Verta Taylor, who painstakingly provided line edits when this was a dissertation, pointed out the viability of this research topic, and facilitated the process. Leila J. Rupp helped me find my way early in this project, and her calm, reassuring guidance gave me the impetus to first put pen to paper. David S. Meyer offered extensive feedback on early chapters and oversaw theoretical shifts that pushed me to see the movement in a new light. Eve Shapiro not only read countless drafts but while I was on Navy bases, in the field, and at my desk gave me much needed pep talks. In a fantastic writing group, Brooke Neeley and Patricia Drew provided edits and pushed my analysis again and again. The book's editor, Jason Weidemann, and reviewers, Morten Ender and Lynne Woehrle, suggested many ideas that improved this book tremendously. I am grateful for my supportive colleague Stella Capek's help, in our writing meetings and in allowing me to carve out time for this book.

Most important, I thank my family, especially my husband, David Dufault, and my parents, Thomas and Kathleen Leitz, for always believing in me. Although combining David's military service with my activism and academic career has never been easy, his love, newfound cooking skills, and encouragement made this book possible. He is the kind of person the military needs, and I hope our country appreciates his dedication and our sacrifices. My family listened, made me laugh when I needed it, and loved me unconditionally, all of which was necessary to bearing both military and academic stress. My success is a testament to their support.

Notes

PREFACE

1. Langton 1984.

2. I use "Iraq War" to designate the 2003–11 U.S.-led war in Iraq and "Gulf War" to designate the war the United States led there from 1990 to 1991.

3. After initial forays into the field from 2002 to 2005, I spent nearly three years consistently attending movement events across the United States from February 2006 to December 2008. I attended most major events from then until the spring of 2011. I logged over one thousand hours in the field as a participant-observer, taking field notes on numerous movement activities, including but not limited to protest demonstrations in Washington, D.C., California, Florida, and the Midwest; a week-long march along the hurricane-ravaged U.S. Gulf Coast; the Camp Casey protests in Texas that catapulted Cindy Sheehan to fame; VFP conventions in Missouri and Minnesota; informational meetings held near military bases and in over a dozen cities; and memorials to American soldiers in numerous cities in the United States. I spent approximately three hundred hours observing the site of VFP's first military cemetery-like memorials—Santa Barbara's Arlington West—and I observed similar memorials for another one hundred hours.

4. Burawoy 1998.

5. Twenty-eight were conducted in person in private spaces found during movement gatherings, and two were conducted over the phone due to time and geographic constraints. I asked questions about the subjects' participation in the movement, the contradictory nature of the military and peace activism, feelings toward other activists in the movement, and whether they believed their activism had affected them. Ten participants were veterans of past wars; ten had joined the military after the September 11, 2001, terrorist attacks; and ten were family members of veterans who had joined since 9/11. The average interview length was an hour and fifteen minutes. Due to my participant observation, I knew particular topics to investigate and was able to follow up after the initial interviews. Through my participation at movement events, I developed a purposive sampling frame to interview a wide range of movement participants. I purposely varied my choice of subject by gender, race, and experiences within the military and within the peace movement.

6. I targeted the survey at IVAW, MFSO, and GSFSO, since they had more direct connections to the wars in Iraq and Afghanistan than did VFP. This follow-up survey focused on the ongoing effects of the wars in 2011 and the continuing antiwar activism of these military veterans and families. Nearly two-thirds of respondents were

military families, some having served in the military themselves during previous wars. Approximately 10 percent no longer considered themselves active participants in the movement.

7. I collected over seven hundred news stories on the movement and several thousand pages of press releases and other written materials from the movement. I was provided access to organizational archives that included photo albums, recordings of events, newsletters, data on membership, videotaped interviews with veterans and military families, meeting minutes, fliers, and other handouts. Additionally, participants often brought additional data, including their own writings about the movement, pictures, videos, and newspaper articles. In analyzing these materials, I used qualitative content coding.

8. More information about the data and methodology is available through correspondence with the author.

9. See Reed-Danahay 1997 for more on autoethnography.

INTRODUCTION

1. Numerous media outlets discussed the intense media coverage given to Sheehan, and many suggested that White House correspondents were typically limited by the ranch's rural setting to reporting President Bush's message of the day. This protest offered something new for them. See FOX News Watch 2005.

2. Sheehan, along with her family and other families of slain servicemembers, met with President Bush at Fort Lewis Army base near Seattle on June 24, 2004. Although a report in her hometown paper, the *Vacaville (Calif.) Reporter,* suggested that at the time Sheehan felt positively about the meeting, she explained that she had since reevaluated it and interpreted it negatively and now felt she was unable to express her opposition to the Iraq War.

3. A few hundred counterprotestors also came to Crawford for up to a half day at a time.

4. Knudson 2009.

5. Feldmann 2005.

6. Dowd 2005.

7. Defense Manpower Data Center 2011.

8. See data collected by CBS News/*New York Times* June 24–28, 2011, January 15–19, 2011, and April 5–12, 2010; Bloomberg National Poll June 17–20, 2011, and October 7–10, 2010; CBS News November 7–10, 2010, and October 1–5, 2010; and the Pew Research Center Survey October 27–30, 2010.

9. Department of Defense 2013; Livingston and Hanlon 2013.

10. This trend began in early 2008. See Perez-Pena 2008; Jurkowitz 2008.

11. See Skocpol 1992; Coy, Woehrle, and Maney 2008; Leitz 2011.

12. WMDs are biological, chemical, nuclear, and radiological weapons that can kill large numbers of people and/or destroy a large area of property or infrastructure.

13. Troop levels come from Defense Department records of boots on the ground, but these numbers do not reflect the full number of servicemembers or contractors

who served in these wars, as additional personnel took part in combat operations but are not listed as boots on the ground in these wars. See Belasco 2011.

14. Belasco 2011.

15. Bilmes 2013.

16. Fletcher 2007.

17. CNN Politics 2005.

18. Although the Iraq War was supported by the majority of Americans at its onset, the antiwar movement amassed the largest prewar protests in history.

19. To get comparable statistics on Vietnam and Iraq, I used Gallup data from both eras and determined the number for approval from those who did not believe the war was a mistake. See *USA Today* 2005.

20. In April 1968, 47 percent disapproved of Nixon's handling of Vietnam (Carroll 2004), whereas 60 percent disapproved of President Bush's handling of the war in April 2006 (*Washington Post* 2006).

21. At the height of the antiwar movement in the early 1970s, the organization's membership peaked at approximately 25,000. See Hunt 1999.

22. Moser 1996.

23. Hunt 1999.

24. Moser 1996; Lewes 2003.

25. Cortwright 2005.

26. Moser 1996.

27. Cortwright 2005.

28. See Lewes 2003; Cortwright 1992, 2005; Moser 1996; Hunt 1999; Anderson 1992; Wells 1994; Stacewicz 1997; Nicosia 2001.

29. See Beamish, Molotch, and Flacks 1995; Lembcke 2000.

30. During an antiwar protest in April 1971, Gold Star mothers were denied access to Arlington National Cemetery, where they intended to lay wreaths to honor the fallen. See Nicosia 2001.

31. Lehr 1999.

32. Coles 1999.

33. Moser 1996.

34. Krueger and Pedraza 2012; Rohall, Ender, and Matthews 2006.

35. Hosek and Martorell 2009.

36. Nicosia 2001.

37. Bobby Muller was paralyzed by a gunshot wound during his service in the Marine Corps during the Vietnam War. He founded Vietnam Veterans of America, a congressionally chartered nonprofit that works on identity and resource issues for Vietnam veterans and families, and Veterans for America (formerly Vietnam Veterans of America Foundation), which aims to help civilians affected by war.

38. Ron Kovic was also a Marine that was paralyzed during his service in Vietnam. He received a Bronze Star for his actions in Vietnam and became heavily involved in VVAW. He wrote the memoir, as well as the screenplay adaptation, *Born on the Fourth of July*.

39. Segal and Segal 2004.

40. Of course, the military draft in the United States more often pulled from poor and minority communities, but this was never exclusive.

41. Nicosia 2001.

42. Cortwright 2005, 50.

43. See Moskos and Chambers, eds., 1993.

44. For more information on these regulations and a discussion of their use from Vietnam to Iraq, see Kiel 2007.

45. Garrett and Hoppin 1998.

46. See Ricks 1997.

47. See Huntington 1957; Ricks 1997; Feaver, 1999; Feaver and Kohn 2000; Feaver and Kohn, eds., 2001; Wiegand and Paletz 2001.

48. See Holsti 1999, 2001. According to polling data, the gap between military servicemembers and civilians was shrinking until the 2004 election. See Teigen 2007; Rohall, Ender, and Matthews 2006. The Swift Boat portrayal of U.S. senator John Kerry, however, which suggested he had received unwarranted commendations for his military service in Vietnam and betrayed his fellow servicemembers by protesting the Vietnam War, profoundly influenced military voters to vote significantly more Republican than their civilian counterparts. See Teigen 2007. An examination of Army soldiers in Iraq found that although servicemembers were more nationalistic and defense oriented, they held diverse views on issues of morality and policy that were not very different from the distribution of attitudes in the American population. See Ender 2009. Data from when the Iraq War was well under way found significantly different attitudes about war and the use of the military between civilians and the military. See Kruger and Pedraza 2012. This gap likely originates, at least in part, from the differences between those who select to enter the military and those who do not. See Bachman et al. 2000.

49. Rohall, Ender, and Mathews 2006.

50. Kruger and Pedraza 2012.

51. Houppert 2005.

52. For more on the collective military memory of Jane Fonda, see Burke 2004; Lembcke 2010.

53. Langton 1984.

54. See Woerhle, Coy, and Maney 2008; Coy, Woerhle, and Maney 2008; Toussaint 2009.

55. Some claim the peace movement contributed to the end of American combat operations in Vietnam. See McAdam and Su 2002.Others argue that the American peace movement went into abeyance after Vietnam. See Heaney and Rojas 2007. For an historical overview of the peace movement see Marullo and Meyer 2004.

56. Meyer and Corrigall-Brown 2005.

57. Heaney and Rojas 2011.

58. Bennett 2004.

59. In 2005 the annual protest was staged near Fort Bragg, an active-duty Army installation in Fayetteville, North Carolina. See Heaney and Rojas 2007.

60. They were held in New York, Boston, Denver, and St. Paul.

61. Maney, Woehrle, and Coy 2005; Woehrle et al. 2008.

62. Coy, Maney, and Woehrle 2003; Woehrle et al. 2008; Maney et al. 2005.

63. Coy, Maney, and Woehrle 2003.

64. See Leitz 2011; Heaney and Rojas 2006.

65. Heaney and Rojas 2011.

66. Heaney and Rojas 2011.

67. This term avoids the branches model that often privileges the moderate, state-focused segment of a movement by equating it with the movement as a whole, whereas other segments whose targets, tactics, goals, or even definitions of the issues differ are relegated to branches of the movement. Although Klawiter suggests that localized iterations of movements produce distinctive cultures of action, I suggest that this term is also useful for understanding national movement subcultures. See Klawiter 1999; 2008.

68. See Taylor and Whittier 1992, 1995; Bernstein 1997, 2008; Earl 2004.

69. Snow et al. 1986; Melucci 1988; Taylor and Whittier 1992; Polletta and Jasper 2001; Hunt and Benford 2004; Klandermans 2004.

70. Polletta and Jasper 2001, 285.

71. Melucci 1989; Klandermans 1992; Hunt, Benford, and Snow 1994; Whittier 1995.

72. See Britt and Heise 2000; Klandermans 2004; Rupp and Taylor 1987; Taylor 1996, 2000; Robnett 1997; Young 2001; Kilshaw 2004.

73. Snow and McAdam 2000.

74. Gamson 1991, 40.

75. Kelly and Breinlinger 1996; Klandermans 2002; Stürmer and Simon 2004a, 2009; Stürmer et al. 2003.

76. Simon and Klandermans 2001; Simon 2004; Stürmer and Simon 2004b.

77. Kelly and Breinlinger 1996; Stüurmer et al. 2003.

78. Bernstein 1997, 2008; Bernstein and Olsen 2009; Dugan 2008; Neuhouser 2008; Schroer 2008; Taylor and Whittier 1992; Whittier 2009; Leitz 2011.

79. Bernstein 1997.

80. Leitz 2011.

81. Similarly, scholars have found that celebrities bring important resources, particularly newsworthiness, to social movement causes (Meyer and Gamson 1995) and to movements mobilized around certain illnesses (Lerner 2006; Taylor and Leitz 2011).

82. Taylor and Raeburn 1995.

83. See Taylor 1995; Aminzade and McAdam 2001; Goodwin, Jasper, and Polletta 2001, 2004; Einwohner 2002; Benford and Hunt 1992; Flam and King 2005; Gould 2009. For several decades before this shift, emotions were ignored by the majority of social movement scholars to promote the idea that participants were rational actors. See Taylor 1995; Robnett 1997; Goodwin, Jasper, and Polletta 2001, 2004. To counter the collective-behaviorist idea that activists behave irrationally due to

anomie (Kornahuser 1959), generalized beliefs (Smelser 1962), or relative deprivation (Gurr 1970), the dominant models in social movements research since the 1970s, resource mobilization (McCarthy and Zald 1977) and political process (McAdam 1982), focused on structural resources or political opportunities, narrowly defined, as determinants of protest.

84. On collective behavior research, see Kornahuser 1959; Smelser 1962; Gurr 1970. Resource mobilization was introduced in McCarthy and Zald 1977. Political process theory was outlined in McAdam 1982 and can be traced to Tilly 1978.

85. Leach and Pedersen 2006; van Zomeren et al. 2004; Rodgers 2010; Frye 1983; Hercus 1999; Gould 2009; Goodwin, Jasper, and Polletta 2000.

86. Goodwin, Jasper, and Polletta 2000; Summers-Effler 2002, 2005.

87. Fraser 1996; Taylor 1996, 2000; Nepstad and Smith 2001; Stein 2001; Gould 2001, 2009.

88. Melucci 1988.

89. Rupp and Taylor 1987; Taylor 1989; Lofland 1996; Whittier 1995; Polletta 2002.

90. Jasper 1998.

91. In the early twentieth century, the international women's movement created a culture that encouraged participants to demonstrate their love for each other, which held the movement together while the world went to war. See Taylor and Rupp 2002.

92. Jasper 1997; Wood 2001; Gould 2009.

93. Rupp and Taylor 1999; Stockdill 2001.

94. The term comes from Hochschild 1979, 1983. For its use in social movements, see Goodwin and Pfaff 2001.

95. See also Britt and Heise 2000; Gould 2009.

96. Summers-Effler 2002.

97. Britt and Heise 2000; Gould 2009; Taylor and Leitz 2010.

98. Britt and Heise 2000; Schrock, Holden, and Reid 2004; Reger 2004; Gould 2009.

99. Similarly, in research on women who had committed infanticide, Taylor and Leitz 2010 found that activism in the postpartum depression movement transformed these women's emotions of guilt into emotions of resistance.

100. Whittier 2001, 2009. Gould 2009. See also Goodwin and Pfaff 2001; Groves 2001.

101. For information on Take Back the Night, see Whittier 1995. On the Clothesline Project, see Ostrowski 1994; Foley 1995; Whittier 2001. On the AIDS Quilt, see Lewis and Fraser 1996; Krouse 1994.

102. Groves 2001; Whittier 2001.

103. Bayard de Volvo 2006.

104. I do not have the space to go into detail on the gendered aspects of this strategy, but media coverage of the military peace movement and the movement's interactions with others reinforced who was allowed to demonstrate which emotions in very gendered ways. See Lemon and Leitz 2011.

105. Bernstein 1997.

1. JOINING THE MILITARY PEACE MOVEMENT

1. McAdam 1986.

2. The modern VFP is unrelated to a group of the same name that formed in 1966 to protest American involvement in Vietnam. VVAW should not be mistaken for the similarly named organization, Vietnam Veterans Against the War Anti-Imperialist, that is affiliated with the Revolutionary Communist Party. In the years following the Vietnam War, VVAW focused mostly on issues related to posttraumatic stress disorder and chemical warfare, including Agent Orange, with five-year reunions and twice-yearly newsletters continuing to address issues of American foreign policy. Members of VFP addressed similar issues while also organizing protests of other aspects of America's foreign policy, such as support for the School of the Americas. Many of the members of VVAW who protest today do so as members of VFP.

3. Such returns often require significant energy and care work, particularly if the servicemember is injured or suffers from psychological trauma.

4. While Massey is a decorated combat veteran of the Iraq War who served in the Marines for more than ten years and was honorably discharged, questions remain about his credibility. In 2006 an embedded journalist for the *Saint Louis Post-Dispatch* claimed that Massey had exaggerated or made up claims of witnessing Marines shooting civilians. The writer said that Massey's stories often changed and were incongruent with that of other Marines' and the journalist's own experiences. Massey disputes Harris's ability, however, to counter his claims since Harris was embedded with a different company than the one to which Massey was assigned.

5. This event was meant to recall Vietnam Veterans Against the War's Winter Soldier Investigation in early 1971, which critiqued military policy for creating war crimes such as the Mai Lai Massacre. IVAW's event also provided personal testimonies, primarily by servicemembers who had fought in these wars, to demonstrate why they were opposed to the war in Iraq.

6. See also Abrams 2007.

7. See Navarro 2001; Athanasiou 2005.

8. One bus route went through northern states, stopping in locations such as Madison, Chicago, Detroit, and Albany. The southern tour stopped in various places in Texas, Alabama, and Georgia. The third bus drove through central states such as Indiana, Ohio, and Pennsylvania.

9. For information on those who did, see Nepstad 2008.

10. American Civil Liberties Union 2007.

11. See Booth et al. 2000; Hosek et al. 2002; Harrell et al. 2004.

12. This is merely a summary of conscientious objection in the U.S. military. More information can be found in branch-specific codes: Air Force Instruction 36-3204; Army Regulation 600-43; Coast Guard Commandant Instruction 1900.8; Marine Corps Order 1306.16E; Navy Military Personnel Manual 1900-020.

13. This is a common practice for military families. The stress of deployments and the lack of physical support from deployed servicemembers mean that military spouses and families must rely on others more frequently. For some military families, this support is best achieved by moving back home with parents.

14. See Moskos and Chambers, eds., 1993.

15. Outside the United States, selective objection has typically resulted in harsh punishment. Israeli soldiers who refused to fight in the second intifada were jailed at very high rates. See Dloomy 2005.

16. See Greene 1989; Lembke 1998.

17. This protest resembled VVAW's Operation Rapid American Withdrawal, which simulated Vietnam War combat conditions for four days in late summer between Morristown, New Jersey, and Valley Forge, Pennsylvania. Both actions were attempts to bring the war home to the American public. For more information on this tactic, see Nicosia 2001.

18. Carlos Arredondo was not criminally charged for setting this fire. The incident and the subsequent formal apology by Arredondo made national news.

19. Ender and Hermsen 1996.

20. See Whittier 2001.

21. Klawiter 1999, 2008.

22. See McAdam 1989; Wiltfang and McAdam 1991.

2. INSIDER–OUTSIDERS

1. Blake spoke before the VA automatically extended health care benefits to Iraq and Afghanistan veterans for five years after their service for issues servicemembers claimed were service related.

2. Servicemembers who spent a year or more in Iraq were allowed a leave of about two weeks during their time in-country.

3. In 2009 and 2010, suicide rates outpaced in-theater casualty rates for military members. The military, particularly the Army, had record-high rates of suicide during the Iraq War, and the suicide rate for veterans, who were prescreened for mental illness prior to joining, was recently suggested to be as high as double the civilian rate among males (see Kaplan et al. 2007) and triple that rate among females (see Farland, Kaplan, and Huguet 2010). For additional information on suicide among veterans and the difficulty of accessing accurate statistics, see Ramchand et al. 2011.

4. Franke 2001; Holsti 1999, 2001, 2004; Kruger and Pedraza 2011.

5. Klandermans 1997; Lofland 1996; Hedstrom 1994.

6. Snow and McAdam 2000.

7. See O'Brien 2004, 2005.

8. Henderson 1985; Moskos 1989; Vaughan and Schum 2001; Rosen, Knudson, and Fancher 2002; King 2006; Siebold 2007.

9. Soldiers could not be sent to Vietnam until they were eighteen.

10. The issue of the war in Afghanistan greatly divided the military peace movement at its onset. With increased rhetoric on troop numbers in Afghanistan coming from presidential candidate Barack Obama, who was described by many in the movement as an antiwar candidate, all three of these organizations began to address this issue in 2008. VFP added opposition to the war in Afghanistan to its platform at its 2008 annual convention; IVAW voted to include it in January 2009; and MFSO

made this decision in early 2010. Several members left each organization with this decision.

11. Mansbridge and Morris 2001.

12. See Moser 1996.

13. See Coy, Maney, and Woehrle 2003; Woehrle, Coy, and Maney 2008.

14. Mansbridge and Morris 2011.

15. PTSD is one specific mental issue that may develop from combat stress. Some of these experiences were likely not traditional psychological disorders but stemmed from traumatic brain injuries. See Vaishnavi, Rao, and Fann 2009.

16. A few companies, such as Sears, Verizon, and Wachovia, and some states do offer what is called military differential pay. This may vary from the full difference in pay and may last only for a limited time.

17. Stop-loss was developed after Vietnam as a way to ensure that the AVF could sustain future military engagements. Stop-loss is provided for in Title 10 of U.S. Code Section 12305(a), which reads, "The President may suspend any provision of law relating to promotion, retirement, or separation applicable to any member of the armed forces who the President determines is essential to the national security of the United States."

18. In 2008 the VA began offering veterans of Iraq and Afghanistan five years of health care without a service-connected disability through VHA Directive 2008-054.

19. McAdam 1986.

20. Collins 2008.

21. VFP verifies veterans' service by requiring a military generated Report of Separation (in military parlance, a DD-214). Like VFP, IVAW verifies its members' military status; potential members are required to submit either the DD-214, a copy of their military ID card, or a handful of other types of military paperwork.

22. Some military peace movement activists are pacifist, however, and a small number do consider themselves opposed to the military, not just militarism.

23. Melucci 1989; Klandermans 1992; Hunt, Benford, and Snow 1994; Whittier 1995.

24. Klawiter 2008.

25. See Taylor 1989; Taylor and Whittier 1992, 1995; Kriesi et al. 1992.

26. Gamson 1991, 40.

3. BUILDING A FAMILY AND TRANSFORMING ACTIVISTS' EMOTIONS

1. Activists thought the phrase was, "Every bomb dropped in Vietnam explodes over Harlem," but that is a combination of the phrase from chapter 31, "Beyond Vietnam," in King's autobiography and words from his speech "Beyond Vietnam," which he delivered April 4, 1967, at Riverside Church in New York City.

2. Some military peace movement activists had brought food in the immediate aftermath of Hurricane Katrina to this church and community.

3. In a written eulogy for VFP president David Cline, titled "A Death in the

Family," MFSO cofounders Nancy Lessin and Charlie Richardson described how David wrote this cadence verse specifically for MFSO before the large national march in Fayetteville, North Carolina, during the 2004 anniversary of the Iraq War.

4. This initiative would thrive in future connections with IVAW. The Warrior Writers project encourages IVAW members to write poems, short stories, and other pieces about their experiences in Iraq and their reintegration into civilian life. Another artistic outlet is Combat Paper, which takes IVAW members' uniforms and transforms them into hand-made paper.

5. See Goodwin and Pfaff 2001.

6. Taylor and Leitz 2010.

7. Faris 1981, 1984; Kilburn and Klerman 1999; Segal and Segal 2004.

8. VVAW was established before VFP, but it was not very active between Vietnam and the Iraq War, and most activists that affiliated with VVAW in the peace movement were also active in VFP.

9. That is also the title of Cindy Sheehan's first book, published in 2006.

10. See Lemon and Leitz 2011.

11. The percentage of women in the U.S. military rose from just over 1 percent in the 1950s to 15 percent in the 2000s. See Segal and Segal 2004.

12. Taylor and Leitz 2010.

13. Iraq Veterans Against the War with Glantz 2008, 217.

14. See Rising-Moore and Oberg 2004.

15. Jasper 1998.

16. See also Gould 2009.

17. Rupp and Taylor 1987; Taylor 1989; Lofland 1996; Whittier 1995; Polletta 2002.

18. See also Summers-Efler 2002.

19. See also Wood 2001; Gould 2009.

20. See reviews of this literature in Earl 2004; Polletta and Jasper 2001.

4. MANAGING AND DEPLOYING THE INSIDER–OUTSIDER IDENTITY

1. Niederer is featured in Michael Moore's documentary *Fahrenheit 9/11*. Lipford received media notoriety after being arrested at a 2004 Bush/Cheney campaign rally for questioning the war in which her son had been killed.

2. The exhibit continued to tour though at least 2013, but after 2007 it was split up by state in order to manage its size. Although originally exclusive to the war in Iraq, many displays later included casualties in Afghanistan, as well.

3. Versions of this display were regularly shown in American cities as an anti–Iraq War protest and frequently featured members of Gold Star family organizations who spoke about the deaths of their family members.

4. A filmmaker appeared to be using the boot display as a backdrop to a documentary about Perle.

5. Bernstein 1997.

6. Bernstein 1997, 2008.

7. See Leitz 2011.

8. Leitz 2011.

9. See Leitz 2011.

10. Sometimes activists substituted "sisters" for "brothers" in this line.

11. Reilly 2007.

12. Leitz 2011, 240.

13. Leitz 2011, 240.

14. See Meyer and Corrigall-Brown 2005; Ravi 2005.

15. Leitz 2011.

16. Leitz 2011; Coy, Woehrle, and Maney 2008.

17. Teachervet 2008.

18. Teachervet 2006.

19. Leitz 2011, 244.

20. Retired Marine major general Smedley Butler died the most highly decorated American Marine after serving in numerous wars. He is famous in the peace movement for writing *War Is a Racket,* which describes the problems of corporate involvement in the military and the growth of the military-industrial complex.

21. In 2009, however, when this same group was again asked to march behind the main parade, it did so with about fifty individuals carrying white VFP flags and no American flags.

22. GSFP was largely defunct before this time, however.

23. VFP already did, and since Cindy Sheehan was the exclusive decision maker for most things in GSFP, that organization quickly moved to support war resisters.

24. The Oscar- and Emmy-nominated documentary short *Poster Girl* is about Robynn Murray's search for healing as she moved from *Army Magazine* cover girl to drug-abusing veteran with posttraumatic stress disorder.

25. IVAW and VFP were particularly outspoken after 2006 about their support of military members who claimed to have suffered from rape or sexual harassment in the military.

26. By and large, before 2013 only VFP had positions on conflicts other than the wars in Iraq and Afghanistan, but the other organizations worried about their affiliation with political tactics that protested a variety of wars internationally.

27. Leitz 2011, 250.

28. For more, see Leitz 2011.

29. See Taylor and Whittier 1992; Bernstein 1997, 2008; Dugan 2008; Einwohner 2008; Neuhouser 2008; Schroer 2008; Bernstein and Olsen 2009; Whittier 2009, 2012; Leitz 2011.

30. Bernstein 1997.

31. See Leitz 2011; Lemon and Leitz 2011.

32. Ryan, Anastario, and Jeffries 2005.

33. See Gamson 2012.

34. Meyer and Gamson 1995.

35. For more on identity deployment for education and critique, see Bernstein 1997, 2008.

36. Heaney and Rojas 2006; Leitz 2011.

37. See Bernstein 1997; Bernstein and Olsen 2009.

38. Coy et al. 2008.

39. Stitka 2005; Denton 2004; Falcous and Silk 2005; Kinnick 2004; Coy, Maney, and Woehrle 2003; Dreier and Flacks 2003; Jensen 2003; Pareniti 2003; Haque 2003; Leitz 2011.

40. See Woehrle, Coy, and Maney 2008.

41. Coy et al. 2008; Coles 1999; Leitz 2011.

42. Leitz 2011.

43. See Kretschmer 2009.

5. USING GRIEF TO CONNECT WITH BYSTANDERS

1. Zoroya 2005; Coddington, Gainer, and Teeuwen 2005; Chawkins 2006; Almedia and Crowley 2008.

2. See Buffton 2005.

3. Jasper 1997, 96.

4. Ennis 1987; Taylor and Van Dyke 2004.

5. See *Arlington West: The Film* by Peter and Sally Dudar and *A Wake on the Pier: Responses to an Iraq War Memorial* by sociologist Thomas Scheff.

6. For more on the importance of modularity of tactics, see Tarrow 1993, 1998.

7. See Soule 1997, 2004; Meyer and Whittier 1994.

8. Leitz 2011; Woehrle et al 2008.

9. On anger's prominence in tactics, see Goodwin, Jasper, and Polletta 2001. For information on anger as potentially alienating audiences, see Kemper 2001.

10. Bystanders and those memorializing loved ones filled eight comment books from 2003 to 2009.

11. See Woehrle et al. 2008.

12. Leitz 2011; Bernstein and Olsen 2009.

13. Standing in social movements is described in Meyer and Gamson 1995.

14. For more on negotiation within identity construction, see Taylor and Whittier 1992.

15. Taylor and Van Dyke 2004; Taylor, Rupp, and Gamson 2004.

16. See Taylor 1996; Goodwin et al. 2001; Taylor and Rupp 2002; Reger 2004.

17. See Reisberg and Hertel, eds., 2003; Uttl, Ohta, and Siegenthaler 2006; McGaugh 2006.

18. See Ahmed 2004; Collins 2001; Kane 2001.

19. Whittier 2001.

20. On the link between emotions and irrationality, see Park 1972. On criticism of anger, see Lutz 1986.

21. See Gould 2009, 253.

22. For information on tactics' role in building collective identity, see Taylor and Van Dyke 2004; Taylor, Rupp, and Gamson 2004.

CONCLUSION

1. Occupy Oakland was an offshoot of the Occupy Wall Street movement, which sought the reduction of financial interests in politics and brought attention to the growing economic inequality in the United States. On October 25, 2011, Scott Olsen was critically injured by Oakland police when he was hit in the head with a tear gas canister. He spent several weeks in the hospital and more in physical therapy regaining his speech and other abilities. His combined injury and veteran status led to a significant amount of media attention and led to the Occupy chant, "We are Scott Olsen."

2. Toribio 2012.

3. Department of Defense 2010.

4. See *Veterans for Common Sense v. Erick K. Shinseki* (originally filed in 2007). Despite agreement from judges that veterans were not receiving promised care and a previous judgment against the Veterans Administration by the same court, the Ninth Circuit Court ruled against veteran advocacy groups in 2012. The Supreme Court refused to hear the case in 2013.

5. See also Ader et al. 2012.

6. Pew Social and Demographic Trends 2011a.

7. McCarthy and Zald 1977.

8. Although Iraq and Afghanistan veterans survived injury more often, a large percentage came home seriously injured or with head and psychological trauma from combat that would have killed previous generations.

9. See Polling Report 2012.

10. Pew Social and Demographic Trends 2011a.

11. See Bachman, Sigelman, and Diamond 1987; Ender 2009.

12. See Jones 2008; Barkley 2012; Weil 2010.

13. Stone and Bello 2009 report that the Army had called up about 27,000 by April 2009, and the DoD documents I examined, which had IRR numbers for deployed servicemembers, indicated that a thousand more were called up by 2012. These numbers are 1.5 times those used in the Gulf War and smaller than the 1961 Berlin crisis mobilization. See Cragg 2008 for numbers from Vietnam, the Gulf War, and Berlin.

14. Private military firms provide the following three types of work done previously by state militaries: (1) troops perform tactical operations; (2) experts offer advice and training; and (3) support personnel offer basic services, logistics, intelligence, and engineering. These workers are what some call contractors and others call mercenaries. For more, see Singer 2007; McCoy 2010, 2012.

15. This may explain the decline of the peace movement as Democrats achieved electoral success in 2006 and 2008, see Heaney and Rojas 2011.

16. See Teigen 2007; Rohall, Ender, and Matthews 2006; Ender 2009; Kruger and Pedraza 2012.

17. Rohall, Ender, and Matthews 2006; Bachman et al. 2000.

18. See Ender and Gibson 2005.

19. Data is from my survey of military peace movement participants, as well as

Pew Social and Demographic Trends 2011a; Blue Star Families Department of Research and Policy 2012.

20. Pew Social and Demographic Trends 2011a.

21. See Stryker, Owens, and White, eds., 2000; Goodwin, Jasper, and Polletta, eds., 2001.

22. See Stryker, Owens, and White, eds., 2000; Polletta and Jasper 2001; Hunt and Benford 2004.

23. For more on identity consolidation, see Snow and McAdam 2000.

24. Leach and Pedersen, 2006; van Zomeren et al. 2004; Rodgers 2010; Frye 1983; Hercus 1999; Gould 2009; Goodwin, Jasper, and Polletta 2000.

25. Stürmer and Simon 2009.

26. Stürmer and Simon 2009.

27. Gamson 1992, 32.

28. Schrock et al. 2004; Summers-Effler 2002.

29. Summers-Effler 2002.

30. Reger 2004.

31. Goodwin et al. 2004.

32. Morgen 2002; Gould 2009.

33. See also Rodgers 2010.

34. See also Adams 2003; Gould 2009.

35. For an exception, see Bernstein and Olsen 2009.

36. See also Ryan, Anastario, and Jeffries 2005.

37. Joshua Gamson demonstrates how this works regarding sexuality issues on modern television talk shows. His findings about the preference of experience versus scientific or other forms of expertise have widespread implications. See Gamson 1998.

38. See Leitz 2011.

39. Kretschmer 2009; Hipsher 2007; Crawford and Olson 2001.

40. Goodwin and Pfaff 2001; Groves 2001; Whittier 2001, 2009; Gould 2009.

41. Goodwin et al. 2004.

42. Thomas, McGarty, and Mavor 2009.

43. See Gould 2009.

44. See also Stürmer and Simon 2009.

45. Gould 2009 eloquently examines the debate over emotion strategies and tactics that elicit anger in the AIDS movement.

46. For complications in using media coverage of protest events, see Oliver and Myers 1999; Oliver and Maney 2000; Maney and Oliver 2001.

47. Taylor and Whittier 1992; Taylor and Raeburn 1995; Einwohner 2006; Simi and Futrell 2009; Whittier 2009, 2012.

48. The commonality of protest has been referred to as a social movement society (see Tarrow 1994; Meyer and Tarrow 1998), but a refutation of the idea that more people are participating in protest today than before is offered in Caren, Ghoshal, and Ribas 2011.

49. See Taylor and VanDyke 2004. For examples of protest how-to materials, see Stevenson 2003; Norton 2007; Clark and Unterberger 2007.

50. Earl 2004.

51. Klawiter 2008.

52. See also Woehrle et al. 2008; Coy et al. 2008.

53. Over 10,000 military contractors remain employed by the United States in Iraq, mostly through the State Department and largely for work related to the embassy in Baghdad.

APPENDIX

1. Except where noted, polling numbers for this timeline come from Holsti 2011, which also provides a more in-depth timeline of the Iraq War.

2. The claims were later admitted to be unfounded, though new forms of al-Qaeda did emerge in the insurgent forces in Iraq after the 2003 invasion.

3. Like the claims of links to al-Qaeda, WMD claims were unfounded, and Powell later called this address a blot on his record. The search for WMDs officially ended unsuccessfully in January 2005.

4. Herein, "troops" refer to military servicemembers who were boots on the ground and does not include civilian contractor forces or additional personnel who served in support capacities at sea or in other countries.

5. Pew Research Center 2008.

6. Pew Research Center 2008.

7. De Pinto 2009.

8. Montopoli 2010.

9. Pew Social and Demographic Trends 2011b.

Bibliography

Adams, Jacqueline. 2003. "The Bitter End: Emotions at a Movement's Conclusion." *Sociological Inquiry* 73, no.1: 84–113.

Ader, Melissa, Robert Cuthbert Jr., Kendall Hoechst, Eliza H. Simon, Zachary Strassburger, and Michael Wishnie. 2012. *Casting Troops Aside: The United States Military's Illegal Personality Disorder Discharge Problem.* New Haven, Conn.: Yale Law School. http://www.law.yale.edu/documents/pdf/Clinics/VLSC_ CastingTroopsAside.pdf.

Ahmed, Sarah. 2004. *The Cultural Politics of Emotion.* New York: Routledge.

Almeida, Monica, and Stephan Crowley. 2008. "Arlington West." *New York Times,* March 4, 2008.

American Civil Liberties Union. 2007. *No Real Threat: The Pentagon's Secret Database on Peaceful Protest.* New York: ACLU National Office.

Aminzade, Ronald, and Doug McAdam. 2001. "Emotions and Contentious Politics." In *Silence and Voice in Contentious Politics,* ed. by Ronald R. Aminzade, Jack A. Goldstone, Doug McAdam, Elizabeth J. Perry, William H. Sewell Jr., Sidney Tarrow, Douglas McAdam, and Charles Tilly, 14–50. New York: Cambridge University Press.

Anderson, Terry H. 1992. "The GI Movement and the Response from the Brass." In *Give Peace a Chance: Exploring the Vietnam Anti-war Movement,* ed. by M. Small and W. D. Hoover, 93–115. Syracuse, N.Y.: Syracuse University Press.

Athanasiou, Athena. 2005. "Reflections on the Politics of Mourning: Feminist Ethics and Politics in the Age of Empire." *Historien* 5:40–57.

Bachman, Jerald G., Peter Freedman-Doan, David R. Segal, and Patrick M. O'Malley. 2000. "Distinctive Military Attitudes among U.S. Enlistees, 1976–1997: Self-Selection versus Socialization." *Armed Forces & Society* 26, no. 4: 561–85.

Bachman, Jerald G., Lee Sigelman, and Greg Diamond. 1987. "Self-Selection, Socialization, and Distinctive Military Values: Attitudes of High School Seniors." *Armed Forces & Society* 2, no. 13: 169–87.

Barkley, Summer. 2012. "A Family Deployed: The Jones Family Supports OEF." *Army Website News,* July 27. http://www.army.mil/article/84448.

Bayard de Volvo, Lorraine. 2006. "The Dynamics of Emotion and Activism: Grief, Gender, and Collective Identity in Revolutionary Nicaragua." *Mobilization* 11, no. 4: 461–74.

Beamish, Thomas D., Harvey Molotch, and Richard Flacks. 1995. "Who Supports the Troops? Vietnam, the Gulf War, and the Making of Collective Memory." *Social Problems* 42, no. 3: 344–60.

Belasco, Amy. 2011. *The Cost of Iraq, Afghanistan, and Other Global War on Terror Operations Since 9/11.* Washington, D.C.: Congressional Research Service. http://www.fas.org/sgp/crs/natsec/RL33110.pdf.

Benford, Robert D., and Scott A. Hunt. 1992. "Dramaturgy and Social Movements: The Social Construction and Communication of Power." *Sociological Inquiry* 62, no. 1: 36–55.

Bernstein, Mary. 1997. "Celebration and Suppression: The Strategic Uses of Identity by the Lesbian and Gay Movement." *American Journal of Sociology* 103, no. 3: 531–65.

———. 2008. "The Analytic Dimensions of Identity: A Political Identity Framework." In *Identity Work in Social Movement,* ed. by J. Reger, D. J. Myers, and R. L. Einwohner, 277–301. Minneapolis: University of Minnesota Press.

Bernstein, Mary, and Kristine A. Olsen. 2009. "Identity Deployment and Social Change: Understanding Identity as a Social Movement and Organizational Strategy." *Sociology Compass* 3, no. 6: 871–83.

Bilmes, Linda J. 2013. "The Financial Legacy of Iraq and Afghanistan: How Wartime Spending Decisions Will Constrain Future National Security Budgets." HKS Faculty Research Working Paper Series RWP13-006. https://research.hks.harvard.edu/publications/getFile.aspx?ID=923.

Blue Star Families Department of Research and Policy. 2012. "2012 Military Family Lifestyle Survey Report." Falls Church, Va.: Blue Star Families. http://bluestarfam.s3.amazonaws.com/42/65/a/1110/CompReport2012.pdf.

Booth, Bradford, William W. Falk, David R. Segal, and Mady Wechsler Segal. 2000. "The Impact of Military Presence in Local Labor Markets on the Employment of Women." *Gender & Society* 14, no. 2: 318–32.

Britt, Lory, and David Heise. 2000. "From Shame to Pride in Identity Politics." In *Self, Identity, and Social Movements,* ed. by Sheldon Stryker, Timothy J. Owens, and Robert W. White, 252–68. Minneapolis: University of Minnesota Press.

Buffton, Deborah. 2005. "Memorialization and the Selling of War." *Peace Review* 17, no. 1: 25–31.

Burawoy, Michael. 1998. "The Extended Case Method." *Sociological Theory* 16, no. 1: 4–33.

Burke, Carol. 2004. *Camp All-American, Hanoi Jane, and the High-and-Tight.* Boston: Beacon Press.

Caren, Neal, Raj Andrew Ghoshal, and Vanesa Ribas. 2011. "A Social Movement Generation: Cohort and Period Trends in Protest Attendance and Petition Signing." *American Sociological Review* 76, no. 1: 125–51.

Carroll, Joseph. 2004. "The Iraq–Vietnam Comparison." *Gallup,* June 15. http://www.gallup.com/poll/11998/iraqvietnam-comparison.aspx.

Chawkins, Steve. 2006. "Crosses Becoming Too Many for Group to Bear." *Los Angeles Times,* November 10.

Clark, Duncan, and Richie Unterberger. 2007. *The Rough Guide to Shopping with a Conscience.* New York: Rough Guides.

CNN Politics. 2005. "Kissinger Finds Parallels to Vietnam in Iraq: Former Diplomat Cites 'Divisions in the United States.'" *CNN Online*, August 15. http://www.cnn.com/2005/POLITICS/08/15/us.iraq/index.html.

Coddington, Ron, Danny Gainer, and Dave Teeuwen. 2005. *USA Today*, May 25. http://www.usatoday.com/news/graphics/arlington_west/flash.htm.

Coles, Roberta L. 1999. "Odd Folk and Ordinary People: Collective Identity Disparities between Peace Groups in the Persian Gulf Crisis." *Sociological Spectrum* 19, no. 3: 325–57.

Collins, Jane. 2008. *For Love of a Soldier*. Lanham, Md.: Rowman and Littlefield.

Cortwright, David. 1992. "GI Resistance during the Vietnam War." In *Give Peace a Chance: Exploring the Vietnam Anti-war Movement*, ed. by M. Small and W. D. Hoover, 116–28. Syracuse, N.Y.: Syracuse University Press.

———. 2005. *Soldiers in Revolt: GI Resistance during the Vietnam War*. New York: Haymarket Books.

Coy, Patrick G., Gregory M. Maney, and Lynne M. Woehrle. 2003. "Contesting Patriotism by the Post-9/11 Peace Movement in the United States." *Peace Review* 15, no. 3: 463–70.

Coy, Patrick G., Lynne M. Woehrle, and Gregory M. Maney. 2008. "Discursive Legacies: The U.S. Peace Movement and 'Support the Troops.'" *Social Problems* 55, no. 2: 161–89.

Cragg, Jennifer. 2008. "Colonel Debunks Individual Ready Reserve Mobilization Myths." *American Forces Press Service*, September 30. http://www.defense.gov/news/newsarticle.aspx?id=51343.

Crawford, Sue E. S., and Laura R. Olson. 2001. *Christian Clergy in American Politics*. Baltimore: Johns Hopkins University Press.

Defense Manpower Data Center. 2011. *Active Duty Military Personnel Strengths by Regional Area and By Country (309A)*. Washington, D.C.: Department of Defense. http://siadapp.dmdc.osd.mil/personnel/MILITARY/history/hst1103.pdf.

Denton, Robert E., Jr. 2004. "Language, Symbols, and Media." *Society* 42, no. 1: 12–18.

Department of Defense. 2010. *Report on the Impact of Deployment of Members of the Armed Forces on Their Dependent Children*. Washington, D.C.: U.S. Department of Defense. http://www.militaryonesource.mil/12038/MOS/Reports/Report_to_Congress_on_Impact_of_Deployment_on_Military_Children.pdf.

———. 2013. *Contractor Support of U.S. Operations in the USCENTCOM Area of Responsibility to Include Iraq and Afghanistan*. Washington, D.C.: U.S. Department of Defense July. http://www.acq.osd.mil/log/PS/CENTCOM_reports.html.

De Pinto, Jennifer. 2009. "Public's Views of Afghanistan War Have Turned Sour." *CBS News*, October 5. http://www.cbsnews.com/8301-503544_162-5363777-503544.html.

Dloomy, Ariel. 2005. "The Israeli Refuseniks: 1982–2003." *Israel Affairs* 11, no. 4: 695–716.

Dowd, Maureen. 2005. "Why No Tea and Sympathy?" *New York Times*, August 10. http://www.nytimes.com/2005/08/10/opinion/10dowd.html.

Dreier, Peter, and Dick Flacks. 2003. "Patriotism and Progressivism." *Peace Review* 15, no. 4: 397–404.

Dugan, Kimberly B. 2008. "Just Like You: The Dimensions of Identity Presentations in an Antigay Contested Context." In *Identity Work in Social Movement*, ed. by J. Reger, D. J. Myers, and R. L. Einwohner, 21–46. Minneapolis: University of Minnesota Press.

Earl, Jennifer. 2004. "Cultural Consequences of Social Movements." In *The Blackwell Companion to Social Movements*, ed. by D. A. Snow, S. A. Soule, and H. Kriesi, 508–30. Oxford: Blackwell Publishers.

Einwohner, Rachel L. 2002. "Motivational Framing and Efficacy Maintenance: Animal Rights Activists' Use of Four Fortifying Strategies." *Sociological Quarterly* 43, no. 4: 509–26.

———. 2006. "Identity Work and Collective Action in a Repressive Context: Jewish Resistance on the 'Aryan Side' of the Warsaw Ghetto." *Social Problems* 53, no. 1: 38–56.

———. 2008. "Passing as Strategic Identity Work in the Warsaw Ghetto Uprising." In *Identity Work in Social Movements*, ed. by J. Reger, D. J. Myers, and R. L. Einwohner, 121–40. Minneapolis: University of Minnesota Press.

Ender, Morten G. 2009. *American Soldiers in Iraq: McSoldiers or Innovative Professionals?* New York: Routledge.

Ender, Morten G., and Joan M. Hermsen. 1996. "Working with the Bereaved: U.S. Army Experiences with Nontraditional Families." *Death Studies* 20, no. 6: 557–75.

Ennis, James G. 1987. "Fields of Action: Structure in Movements' Tactical Repertoires." *Sociological Forum* 2, no. 3: 520–33.

Falcous, Mark, and Michael Silk. 2006. "Global Regimes, Local Agendas: Sport, Resistance, and the Mediation of Dissent." *International Review for the Sociology of Sport* 41, no. 3/4: 317–38.

Feaver, Peter D. 1999. "Civil–Military Relations." *Annual Review of Political Science* 2:211–41.

Feaver, Peter D., and Richard H. Kohn. 2000. "The Gap: Soldiers, Civilians, and Their Mutual Misunderstanding." *National Interest* 61:29–37.

———. eds. 2001. *Soldiers and Civilians: The Gap between the Military and American Society and What It Means for National Security.* Cambridge, Mass.: MIT Press.

Feldmann, Linda. 2005. "Did the Cindy Sheehan Vigil Succeed?" *Christian Science Monitor,* August 29. http://www.csmonitor.com/2005/0829/p01s03-uspo.html.

Flam, Helena, and Debra King, eds. 2005. *Emotions and Social Movements.* New York: Routledge.

Fletcher, Michael A. 2007. "Bush Compares Iraq to Vietnam: He Says Pullout Would Be Disastrous." *Washington Post,* August 23.

Foley, Sally Lee. 1995. "First National Clothesline Project Display." *Women Lawyers Journal* 81, no. 3: 18–19.

FOX News Watch. 2005. "Media Coverage of Cindy Sheehan's Vigil." *FOX News,* August 19. http://www.foxnews.com/story/0,2933,166231,00.html.

Franke, Volker C. 2001. "Generation X and the Military: A Comparison of Attitudes and Values between West Point Cadets and College Students." *Journal of Political and Military Sociology* 20, no. 19: 92–119.

Fraser, Skye. 1996. "Reclaiming Our Power, Using Our Anger: Working in the Field of Sexual Violence." In *Women and Violence: Working for Change,* ed. by R. Thorpe and J. Irwin, 162–72. Sydney, Australia: Hale and Iremonger.

Frye, Marilyn. 1983. "A Note on Anger." In *The Politics of Reality: Essays in Feminist Theory.* Trumansburg, N.Y.: The Crossing Press.

Gamson, William A. 1991. "Commitment and Agency in Social Movements." *Sociological Forum* 6, no. 1: 27–50.

———. Gamson, William A. 1992. *Talking Politics.* New York: Cambridge University Press.

———. 2012. "Reflections Ten Years Later." *Mobilizing Ideas,* July 2. http://mobilizingideas.wordpress.com/2012/07/02/reflections-ten-years-later.

Gamson, Joshua. 1998. *Freaks Talk Back: Tabloid Talk Shows and Sexual Nonconformity.* Chicago: University of Chicago Press.

Garrett, Sheryl, and Sue Hoppin. 1998. *A Family's Guide to the Military for Dummies.* Hoboken, N.J.: For Dummies.

Goodwin, Jeff, James Jasper, and Francesca Polletta. 2000. "The Return of the Repressed: The Fall and Rise of Emotions in Social Movement Theory." *Mobilization* 5, no. 1: 65–83.

———. eds. 2001. *Passionate Politics: Emotions and Social Movements.* Chicago: University of Chicago Press.

———. 2004. "Emotional Dimensions of Social Movements." In *The Blackwell Companion to Social Movements,* ed. by David A. Snow, Sarah A. Soule, and Hanspeter Kriesi, 413–32. Oxford: Blackwell Publishers.

Goodwin, Jeff, and Stephan Pfaff. 2001. "Emotion Work in High-Risk Social Movements: Managing Fear in the U.S. and East German Civil Rights Movements." In *Passionate Politics,* ed. by Jeff Goodwin, James M. Jasper, and Francesca Polletta, 282–302. Chicago: University of Chicago Press.

Gould, Deborah B. 2001. "Rock the Boat, Don't Rock the Boat, Baby: Ambivalence and the Emergence of Militant AIDS Activism." In *Passionate Politics: Emotions and Social Movements,* ed. by Jeff Goodwin, James Jasper, and Francesca Polletta, 135–57. Chicago: University of Chicago Press.

———. 2009. *Moving Politics: Emotion and ACT UP's Fight against AIDS.* Chicago: University of Chicago Press.

Greene, Bob. 1989. *Homecoming: When Soldiers Returned from Vietnam.* New York: Putnam.

Groves, Julian McAllister. 2001. "Animal Rights and the Politics of Emotion: Folk Constructions of Emotion in the Animal Rights Movement." In *Passionate Politics: Emotions and Social Movements,* ed. by Jeff Goodwin, James Jasper, and Francesca Polletta, 212–29. Chicago: University of Chicago Press.

Gurr, Ted. 1970. *Why Men Rebel.* Princeton, N.J.: Princeton University Press.

Haque, M. Shamsul. 2003. "Patriotism versus Imperialism." *Peace Review* 15, no. 3: 451–56.

Harrell, Margaret C., Nelson Lim, Laura Werber Castaneda, and Daniela Golinelli. 2004. *Working around the Military: Challenges to Military Spouse Employment and Education*. Santa Monica, Calif.: RAND.

Heaney, Michael T., and Fabio Rojas. 2006. "The Place of Framing: Multiple Audiences and Antiwar Protests near Fort Bragg." *Qualitative Sociology* 29, no. 4: 485–505.

———. 2011. "The Partisan Dynamics of Contention: Demobilization of the Antiwar Movement in the United States, 2007–2009." *Mobilization* 16, no. 1: 45–64.

Hedstrom, Peter. 1994. "Contagious Collectivities: On the Spatial Diffusion of Swedish Trade Unions, 1890–1940." *American Journal of Sociology* 99, no. 5: 1157–79.

Henderson, William Darryl. 1985. *Cohesion: The Human Element*. Washington, D.C.: National Defense University Press.

Hercus, Cheryl. 1999. "Identity, Emotion, Feminist Collective Action." *Gender & Society* 13, no. 1: 34–55.

Hipsher, Patricia L. 2007. "Heretical Social Movement Organizations and Their Framing Strategies." *Sociological Inquiry* 77, no. 2: 241–63.

Hochschild, Arlie. 1979. "Emotion Work, Feeling Rules, and Social Structure." *American Journal of Sociology* 85, no. 3: 551–75.

———. 1983. *The Managed Heart: Commercialization of Human Feeling*. Berkeley: University of California Press.

Holsti, Ole R. 1999. "A Widening Gap between the U.S. Military and Civilian Society? Some Evidence, 1976–1996." *International Security* 23, no. 3: 5–42.

———. 2001. "Of Chasms and Convergences: Attitudes and Beliefs of Civilians and Military Elites at the Start of a New Millennium." In *Soldiers and Civilians: The Civil–Military Gap and American National Security*, ed. by Peter D. Feaver and Richard H. Kohn, 15–100. Cambridge, Mass.: MIT Press.

———. 2004. "Identity of the U.S. Military: Comments on 'An N of 1.'" *Perspectives on Politics* 2, no. 3: 557–60.

Hosek, James, and Paco Martorell. 2009. *How Have Deployments during the War on Terrorism Affected Reenlistment?* Santa Monica, Calif.: RAND. http://www.rand.org/pubs/monographs/MG873.

Hosek, James, Beth Asch, C. Christine Fair, Craig Martin, and Michael Mattock. 2002. *Married to the Military: The Employment and Earnings of Military Wives Compared with Those of Civilian Wives*. Santa Monica, Calif.: RAND.

Houppert, Karen. 2005. *Home Fires Burning: Married to the Military for Better or Worse*. New York: Ballantine Books.

Hunt, Andrew E. 1999. *The Turning: A History of Vietnam Veterans Against the War*. New York: New York University Press.

Hunt, Scott A., and Robert D. Benford. 2004. "Collective Identity, Solidarity, and Commitment." In *The Blackwell Companion to Social Movements*, ed. by David A. Snow, Sarah A. Soule, and Hanspeter Kriesi, 433–57. Oxford: Blackwell Publishers.

Hunt, Scott A., Robert D. Benford, David A. Snow. 1994. "Identity Fields: Framing Processes and the Social Construction of Movement Identities." In *New Social*

Movements: From Ideology to Identity, ed. by Laraña, E. H. Johnston, and J. R. Gusfield, 185–208. Philadelphia: Temple University Press.

Huntington, Samuel P. 1957. *The Soldier and the State: The Theory and Politics of Civil–Military Relations.* New York: Vintage Books.

Iraq Veterans Against the War, with Aaron Glantz. 2008. *Winter Soldier Iraq and Afghanistan: Eyewitness Accounts of the Occupations.* New York: Haymarket Books.

Jasper, Jim. 1997. *The Art of Moral Protest: Culture, Biography, and Creativity in Social Movements.* Chicago: University of Chicago Press.

———. 1998. "The Emotions of Protest: Affective and Reactive Emotions in and around Social Movements." *Sociological Forum* 13, no. 3: 394–424.

Jennings, M. Kent, and Gregory B. Markus. 1977. "The Effect of Military Service on Political Attitudes: A Panel Study." *American Political Science Review* 71, no. 1: 131–47.

Jensen, Robert. 2003. "Patriotism's a Bad Idea at a Dangerous Time." *Peace Review* 15, no. 4: 389–96.

Jones, Shawn. 2008. "Airman Earns Purple Heart on Twelfth Deployment." *U.S. Air Forces Central Public Affairs.* http://www.acc.af.mil/news/story .asp?id=123093622.

Jurkowitz, Mark. 2008. "Why News of Iraq Dropped." *Pew Research Center's Project for Excellence in Journalism,* March 26. http://www.journalism.org/ commentary_backgrounder/why_news_iraq_dropped.

Kaplan, Mark S., Nathalie Huguet, Bentson H. McFarland, and J. Newsom. 2007. "Suicide among Male Veterans: A Prospective Population-Based Study." *Journal of Epidemiology and Community Health* 61, no. 7: 619–24.

Kelly, Caroline, and Sara Breinlinger. 1996. *The Social Psychology of Collective Action: Identity, Injustice, and Gender.* Philadelphia: Taylor and Francis.

Kemper, Theodore. 2001. "A Structural Approach to Social Movement Emotions." In *Passionate Politics. Emotions and Social Movements,* ed. by Jeff Goodwin, James M. Jasper, and Francesca Polletta, 58–73. Chicago: University of Chicago Press.

Kiel, John Loran, Jr. 2007. "When Soldiers Speak Out: A Survey of Provisions Limiting Freedom of Speech in the Military." *Parameters: Army War College Quarterly* 37, no. 3: 69–82.

Kilshaw, Susie. 2004. "Friendly Fire: The Construction of Gulf War Syndrome Narratives." *Anthropology and Medicine* 11, no. 2: 149–60.

King, A. 2006. "The Word of Command: Communication and Cohesion in the Military." *Armed Forces & Society* 32, no. 4: 493–512.

Kinnick, Katherine N. 2004. "Advertising Responses to Crisis." *Society* 42, no. 1: 32–36.

Klandermans, Bert. 1992. "The Social Construction of Protest and Multi-organizational Fields." In *Frontiers in Social Movement Theory,* ed. by Aldon Morris and Carol Mueller, 77–103. New Haven, Conn.: Yale University Press.

———. 1997. *The Social Psychology of Protest.* Oxford: Blackwell Publishers.

———. 2002. "How Group Identification Helps to Overcome the Dilemma of Collective Action." *American Behavioral Scientist* 45, no. 5: 887–900.

————. 2004. "The Demand and Supply of Participation: Social Psychological Correlates of Participation in Social Movements." In *The Blackwell Companion to Social Movements*, ed. by David A. Snow, Sarah A. Soule, and Hanspeter Kriesi, 360–79. Oxford: Blackwell Publishers.

Klawiter, Maren. 1999. "Racing for the Cure, Walking Women, and Toxic Touring: Mapping Cultures of Action within the Bay Area Terrain of Breast Cancer." *Social Problems* 46, no. 1: 104–26.

————. 2008. *The Biopolitics of Breast Cancer: Changing Cultures of Disease and Activism*. Minneapolis: University of Minnesota Press.

Kornhauser, William. 1959. *The Politics of Mass Society*. New York: Free Press.

Kretschmer, Kelsey. 2009. "Contested Loyalties: Dissident Identity Organizations, Institutions, and Social Movements." *Sociological Perspectives* 52, no. 4: 433–54.

Kriesi, Hanspeter, Ruud Koopmans, Jan Willem Duyvendak, and Marco G. Giugni, eds. 1992. *New Social Movements in Western Europe: A Comparative Analysis*. London: UCL Press.

Krouse, Mary Beth. 1994. "The AIDS Memorial Quilt as Cultural Resistance for Gay Communities." *Critical Sociology* 20, no. 3: 65–80.

Kruger, James S., and Francisco I. Pedraza. 2012. "Missing Voices: War Attitudes among Military Service-Connected Civilians." *Armed Forces & Society* 38, no. 3: 391–412.

Langton, Kenneth P. 1984. "The Influence of Military Service on Social Consciousness and Protest Behavior." *Comparative Political Studies* 16, no. 4: 479–504.

Lawston, Jodie. 2009. "Managing Organizational Emotions: Framing Feelings of Illegitimacy in the Radical Women's Prison Movement." *Sociological Focus* 42, no. 4: 350–72.

Leach, Colin Wayne, A. Iyer, and A. Pedersen. 2006. "Anger and Guilt about In-Group Advantage Explain the Willingness for Political Action." *Personality and Social Psychology Bulletin* 32, no. 9: 1232–45.

Lehr, Doreen Drewry. 1999. "Military Wives: Breaking the Silence." In *Gender Camouflage: Women and the U.S. Military*, ed. by Francine D'Amico and Laurie Weinstein, 117–31. New York: New York University Press.

Leitz, Lisa. 2011. "Oppositional Identities: The Military Peace Movement's Challenge to Pro–Iraq War Frames." *Social Problems* 58, no. 2: 235–56.

Lembcke, Jerry. *The Spitting Image: Myth, Memory, and the Legacy of Vietnam*. New York: New York University Press.

————. 2010. *Hanoi Jane: War, Sex, and Fantasies of Betrayal*. Boston: University of Massachusetts Press.

Lemon, Maya, and Lisa Leitz. 2011. "Media Portrayals of Women in the U.S. Peace Movement." Presentation at the Mid-South Sociological Association Annual Meeting.

Lerner, Barron H. 2006. *When Illness Goes Public: Celebrity Patients and How We Look at Medicine*. Baltimore: Johns Hopkins University Press.

Lewes, James. 2003. *Protest and Survive: Underground GI Newspapers during the Vietnam War*. Westport, Conn.: Praeger.

Lewis, Jacqueline, and Michael R. Fraser. 1996. "Patches of Grief and Rage: Visitor

Responses to the NAMES Project AIDS Memorial Quilt." *Qualitative Sociology* 19, no. 4: 433–51.

Livingston, Ian S., and Michael O'Hanlon. "Afghanistan Index." Brookings Institute, August 27. http://www.brookings.edu/about/programs/foreign-policy/afghanistan-index.

Lofland, John. 1996. *Social Movement Organizations: Guide to Research on Insurgent Realities.* New York: Aldine de Gruyter.

Lutz, Catherine. 1986. "Emotion, Thought, and Estrangement: Emotion as a Cultural Category." *Cultural Anthropology* 1, no. 3: 287–309.

Maney, Gregory M., and Pamela E. Oliver. 2001. "Finding Event Records: Timing, Searching, Sources." *Sociological Methods and Research* 30, no. 2: 131–69.

Maney, Gregory M., Lynne M. Woehrle, Patrick G. Coy. 2005. "Harnessing and Challenging Hegemony: The U.S. Peace Movement after 9/11." *Sociological Perspectives* 48, no. 3: 357–81.

Mansbridge, Jane, and Aldon Morris, eds. 2001. *Oppositional Consciousness: The Subjective Roots of Social Protest.* Chicago: University of Chicago Press.

Marullo, Sam, and Meyer, David S. 2004. "Antiwar and Peace Movements." In *The Blackwell Companion to Social Movements,* ed. by David A. Snow, Sarah A. Soule, and Hanspeter Kriesi, 641–65. Oxford: Blackwell Publishers.

McAdam, Doug. 1982. *Political Process and the Development of Black Insurgency, 1930–1970.* Chicago: University of Chicago Press.

———. 1986. "Recruitment to High-Risk Activism: The Case of Freedom Summer." *American Journal of Sociology* 92, no. 1: 64–90.

———. 1989. "The Biographical Consequences of Activism." *American Sociological Review* 54, no. 5: 744–60.

McAdam, Doug, and Yang Su. 2002. "The War at Home: Antiwar Protests and Congressional Voting, 1965–1973." *American Sociological Review* 67, no. 5: 696–721.

McCarthy, John D., and Mayer N. Zald. 1977. "Resource Mobilization and Social Movements: A Partial Theory." *American Journal of Sociology* 82, no. 6: 1212–41.

McCoy, Katerhine E. 2010. "Beyond Civil–Military Relations: Reflections on Civilian Control of a Private, Multinational Workforce." *Armed Forces & Society* 36, no. 4: 671–94.

———. 2012. "Organizational Frames for Professional Claims: Private Military Corporations and the Rise of the Military Paraprofessional." *Social Problem* 59, no. 3: 322–40.

McFarland, Bentson H., Mark S. Kaplan, and Nathalie Huguet. 2010. "Self-Inflicted Deaths among Women with U.S. Military Service: A Hidden Epidemic?" *Psychiatric Services* 61, no. 12: 1177.

Melucci, Alberto. 1988. "Getting Involved: Identity and Mobilization in Social Movements." *International Social Movements Research* 1:329–48.

———. 1989. *Nomads of the Present: Social Movements and Individual Needs in Contemporary Society.* Philadelphia: Temple University Press.

Meyer, David S., and Catherine Corrigall-Brown. 2005. "Coalitions and Political Context: U.S. Movements against Wars in Iraq." *Mobilization* 10, no. 3: 327–44.

Meyer, David S., and Joshua Gamson. 1995. "The Challenge of Cultural Elites: Celeb-rities and Social Movements." *Sociological Inquiry* 65, no. 2: 181–206.

Meyer, David S., and Nancy Whittier. 1994. "Social Movement Spillover." *Social Problems* 41, no. 2: 277–98.

Morgen, Sandra. 2002. *Into Our Own Hands: The Women's Health Movement in the United States, 1969–1990.* New Brunswick, N.J.: Rutgers University Press.

Montopoli, Brian. 2010. "Poll: Afghanistan Troop Increase Unpopular." *CBS News*, June 24. http://www.cbsnews.com/stories/2009/09/24/opinion/polls/main5337753.shtml?tag=contentMain;contentBody.

Moser, Richard R. 1996. *The New Winter Soldiers: GI and Veteran Dissent during the Vietnam Era.* New Brunswick, N.J.: Rutgers University Press.

Moskos, Charles C. 1989. *Soldiers and Sociology.* Alexandria, Va.: Army Research Institute.

Moskos, Charles C., and John Whiteclay Chambers II. 1993. *The New Conscientious Objection: From Sacred to Secular Resistance.* New York: Oxford University Press.

Navarro, Marysa. 2001. "The Personal Is Political: Las Madres de Plaza de Mayo." In *Power and Popular Protest: Latin American Social Movements*, rev. ed., ed. by Susan Eckstein, 241–58. Berkeley: University of California Press.

Nepstad, Sharon Erickson. 2008. *Religion and War Resistance in the Plowshares Move-ment.* New York: Cambridge University Press.

Nepstad, Sharon Erickson, and Christian Smith. 2001. "The Social Structure of Moral Outrage in Recruitment to the U.S. Central America Peace Movement." In *Passionate Politics: Emotions and Social Movements*, ed. by Jeff Goodwin, James M. Jasper, and Francesca Polletta, 158–74. Chicago: University of Chicago Press.

Neuhouser, Kevin. 2008. "I Am the Man and Woman in This House: Brazilian Jeito and the Strategic Framing of Motherhood in a Poor, Urban Community." In *Identity Work in Social Movement*, ed. by J. Reger, D. J. Myers, and R. L. Einwohner, 141–66. Minneapolis: University of Minnesota Press.

Nicosia, Gerald. 2001. *Home to War: A History of the Vietnam Veterans' Movement.* New York: Crown Publishers.

Norton, Michael. 2007. *365 Ways to Change the World: How to Make a Difference, One Day at a Time.* New York: Free Press.

Oliver, Pamela E., and Gregory M. Maney. 2000. "Political Cycles and Local News-paper Coverage of Protest Events: From Selection Bias to Triadic Interactions." *American Journal of Sociology* 106, no. 2: 463–505.

Oliver, Pamela E., and Daniel J. Myers. 1999. "How Events Enter the Public Sphere: Conflict, Location, and Sponsorship in Local Newspaper Coverage of Public Events." *American Journal of Sociology* 105, no. 1: 38–87.

Ostrowski, Constance J. 1994. "The Clothesline Project: Women's Stories of Gender-Related Violence." *Women and Language* 19, no. 1: 37–41.

Pareniti, Michael. 2003. "What Does It Mean to Love One's Country?" *Peace Review* 15, no. 4: 385–88.

Park, Robert. 1972. *The Crowd and the Public, and Other Essays.* Chicago: University of Chicago Press.

Perez-Pena, Richard. 2008. "The War Endures, but Where's the Media?" *New York Times,* March 24. http://www.nytimes.com/2008/03/24/business/media/24press.html.

Pew Research Center. 2008. *Public Attitudes toward the War in Iraq: 2003–2008.* Washington, D.C.: Pew Research Center. http://www.pewresearch.org/2008/03/19/public-attitudes-toward-the-war-in-iraq-20032008.

Pew Social and Demographic Trends. 2011a. *The Military-Civilian Gap: War and Sacrifice in the Post-9/11 Era.* Washington, D.C.: Pew Research Center. http://www.pewsocialtrends.org/files/2011/10/veterans-report.pdf.

———. 2011b. *Obama Job Approval Improves, GOP Contest Remains Fluid.* Washington, D.C.: Pew Research Center. http://www.people-press.org/files/legacy-pdf/11-17-11%20Politics%20Release.pdf.

Polletta, Francesca. 2002. *Freedom Is an Endless Meeting: Democracy in American Social Movements.* Chicago: University of Chicago Press.

Polletta, Francesca, and James M. Jasper. 2001. "Collective Identity and Social Movements." *Annual Review of Sociology* 27:283–305.

Polling Report. 2012. "Problems and Priorities." PollingReport.com. http://www.pollingreport.com/prioriti.htm.

Ramchand, Rajeev, Joie Acosta, Rachel M. Burns, Lisa H. Jaycox, and Christopher G. Pernin. 2011. *The War Within: Preventing Suicide in the U.S. Military.* Santa Monica, Calif.: RAND. http://www.rand.org/pubs/monographs/MG953.

Ravi, Narasimhan. 2005. "Looking beyond Flawed Journalism: How National Interests, Patriotism, and Cultural Values Shaped the Coverage of the Iraq War." *Harvard International Journal of Press/Politics* 10, no. 1: 45–62.

Reed-Danahay, D. 1997. *Auto/Ethnography.* New York: Berg.

Reger, Jo. 2004. "Organizational 'Emotion Work' through Consciousness-Raising: An Analysis of a Feminist Organization." *Qualitative Sociology* 27, no. 2: 205–22.

Reilly, Ward. 2007. "The Game of the Century: IVAW vs. the Neocons." Vietnam Veterans Against the War. http://www.vvaw.org/veteran/article/?id=799andhilite=.

Reisberg, Daniel, and Paula Hertel, eds. 2003. *Memory and Emotion.* New York: Oxford University Press.

Ricks, Thomas E. 1997. "The Widening Gap between the Military and Society." *Atlantic Monthly* 280, no. 1: 66–78.

Rising-Moore, Carl, and Becky Oberg. 2004. *Freedom Underground: Protesting the Iraq War in America.* New York: Chamberlain Bros.

Robnett, Belinda. 1997. *How Long? How Long? African American Women in the Struggle for Civil Rights.* New York: Oxford University Press.

Rohall, David E., Morten G. Ender, and Michael D. Matthews. 2006. "The Role of Military Affiliation, Gender, and Political Ideology in the Favoring of War in Afghanistan and Iraq." *Armed Forces & Society* 33, no. 1: 1–19.

Rodgers, Kathleen. 2010. "'Anger Is Why We're All Here': Mobilizing and Managing Emotions in a Professional Activist Organization." *Social Movement Studies* 9, no. 3: 273–91.

Rosen, Leora N., Kathryn H. Knudson, and Peggy Fancher. 2002. "Cohesion and the

Culture of Hypermasculinity in the U.S. Army Units." *Armed Forces & Society* 29, no. 3: 325–52.

Rupp, Leila J., and Verta Taylor. 1987. *Survival in the Doldrums: The American Women's Rights Movement, 1945 to the 1960s.* New York: Oxford University Press.

———. 1999. "Forging Feminist Identity in an International Movement: A Collective Identity Approach to Feminism." *Signs* 24, no. 2: 363–86.

Ryan, Charlotte, Michael Anastario, and Karen Jeffries. 2005. "Start Small, Build Big: Negotiating Opportunities in Media Markets." *Mobilization* 10, no. 1: 111–28.

Schrock, Douglas, Daphne Holden, and Lori Reid. 2004. "Creating Emotional Resonance: Interpersonal Emotion Work and Motivational Framing in a Transgender Community." *Social Problems* 51, no. 1: 61–81.

Schroer, Todd. 2008. "Technical Advances in Communication: The Example of White Racialist 'Love Groups' and 'White Civil Rights Organizations.'" In *Identity Work in Social Movement,* ed. by J. Reger, D. J. Myers, and R. L. Einwohner, 77–100. Minneapolis: University of Minnesota Press.

Scokpol, Theda. 1992. *Protecting Soldiers and Mothers: The Political Origins of Social Policy in the United States.* Cambridge, Mass.: Harvard University Press.

Segal, David R., and Mady Wechsler Segal. 2004. "America's Military Population." *Population Bulletin* 59, no. 4.

Sheehan, Cindy. 2006. *Peace Mom: A Mother's Journey through Heartache to Activism.* New York: Atria Books.

Siebold, Guy L. 2007. "The Essence of Military Group Cohesion" *Armed Forces & Society* 33, no. 2: 286–95.

Simi, Pete, and Robert Futrell. 2009. "Negotiating White Power Activist Stigma." *Social Problems* 56, no. 1: 89–110.

Simon, Bernd. 2004. *Identity in Modern Society: A Social Psychological Perspective.* Oxford: Blackwell Publishers.

Simon, Bernd, and Bert Klandermans. 2001. "Politicized Collective Identity: A Social Psychological Analysis." *American Psychologist* 56, no. 4: 319–31.

Singer, P.W. 2007. *Corporate Warriors: The Rise of the Privatized Military Industry.* Ithaca, N.Y.: Cornell University Press.

Smelser, Neil. 1962. *Theory of Collective Behavior.* New York: Free Press.

Snow, David, and Doug McAdam. 2000. "Identity Work Processes in the Context of Social Movements: Clarifying the Identity/Movement Nexus." In *Self, Identity, and Social Movements,* ed. by S. Stryker, T. Owens, and R. White, 41–67. Minneapolis: University of Minnesota Press.

Snow, David A., E. Burke Rochford Jr., Steven K. Worden, Robert D. Benford. 1986. "Frame Alignment Processes, Micromobilization, and Movement Participation." *American Sociological Review* 51, no. 4: 464–81.

Soule, Sarah. 1997. "The Student Divestment Movement in the United States and the Tactical Diffusion: The Shantytown Protest." *Social Forces* 75, no. 3: 855–83.

———. 2004. "Diffusion Processes within and across Movements." In *The Blackwell Companion to Social Movements,* ed. by David A. Snow, Sarah A. Soule, and Hanspeter Kriesi, 294–310. Oxford: Blackwell Publishers.

Stacewicz, Richard. 1997. *Winter Soldiers: An Oral History of the Vietnam Veterans Against the War.* New York: Twayne Publishers.

Stein, Arlene. 2001. "Revenge of the Shamed: The Christian Right's Emotional Culture War." In *Passionate Politics: Emotions and Social Movements,* ed. by Jeff Goodwin, James M. Jasper, and Francesca Polletta, 115–31. Chicago: University of Chicago Press.

Stevenson, Micha. 2003. *Everyday Activism: A Handbook for Lesbian, Gay, and Bisexual People and Their Allies.* New York: Routledge.

Stitka, Linda J. 2005. "Patriotism or Nationalism? Understanding Post-September 11, 2001, Flag-Display Behavior." *Journal of Applied Social Psychology* 35, no. 10: 1995–2011.

Stockdill, Brett. 2001. "Forging Multidimensional Oppositional Consciousness: Lessons from Community-Based Activism." In *Oppositional Consciousness: The Subjective Roots of Social Protest,* ed. by Jane Mansbridge and Aldon Morris, 204–37. Chicago: University of Chicago Press.

Stone, Andrea, and Marisol Bello. 2009. "Mom's Plight Shows Army Strain." *USA Today,* March 4. http://www.usatoday.com/news/military/2009-03-03-reserve_N.htm.

Stryker, Sheldon, Timothy J. Owens, and Robert W. White, eds. 2001. *Self, Identity, and Social Movements.* Minneapolis: University of Minnesota Press.

Stürmer, Stefan, and Bernd Simon. 2004a. "The Role of Collective Identification in Social Movement Participation: A Panel Study in the Context of the German Gay Movement." *Personality and Social Psychology Bulletin* 30, no. 3: 263–77.

———. 2004b. "Collective Action: Towards a Dual-Pathway Model." *European Review of Social Psychology* 15:59–99.

———. 2009. "Pathways to Collective Protest: Calculation, Identification, or Emotion? A Critical Analysis of the Role of Group-Based Anger in Social Movement Participation." *Journal of Social Issues* 65, no. 4: 681–705.

Stürmer, Stefan, Bernd Simon, Michael Loewy, and Heike Jörger. 2003. "The Dual-Pathway Model of Social Movement Participation: The Case of the Fat Acceptance Movement." *Social Psychology Quarterly* 66, no. 1: 71–82.

Summers-Effler, Erika. 2002. "The Micro Potential for Social Change: Emotion, Consciousness, and Social Movement Formation." *Sociological Theory* 20, no. 1: 41–60.

———. 2005. "The Role of Emotions in Sustaining Commitment to Social Movement Activity: Building and Maintaining Solidarity in a Catholic Worker House." In *Emotions and Social Movements,* ed. by Helena Flam and Debra King, 35–149. New York: Rutledge.

Tarrow, Sidney. 1992. "Mentalities, Political Cultures, and Collective Action Frames." In *Frontiers in Social Movement Research,* ed. by A. Morris and C. Mueller, 174–202. New Haven, Conn.: Yale University Press.

———. 1993. "Modular Collective Action and the Rise of the Social Movements: Why the French Revolution Was Not Enough." *Politics and Society* 21, no. 1: 69–90.

———. 1998. *Power in Movements, Social Movements, and Contentious Politics.* New York: Cambridge University Press.

Taylor, Verta. 1989. "Social Movement Continuity: The Women's Movement in Abeyance." *American Sociological Review* 54, no. 5: 761–75.

———. 1995. "Watching for Vibes: Bringing Emotions into the Study of Feminist Organizations." In *Feminist Organizations: Harvest of the New Women's Movement*, ed. by Myra Marx Ferree and Patricia Yancey Martin, 223–33. Philadelphia: Temple University Press.

———. 1996. *Rock-a-By Baby: Feminism, Self-Help, and Postpartum Depression*. New York: Routledge.

———. 2000. "Emotions and Identity in Women's Self-Help Movements." In *Self, Identity, and Social Movements*, ed. by Sheldon Stryker, Timothy J. Owens, and Robert W. White, 271–99. Minneapolis: University of Minnesota Press.

Taylor, Verta, and Lisa Leitz. 2010. "From Infanticide to Activism: Emotions and Identity in Self-Help Movements." In *Social Movements and the Transformation of American Health Care*, ed. by Mayer Zald, Jane Banaszak-Holl, and Sandy Levitsky, 266–83. New York: Oxford University Press.

Taylor, Verta, and Nicole C. Raeburn. 1995. "Identity Politics as High-Risk Activism: Career Consequences for Lesbian, Gay, and Bisexual Sociologists." *Social Problems* 42, no. 2: 252–73.

Taylor, Verta, and Leila J. Rupp. 2002. "Loving Internationalism: The Emotion Culture of Transnational Women's Organizations, 1888–1945." *Mobilization* 7, no. 2: 125–44.

Taylor, Verta, Leila J. Rupp, and Joshua Gamson. 2004. "Performing Protest: Drag Shows as Tactical Repertoires of the Gay and Lesbian Movement." *Research in Social Movements, Conflict and Change* 25:105–37.

Taylor, Verta, and Nella Van Dyke. 2004. "Tactical Repertoires, Action, and Innovation." In *The Blackwell Companion to Social Movements*, ed. by David A. Snow, Sarah A. Soule, and Hanspeter Kriesi, 262–93. Oxford: Blackwell Publishers.

Taylor, Verta, and Nancy Whittier. 1992. "Collective Identity in Social Movement Communities: Lesbian Feminist Mobilization." In *Frontiers in Social Movement Theory*, ed. by Aldon Morris and Carol Mueller, 104–29. New Haven, Conn.: Yale University Press.

———. 1995. "Analytical Approaches to Social Movement Culture: The Culture of the Women's Movement." In *Social Movements and Culture*, ed. by Hank Johnston and Bert Klandermans, 163–87. Minneapolis: University of Minnesota Press.

Teachervet. 2006. "Returning from Iraq." *Daily Kos*, October 21. http://www.dailykos.com/story/2006/10/21/260263/-Returning-from-Iraq?via=user.

Teachervet. 2008. "The PTSD Coma." *Daily Kos*, December 21. http://www.dailykos.com/story/2008/12/21/675919/-The-PTSD-Coma.

Teigen, Jeremy M. 2007. "Veterans' Party Identification, Candidate Affect, and Vote Choice in the 2004 U.S. Presidential Election." *Armed Forces & Society* 33, no. 3: 414–37.

Thomas, Emma F., Craig McGarty, and Kenneth I. Mavor. 2009. "Transforming

Apathy into Movement: The Role of Prosocial Emotions in Motivating Action for Social Change." *Personality and Social Psychology Review* 13, no. 4: 310–33.

Tilly, Charles. 1978. *From Mobilization to Revolution.* Reading, Mass.: Addison-Wesley.

Toribio, Elyse. 2012. "Activists Mark U.S. War Deaths with Teaneck Peace Vigil." *Teaneck Patch,* June 7. http://teaneck.patch.com/articles/activists-mark-u-s-war-deaths-with-teaneck-peace-vigil#photo-10208884.

Toussaint, Laura L. 2009. *The Contemporary U.S. Peace Movement.* New York: Routledge.

USA Today. 2005. "USA Today/CNN Gallup Poll." *USA Today,* November 15. http://www.usatoday.com/news/polls/2005-11-15-iraq-poll.htm.

Vaishnavi, S., V. Rao, and J. Fann. 2009. "Neuropsychiatric Problems after Traumatic Brain Injury, Unraveling the Silent Epidemic." *Psychosomatics* 50, no. 3: 198–205.

van Zomeren, Martijn, Russell Spears, Agneta H. Fischer, and Colin Wayne Leach. 2004. "Put Your Money Where Your Mouth Is! Explaining Collective Action Tendencies through Group-Based Anger and Group Efficacy." *Journal of Personality and Social Psychology* 87, no. 5: 649–64.

Vaughan, David K., and William A. Schum. 2001. "Motivation and U.S. Narrative Accounts of the Ground War in Vietnam." *Armed Forces & Society* 28, no. 1: 7–31.

Washington Post. 2006. "Washington Post–ABC News Poll." *Washington Post,* April 10. http://www.washingtonpost.com/wp-srv/politics/polls/postpoll_immigration_041006.htm.

Weil, Martin. 2010. "Army Sgt. 1st Class Lance Vogeler of Frederick is Killed in Afghanistan." *Washington Post,* October 4. http://www.washingtonpost.com/wp-dyn/content/article/2010/10/04/AR2010100407375.html.

Wells, Tom. 1994. *The War Within: America's Battle over Vietnam.* Berkeley: University of California Press.

Whittier, Nancy. 1995. *Feminist Generations: The Persistence of the Radical Women's Movement.* Philadelphia: Temple University Press.

———. 2001. "Emotional Strategies: The Collective Reconstruction and Display of Oppositional Emotions in the Movement against Child Sexual Abuse." In *Passionate Politics: Emotions and Social Movements,* ed. by Jeff Goodwin, James M. Jasper, and Francesca Polletta, 233–50. Chicago: University of Chicago Press.

———. 2009. *The Politics of Child Sexual Abuse: Feminism, Social Movements, and The Therapeutic State.* New York: Oxford University Press.

———. 2012. "The Politics of Visibility: Coming Out and Individual and Collective Identity." In *Strategies for Change,* ed. by Gregory M. Maney, Rachel V. Kutz-Flamenbaum, Deana A. Rohlinger, and Jeff Goodwin, 145–69. Minneapolis: University of Minnesota Press.

Wiegand, Krista, and David Paletz. 2001. "The Elite Media and the Military-Civilian Culture Gap." *Armed Forces & Society* 27, no. 2: 183–204.

Wiltfang, Gregory L., and Doug McAdam. 1991. "The Costs and Risks of Social Activism: A Study of Sanctuary Movement Activism." *Social Forces* 69, no. 4: 987–1010.

Woehrle, Lynne M., Patrick G. Coy, and Gregory M. Maney. 2008. *Contesting Patriotism: Culture, Power, and Strategy in the Peace Movement*. Lanham, Md.: Rowman and Littlefield.

Wood, Elisabeth Jean. 2001. "The Emotional Benefits of Insurgency in El Salvador." In *Passionate Politics: Emotions and Social Movements*, ed. by Jeff Goodwin, James M. Jasper, and Francesca Polletta, 267–81. Chicago: University of Chicago Press.

Young, Michael P. 2001. "A Revolution of the Soul: Transformative Experiences and Immediate Abolition." In *Passionate Politics: Emotions and Social Movements*, ed. by Jeff Goodwin, James M. Jasper, and Francesca Polletta, 99–114. Chicago: University of Chicago Press.

Zoroya, Gregg. 2005. "Modern Memorials Stand for the Warriors, Not the War." *USA Today*, May 26.

Index

Page numbers in italics refer to photographs or other illustrations.

Arredondo, Alexander S. (son of Carlos and Mélida), 68, 157
Arredondo, Brian, 70
Arredondo, Carlos, 68, 69, 133, 157, 266n18
Arredondo, Mélida, *xii,* 68, 133
art therapy, *119,* 127, 247–48, 268n4 (chap. 3)
Ashcroft, Evan, 44
audiences: connecting emotionally with, 20, 26–27, 67, 71, 124, 153, 162, 208, 225–26, 246; identities presented to, 23–24, 171, 198–99, 200, 242–43; mobilizing new, 168, 238; reaching diverse, 78, 154, 183–89, 191, 210, 242, 247–48
AVF. *See* all-volunteer force (AVF)
AWOL (absent without leave), 29–31, 41–42, 43, 54–55, 151, 173, 194–95, 207

Baker, Sherwood (son of Alfred and Celeste Zappala), 44, 48, 161, 230
Bake Sales for Body Armor, 113–14
Ballard, Kenneth (son of Karen Meredith), 46, 163; Arlington West cross, *212*
Bannerman, Stacy, *xii,* 69, 163
Barfield, Ellen, 104
Bello, Marisol, 271n13
beneficiaries, of peace movement, 14, 93, 135–37, 150, 155, 176, 234, 236, 246
Bennett, Terry, 100
Bernstein, Mary, 23, 164, 198, 199, 215
betrayal, feelings of, 67–68, 70–71, 73, 91, 100, *121,* 126, 140
Biden, Jill, 37
Bin Laden, Osama, 87
Blake, Michael, 52, 73–77, 74, 82, 266n1
Blue Star Families for Obama, *35,* 37
Bolger, Leah, 183
bonding and bonds, peace activists', 14, 122, 134–35, 144–45, 153–56, 224. *See also* emotion(s): reciprocal; love, among peace activists; solidarity

Boston Veteran's Day parades, 186–87, 269n21
Bright, Jane and Jim, 44
Bring Them Home Now Tour (2005), 46–50, 251, 265n8
Brinson, Thomas, 104
Brower, Elaine, 194–95
Brown, Peter, 53
Brown, Rod, 219–20, 222, 227
Buonomo, Thomas J., 56–57
Bush, George W., xiii, 8–11, 18, 35, 45, 63, 249, 250, 251, 260n2, 261n20, 268n1; administration of, 9, 20, 91, 100, 175, 181; as target of activists, 39, 60, 87, 91, 100, 160, 168, 186–87, 205, 253. *See also* Crawford, Texas, protests in
Butler, Smedley, 269n20; protest group named after, 186

cadences, military, 17; use in protests, 125–27, 170–72, 186, 229, 267–68n3
Calamar, Don, 216
Camp Casey. *See* Crawford, Texas, protests in
Capps, Chris, 43
Carbonaro, Alessandro (son of Gilda), 162
Carbonaro, Gilda, 162, *230*
care work: in activism, 117–20, 139, 140, 145, 146; by GSFSO, 119, 232–33; by IVAW, 101, 117–19, 128; by MFSO, 101, 119; resulting from war injuries, 66–67, 96–97, 144–45, 146–47, 149–50, 265n3
Caruth, Debbie, 5
Casteel, Joshua, 52
casualties. *See* death(s)
Cervantes, Michael, 85–86, 141, 217–19
Chicago, Illinois, anti–Iraq War protest (2002), 19
Chiroux, Matthis, 194–95
civilians: Afghan, 206, 254; Iraqi, 9, 43, 65, 88, 93, 94, 114, 117, 124, 141, 149, 159–60, 166, 167, 173–74, 206, 247,

252, 265n4; peace activists' efforts
to convert, 165, 170–76, 177–79, 181,
183–85, 215–19, 237. *See also* contractors, private military; death(s):
civilian; military–civilian divide;
peace activism and activists
Clements, Richard, 179–80
Cline, David, 123, 126, 127, 136, 267–68n3
clothing, as protest symbol, 3, 49, 160,
170, 172, 194, 204, 213, 215, 222, 230,
244; military uniforms, 160, 162–63,
173, 183, 185–87, 229
coalition forces, 8, 9
CodePink: Women for Peace, 29, 197
cohesion: military, 82. *See also*
solidarity
collective identity: boundaries of,
107–8, 110–11, 113, 125, 129, 131, 226,
240; conflicts over, 164, 190–97;
construction of, 21–23, 25, 124–25,
191, 208, 226–27, 240–41; culture-of-action level, 107–11, 120,
121–22, 129, 130–35, 153–56, 191,
245–46; layers of, 21–22, 121–22; of
military peace movement, 18, 22–23,
77–82, 106–7, 111–22, 130–35, 182–83,
208, 221; negotiation of, 112, 222–24,
227, 270n14; organizational, 134–35;
peace activists', 7, 23, 38, 155, 241,
263–64n83. *See also* consciousness:
collective; identity; identity deployment strategies; insider–outsider
identities
Collins, Henry, *169*
Collins, Jane, 104–5
combat: in Afghanistan and Iraq, 11, 13,
32, 247; trauma from, 152, 157–58,
168, 179, 232–33, 267n15, 271n8;
veterans of, 38, 75, 85, 123, 178, 180; in
Vietnam, 12, 13, 262n55, 266n17. *See
also* posttraumatic stress disorder
(PTSD); war(s)
Combat Paper Project, 247, 268n4
(chap. 3)

communism, 195–96
conformity, military, 15, 16, 82
conscience, 31–32, 53–54, 231
conscience constituents, 93, 234, 236, 243
conscientious objection, 15, 52–56,
63, 73, 76, 106, 173, 265n12. *See also*
selective objection
consciousness: collective, 111, 112, 120;
oppositional, 89, 93, 114, 155; peace
movement's, 231; shared, 77–78,
182, 241
Constitution, U.S., war protest as
defense of, 89, 91–93, 181; servicemember's oath to, 91, 178, 181–82;
patriotic symbol, 181–82
contractors, private military, 5, 10, 172,
236, 271n14, 273n53, 273n4
Coppa, Selena, 90, 116–17, 196
Cortwright, David, 15
Coy, Patrick G., 199
Crawford, Texas, protests in, 2–4,
29–32, 45–47, 67, 86, 140, 167–68,
176, 207–8, 223, 260n1, 260n3;
referred to as Camp Casey, 3, 29, *30*,
49, 95, 102, 128, 151, 153, 167, 251, 252,
259n3
Crowell, Ethan, 127
culture of action: 20, 244, 245–46,
263n67; definition, 20, 245; emotion's role in, 24–27, 121, 144–46;
family structure of, 128, 130–44;
identity and, 20–24, 28; military
peace movement as, 32, 37–38, 47,
49–50, 71–72, 107–20, 121–22, 125,
131–35, 150, 153–54, 244–46. *See also*
collective identity: culture-of-action level

Davis, Chaz, *30*
Dawson, Josh, 127
Dawson, Theresa, 86–87, 131, 140, 180
death(s), 102–3, 141, 178, 204, 226, 235;
civilian, 8, 70, 75, 160, 166, 168–69,
249; servicemembers', 12, 44, 46,

Hafley, Stacy, 61–63, 105–6, 132
Hatcher, Joe, 127
health care, servicemembers' lack of
access to, 44, 74, 94, 96, 102, 121, 189,
229, 233, 238, 243, 247, 266n1, 267n18.
See also military peace movement:
healing or therapy through; Veterans
Administration, U.S. (VA)
Hearington, Mike, 83–84, 139, 151–52
hippies. *See* peace activism and activists: military's stereotypes of
Hitz, Carla, 101
Hoffman, Mike, 42
Hogg, Jen, 84, 92–93
Hurricane Katrina: inadequate government response to, 47, 98, 123,
124, 251; military peace movement's
assistance, 267n2
Hussein, Saddam, 9, 249, 250, 252
Hutto, Jonathan, 82

IAVA. *See* Iraq and Afghanistan Veterans of America (IAVA)
identity, 7, 18, 64, 70, 110, 156, 244, 246;
activist, 60, 138, 190, 246; American, 19; in culture of action, 20–24,
154, 245; emotion and, 21, 26–27,
238–44; military, 4, 26, 32, 36, 60,
180, 182–83, 188, 229; peace-related,
191, 214–24; role in mobilization,
226–27, 231. *See also* collective
identity; insider–outsider identities,
military peace activists'; military
peace movement: combining military affiliations with peace
identity deployment strategies, 4, 27–28,
156, 160, 163–200, 204, 208, 214–27,
242, 248; authority, 23–24, 164,
170–76, 199–200, 204, 215–17, 224–25,
226, 242, 244; enhancing credibility,
242–44; navigating, 190–97; novelty,
27–28, 164, 165–69, 176–82, 198, 200,
226, 239, 242; oppositional, 23, 24,
164, 165, 176–82, 200, 226, 243, 244,

246; reaching the unconverted, 165,
182–89, 217, 225. *See also* Bernstein,
Mary; clothing, as protest symbol
Improvised Explosive Devices (IEDs),
103, 162, 173
Individual Ready Reserve (IRR) status,
57, 58, 94, 98, 100–101, 236, 271n13
injustice, fighting against, 25, 90–91, 155,
200, 240–41, 243
insider–outsider identities, military
peace activists': authority, 170–76,
204, 224, 225; care work central to,
117–20; collective, 22–23, 78–82,
120–22, 131, 135, 238; contradictions
in, 78–82, 190–97; credibility of,
198, 242–43; information leading
to formation, 83–89, 238; insider
characteristics, 111–20; of military
families, 79–82, 108, 167–69, 170–72,
175; novel, 164, 165–69, 176, 198, 226,
239; oppositional, 164, 176–82, 198,
200, 226; outsider characteristics,
107–11, 127, 137, 144, 145; personal
grievances leading to, 93–103;
politics of, 103–7, 164; reaching the
unconverted, 182–89, 198, 217, 225,
231; social psychological motivations, 120–21, *121*; value redefinition
leading to, 89–93, 129
International Security Assistance Force
(ISAF, NATO), 8, 249, 250, 251
Iraq and Afghanistan Veterans of
America (IAVA), 36
Iraq Veterans Against the War (IVAW),
xiv, 2, *30*, *35*, 42–44, 66, 74, *142*, *158*,
159, *169*; Afghanistan War opposition, 87, 192, 266–67n10; Appeal for
Redress sponsored by, 82, 187–88;
artistic projects, 127–28, 247, 268n4
(chap. 3); care work of, 101, 117–19,
128; combining military affiliation
and peace activism, 80, 81, 84, 114; at
Crawford, Texas, protests, 29, 47, 55;
disagreements in, 193–95; founding

of, 36, 42–43, 136, 140–41, 143; gender
roles in, 133, 138, 139; identity of, 14,
38, 77, 110, 170, 190; insider–outsider
identity, 170–71, 172–73, 175–76, 231;
and military-related sexual traumas,
269n25; at Mother's Day weekend
events, 157; at NATO conference
protests, 229; Operation First Casualty protests, 65–66, 66, 173–74, 204;
Operation Recovery, 118–19, 119; on
patriotism, 90, 91–92; politics of, 105,
106–7, 195–97; reasons for activism
of, 75–76, 96, 116–17, 146; regional/
local chapters, 31, 43, 133–35, 154, 187,
192; risks faced by, 50, 51–53, 56–58,
65–66, 67; stop-loss protests, 99,
100; Tri-folded Flag Campaign, 178;
Truth in Recruiting, 187; veterans
status required for, 113; Walkin' to
New Orleans march, 74, 123–29, 124,
153, 170, 230; Winter Soldier events,
43, 149–51, 265n5; work with UFPJ,
177–78. See also Combat Paper
Project; military peace movement;
Warrior Writers; and individual
activists
Iraq War, 8–11; Afghanistan War dif-
ferentiated from, 13, 87–89; civilian
casualties, 94, 124, 149, 173–74,
192, 206, 231, 252; costs of, 10–11,
123, 160, 162, 235; countermovement support for, 104, 243, 260n3;
critical military politics during, 32,
33–37; disillusionment with, 73–75,
93, 94; drawdown, 232, 253, 254;
experiences of, 23, 154; ground truth
of, 141–42, 170, 174, 175, 239–40;
illegality of, 9, 29, 31, 32, 74, 75, 87,
88, 117, 157, 174, 181, 186, 193, 240;
lies associated with, 74, 85–87, 88,
92, 191; media coverage of, 6–7,
114; military casualties, 10, 86–87,
114, 201, 231, 234, 250, 252, 268n2;
as preemptive war, 9, 85, 88, 92–93,

249; public opinion of, 2, 7, 8, 11, 48,
213, 234, 249–54; seeking end to,
47, 49, 65, 85, 98, 112–13, 117–20, 124,
126, 149–50, 157, 162, 180, 208, 213,
225, 227, 231; troop levels, 5, 98–100,
227, 250–54, 260–61n13; unconsti-
tutionality of, 92, 181–82; Vietnam
War compared with, 11–15, 85–86,
234–36; as violation of American
values, 89–93; withdrawal of U.S.
forces from, 5, 10, 231–32, 254. See
also anti–Iraq War movement
IRR. See Individual Ready Reserve
(IRR) status
IVAW. See Iraq Veterans Against the
War (IVAW)

Jasper, James, 21, 204
Joining Forces, 37
Jones, Walter, 48
Justseeds Artists' Cooperative, 119

Kahlor, Ryan (son of Tim), 146–47
Kahlor, Tim, xii, 133, 146–47, 148
Kerry, John, xii–xiii, 33, 34, 182, 189, 251,
262n48
Key, Jeff, 142
King, Martin Luther, Jr., 123, 267n1
Klawiter, Maren, 20, 71, 245, 263n67
Kokesh, Adam, 57, 178, 181
Kovic, Ron, 14; Born on the Fourth of
July, 261n38
Kubein, Adele, 166
Kyne, Dennis, 114, 140

leaders and leadership: military and
government/political, 8, 13, 17, 52,
68, 87, 96, 106, 109, 116, 124, 147, 149,
172, 173, 188–90, 191, 229, 236, 238,
250, 253; military peace movement,
3, 14, 19, 36–37, 41, 68, 113, 117, 132,
136, 140, 141, 143, 155, 165, 171, 175,
190, 197, 203, 238. See also individual
activists

servicemembers, military participation in antiwar activities; troops

military–civilian divide, 1, 6–7, 15–18, 227, 234–38, 248, 262n48

military culture, 15–18, 82, 95; stereotypes of peace activists, 58, 59, 107, 164, 184, 185

military families: critical organizations, 35, 36–37; Gulf War protests, 12–13; insider–outsider identity, 79–82, 108, 167, 168–69, 170–72, 175; percentage of population as, 14, 234; personal grievances of, 65–67, 89, 92, 93–103, 167–68; political activities, 34, 36–37; PTSD's effects on, 1, 95, 96–98, 105–6, 146, 147, 189, 229; risks of protest activities, 58–64, 67–71, 99; stop-loss protests, 99–100; supporting troops, 18, 19, 117–18, 147, 265n13; wars' impact on, 1–2, 14, 163, 237–38. *See also* Gold Star families; military peace movement; parents, military; spouses, military

Military Families Speak Out (MFSO), *xii*, xiii, xiv, *30*, 39–42, *148, 158, 159, 212*; Afghanistan War opposition, 190–91, 192, 266–67n10; Appeal for Redress sponsored by, 82; bus tour protests, 46–49; cadences written for, 126, 267–68n3; care work of, 101, 119; chapters, 37, 45, 71, 118, 132, 133–35, 154, 157, 192; combining military affiliation and peace activism, 80–81, 146; at Crawford, Texas, protests, 29–30, 45; disagreements in, 194–95; hate mail directed at, 107–8; insider–outsider identity, 165–66, 188–89; loss of military support networks, 59, 60–63, 64; at Mother's Day weekend events, 157, 160, 163; Native American healing retreat, 119; at NATO conference protests, 229; politics of, 36–37, 105, 106; protest activities, 105, 197, 232;

reasons for protesting, 39–40, 85, 86–87, 90, 92, 94, 97–98, 99–102, 103, 104–6; risks faced by, 50–51, 56–58, 60–64, 65, 67–68; at Santa Barbara Veterans' Day parade, 109; stop-loss protests, 99; Vietnam War protests, 104–5; Walkin' to New Orleans march, 125, 126; work with other organizations, 38, 43, 90, 136–38, 140, 177–78. *See also* military peace movement; Operation House Call (MFSO)

Military Family Support Network, 13, 40

military–industrial complex, 269n20

military occupational specialty (MOS), 139

military peace movement: activism encouraged by, 33–37, 151; civilian peace movement's differences from, 31–33, 239; coalition building, 46–50, 71, 127, 129–30, 131–35; combining military affiliations with peace, 3–4, 5, 15–18, 19, 22–23, 59, 75–82, 84, 105, 106–13, 114, 125–26, 129, 137, 146, 160, 163–69, 194, 198–200, 220, 203–4, 211–27, 238, 239–40, 243; community building in, 4, 33–37; context of, 7–20; contradictions in, 78–82, 239–40, 244; credibility of, 164, 172, 173, 174–75, 188, 198–200, 215, 217–21, 222, 243; developing community, 107–11, 121–22; family-like structure, 25–26, 128, 129–30, 130–44, 153–54; general peace movement distinguished from, 31–32, 96, 107–11, 122, 214–24, 229, 239; healing or therapy through, 117–20, 123, 128–29, 144–53, 155–56, 231, 232–33, 245, 247–48, 269n24; intergenerational character, 139–44, 151–53, 154; organizations comprising, 2, 35, 37–50, 131–35; overcoming military–civilian divide, 237–38; as

Operation Free (PAC), 34
Operation House Call (MFSO), 70, 85, 252
Operation Iraqi Freedom. *See* Iraq War
Operation New Dawn. *See* Iraq War: drawdown
Operation Rapid American Withdrawal (VVAW), 266n17
Operation Recovery (IVAW), 118–19, *119*, 254
Operation Truth, *35*, 36
OPTEMPO (operational tempo), 10, 99, 232, 235. *See also* deployments/tours: pace of

pacifism and pacifists, 18, 39, 89, 114, 190, 267n22. *See also* peace activism and activists
Pallos, Isaiah, 42
parents, military, 2, 40, 54, 64, 75–76, 83, 105, 124, 265n13; protest activities, 36, 37, 41, 45, 48, 55, 56, 68, 77, 80–81, 92, 99, 103, 104, 106, 133, 137, 138–39, 160, 162, 182. *See also* military families; Military Families Speak Out (MFSO)
paranoia, resulting from war, 55. *See also* fear(s): war-related
patriotism: discourses on, 176, 179, 191, 193–95, 197–98; peace activism as, 73, 83, 97, 122, 164, 179–82, 186, 190; redefining/reframing, 4, 19, 76, 78, 82, 89–93, 121, 180; symbols of, 181–82, 199. *See also* September 11, 2001, terrorist attacks; troops: peace activism as support for
Paul, Ron, 181
peace activism and activists: anti–Iraq War movement distinguished from, 31–32, 190–91, 197; benefits for the military, 86–87, 113–14, 116–17; collective identity of, 7, 23, 38, 155, 241, 263–64n83; emotions' role in, 24–26, 145, 153–56, 239–44; growing into,

83–89; military activists differing from, 31–33, 107–11, 239; military's stereotypes of, 17–18, 58, 59, 107, 164, 184, 185; radicalization of, 12, 20, 44, 190, 194, 196–97, 226, 243; risks associated with, 32–33, 50–72, 81–82. *See also* insider–outsider identities, military peace activists'; militarism, opposition to; military peace movement; mobilization; pacifism and pacifists; patriotism: peace activism as; social movement(s); troops: peace activism as support for; *and individual organizations*
peace-keeping forces, 73, 105, 249
Pederson, Michael, 44
Perle, Richard, 163, 268n4 (chap. 4)
personalized political strategies, 24, 244–45
police: at demonstrations, 175, 229, 230, 271n1; military, 8, *115*, 173, 175
political action committees (PACs), 33, 34, *35*
politics: critical military, 32, 33–37, *35*; everyday, 244–46; left-leaning, 75, 78, 103–4, 184, 194, 195–97, 240; of social movements, 263–64n83; of war, 128. *See also* targets, movement
Polletta, Francesca, 21
Porter, Casey, 99
Poster Girl (documentary, Nesson), 247, 269n24
posttraumatic stress disorder (PTSD): activism's worsening of, 64, 65–67; effects on families, 1, 95, 96–98, 105–6, 147, 189, 229; experiences of, 128, 269n24; healing from, 76, 140, 146–47, 231, 247; lack of care for, 118–19, 233; as reason for protesting, 94–98, 234; secondary, 146, 189; suicides related to, 96, 147, 150–51, 266n3. *See also* combat: trauma from; traumatic brain injuries (TBIs)
Potter, Bob, *109*, 170, 201, 224

Potts, Stephen, 52, 63–64, 80, 84, 106, 127
Powell, Colin, 19, 88, 250, 273n3
Powell, Woody, 137
powerlessness, emotions of, 124, 242; transforming into resistance, 25–26, 27, 124, 128, 129–30, 144–53, 155, 241. *See also* resistance, emotions of
protests. *See* anti–Iraq War movement; military peace movement; peace activism and activists; tactics, military peace movement
PTSD. *See* posttraumatic stress disorder (PTSD)

racial issues, 13, 25, 44. *See also* Act Now to Stop War and End Racism (ANSWER)
radicalization, of activists, 12, 20, 44, 190, 194, 196–97, 226, 243
recession of 2007, 4, 5, 20, 227
reenlistment/retention, 10, 13–14, 165, 187–88
Reilly, Ward, 127, 175
reintegration, from deployment into civilian life, 5, 6–7, 37, 51, 102, 152, 265n3
Reppenhagen, Garrett, 127, 140, 141, 173
Republican Party, 19, 34, 252, 253, 262n48
Reserve forces: in Iraq War, 47, 98, 236; lack of family support system, 99, 101–2, 188–89; multiple deployments, 98, 235
resistance, emotions of, 26, 27, 129–30, 144, 149, 150, 151, 154, 155, 241, 264n99
resisters, war, military peace movement's support for, 30, 31–32, 41–42, 44, 193–194, 252, 269n23
Richards, Cloy, 59–60, 150–51, 167–68, 169
Richards, Tina, 60, 132
Richardson, Charlie, 39, 40, 41, 136–37, 267–68n3

Richmond, Virginia, courthouse vigil, 1–2
rights: gay, 44, 106, 243, 246; servicemembers', 114, *115*, 132, 201; survivors', 123
Rising-Moore, Carl, 141, 151
risks, of activism: of conscientious objectors, 15, 52–56, 63, 73, 76, 106; distinguishing military from general peace movement, 31–33, 239; emotional, 72; estrangement, 58–64, 72; financial, 70, 72, 99; official military punishment, 51–58, 71–72, 90; psychological, 64–71, 72
Roesler, Anne, 66–67
Rogovin, Paula, 98
Rosenleaf, Tammara, 48, 56, 113
Ruger, Lietta, xiii, 85
Rupp, Leila, 225
Ryabov, Alex, 42

sabotage, of military equipment, 12, 193
Santa Barbara, California, protest events, *xii*, 19, *69*, 109, *109*, 133–34. *See also* Arlington West (Santa Barbara, California)
Seattle, Washington, protest activities in, 181
selective objection, 52, 56, 266n15
Seligman, Mischa, *109*
September 11, 2001, terrorist attacks, 8, 19, 74, 192, 210, 249; increasing patriotism, 91, 176, 199; reason for joining military, 92; relationship to activism, 37, 43, 86, 181, 192; relationship to policy, 34; victims' families' organization, 157
servicemembers, military participation in antiwar activities: benefits of, 44, 52, 53, 116–17; personal grievances of, 50–51, 93–103; regulations limiting, 15–18, 32, 51–52, 81; risks faced by, 29–30, 30–32, 51–52, 81–82. *See also* AWOL (absent without

Stürmer, Stefan, 240
suicide: attempted, 68, 95, 150; avoiding,
150–51, 155; committed, 46, 70,
96–97; at Fort Hood, 118–19; idea-
tion, 76, 95, 168; PTSD as cause of,
96, 147, 150–51, 231, 232–33; rates of,
76, 233, 238, 266n3
Summers-Effler, Erika, 241
Support and Defend the Constitution
Campaign (2006–7), 91
symbols, 12, 20, 24, 118, 165, 182, 198,
215, 244; grieving mother, 45. *See
also* clothing, as protest symbol;
death(s): symbols of; patriotism:
symbols of; signs
Syverson, Larry, 1–2, 5–6, 145

tactics, military peace movement: 4,
47, 200, 204; artistic, 127–28, 247,
268n4; counterrecruitment (truth
in recruiting), 39, 173, 187; educational, 35, 90, 155, 254; emotions'
role in, 26–27, 149–50, 153, 174–75,
178, 203–4, 208–13, 215–17, 238;
march, 1, 2, 19, 35, 39, 49, 63, 74, 98,
109, 133, 134, 136–37, 138, 141, 142,
148, 157, *158, 159,* 160, 166, 170–72, 177,
184, 186–87, 204, 208, 229, 252; memorial, 27, 28, 29, 47, 68, 157, 161–62,
200, 231, 237, 243–44, 251, 252,
259n3, 270n5; storytelling, 40, 46,
48, 64, 66–67, 72, 76, 124, 138–39,
149, 153, 167–69, 177, 237, 243; street
theater, 65–66, *66,* 172–74, 204,
237, 243; therapy through, 149–51;
vigil, 1–3, 39. *See also* Arlington
West memorial (Santa Barbara,
California); Bake Sales for Body
Armor; Bring Them Home Now
Tour (2005); Crawford, Texas, protests in; NATO conference protests
(Chicago, 2012); Operation First
Casualty protests (IVAW); Silence
of the Dead, Voices of the Living;

strategies, military peace movement; Tri-folded Flag Campaign;
Walkin' to New Orleans Veterans
and Survivors March (2006)
Taliban, 8–9, 192
targets, movement: activists themselves, 144–53; government officials,
48, 57, 70, 82, 162, 165, 177–78, 180,
182, 188–89, 252, 253; public opinion,
2, 7, 23, 48, 150, 203–5, 225, 243; *See
also* Bush, George W.: as a target of
protest; civilians: peace activists'
efforts to convert; media coverage
Taylor, Verta, 130, 144, 225, 264n99
TBIs. *See* traumatic brain injuries
(TBIs)
Totten, Michael, 149
training, military, lack of, 51, 54, 74, 86,
99, 100–102, 114
traumatic brain injuries (TBIs), 118–19,
146–47, 254, 267n15, 271n8
Tri-folded Flag Campaign (IVAW), 178
troops: peace activism as support for,
87, 112–13, 117–18, 128–29, 146–47,
164–65, 168, 177–79, 191, 211, 238;
society's support for, 19, 128, 176,
199–200, 221, 238; war's negative
effects on, 177, 198, 234. *See also* military, the; servicemembers, military
participation in antiwar activities

Uniform Code of Military Justice
(UCMJ), 16, 56–57. *See also* military,
the: regulations
United for Peace and Justice (UFPJ),
49, 177–78
United Nations (UN), 19, 39, 182, 249,
250
United States (U.S.). *See* Constitution,
U.S., war protest as defense of;
government policies, U.S.; Veterans
Administration, U.S. (VA)
Urban, Tom, 214
U.S. Social Forum, 2010, *142*

values: Army's core, 116–17; redefining, 89–93, 129

VCS. *See* Veterans for Common Sense (VCS)

veterans: authority identity of, 170, 215, 216–17; benefits for, 34, 36, 44, 57, 112, 117–18, 188, 206, 233, 266n1; caring for, 101, 117–20, 146–47, 176, 179, 232; credibility of, 198–200, 217–19, 222, 243; critical organizations of, 35, 35–36; fears of, 95, 150, 152–53; insider–outsider identity of, 108, 167, 170–72, 175; in military peace movement, 2–4, 22, 129, 225–26; personal grievances of, 93–103, 237–38; stresses of activism on, 58–59, 63–67, 243. *See also* military peace movement; Veterans Administration, U.S. (VA)

veterans, Gulf War, 36

veterans, Iraq and Afghanistan: and Arlington West memorial, 219–21, 224–25; critical organizations, 35; effects of war on, 126–27, 146–47, 266n3, 271n8; movement support for, 36, 132; PTSD's effects on, 95–96, 118–19, 229; rate of antiwar organizing, 14–15. *See also* Afghanistan War; Iraq Veterans Against the War (IVAW); Iraq War; NATO conference protests (Chicago, 2012); suicide; veterans

veterans, Korean War, 19, 38, 109, 137, 191, 216

veterans, Vietnam War, 19, 35, 38, 93, 109; personal stories of, 65–67, 124; postwar treatment of, 176, 199–200; protest activities, 11, 14–15, 261n37, 265n2; Walkin' to New Orleans march, 126, 127. *See also* Vietnam War

veterans, World War II, 12, 14, 19, 38, 109, 205, 216

Veterans Administration, U.S. (VA):

difficulties getting treatment from, 6, 94, 96, 97; health care benefits for Iraq and Afghanistan veterans, 266n1, 267n18; lawsuits against, 97, 233, 271n4

Veterans and Military Families for Progress (VMFP), 34, 35

Veterans Day parades: Boston, Massachusetts, 186; Santa Barbara, California, 109, 109

Veterans for America, 261n37

Veterans for Common Sense (VCS), 35, 36, 97, 271n4

Veterans for Peace (VFP), xiv, 38–39, 158, 159, 265n2; Afghanistan War opposition, 190, 192, 266–67n10; Appeal for Redress sponsored by, 82; Arlington West memorial, 206–8, 212, 214, 216, 222, 224–27; chapter(s), 39, 85, 109, 123, 133–35, 181, 186–87, 201, 205, 206, 207, 208, 224; combining military affiliation and peace activism, 81, 91, 109, 183; at Crawford, Texas, protests, 29, 45; as culture of action, 70, 131–33; establishment of, 135–36; handling addictions, 151–52; insider–outsider identity of, 170–71, 181–82, 186–87, 269n21; members of, 30, 109, 110–11, 268n8; and military-related sexual traumas, 269n25; national conventions, 42, 45, 100, 105, 133, 136, 168, 172, 192, 193, 250, 259n3, 266n10; at NATO conference protests, 229; politics of, 35, 106, 269n26; pre–Iraq War activism, 104, 125–26, 136–37; risks faced by, 50, 65, 67; veterans status required for full membership, 113, 267n21; war resisters supported by, 194, 269n23. *See also* military peace movement; Walkin' to New Orleans Veterans and Survivors March (2006)

Veterans for Peace/Veterans for Peace in Viet-Nam, 12

LISA LEITZ is assistant professor of sociology and director of Project Pericles at Hendrix College.

(continued from page ii)

Volume 6 Donatella della Porta and Herbert Reiter, editors, *Policing Protest: The Control of Mass Demonstrations in Western Democracies*

Volume 5 Hanspeter Kriesi, Ruud Koopmans, Jan Willem Duyvendak, and Marco G. Giugni, *New Social Movements in Western Europe: A Comparative Analysis*

Volume 4 Hank Johnston and Bert Klandermans, editors, *Social Movements and Culture*

Volume 3 J. Craig Jenkins and Bert Klandermans, editors, *The Politics of Social Protest: Comparative Perspectives on States and Social Movements*

Volume 2 John Foran, editor, *A Century of Revolution: Social Movements in Iran*

Volume 1 Andrew Szasz, *EcoPopulism: Toxic Waste and the Movement for Environmental Justice*